THE NOVELS OF MAX FRISCH

THE NOVELS OF
MAX FRISCH

by

MICHAEL BUTLER

OSWALD WOLFF
London

ISBN 0 85496 059 7

MADE AND PRINTED IN GREAT BRITAIN BY
THE GARDEN CITY PRESS LIMITED
LETCHWORTH, HERTFORDSHIRE
SG6 1JS

for
JEAN, JULIAN
and EMMA

Note on References

All page references to Frisch's work are taken from the new standard
Suhrkamp edition in six volumes (1976). Roman numerals refer to
the volume, Arabic to the page. In the case of double references, the
italicised figures refer to the official translations by Michael Bullock
as listed in the Bibliography.

Contents

Preface

In writing this book I have tried to reconcile the differing needs of specialist and general reader. My aim has been to present a clear and concise interpretation of Max Frisch's novels which does justice to their individual emphases but at the same time establishes them as belonging to one distinctive thematic complex. My analyses are firmly based on the texts themselves and supported by ample quotation both in the original German and in English translation. For the benefit of those readers who do not wish to follow the argument into secondary areas, all Notes have been grouped together and placed at the end of the volume where they can be conveniently by-passed. The Bibliography, on the other hand, has been compiled with the specialist in mind; it is a comprehensive record of the secondary literature in German and English on Frisch's work as a novelist.

I wish to thank the following for permission to quote from Frisch's published work : in German, the Atlantis Verlag, Zürich (*Die Schwierigen*), and the Suhrkamp Verlag, Frankfurt am Main (all other quotations); in English, Michael Bullock (*I'm not Stiller* and *A Wilderness of Mirrors*), Eyre Methuen Ltd. and Michael Bullock (*Homo Faber*).

I should like to express my gratitude to the *Stiftung Pro Helvetia* for a generous subsidy towards the costs of publishing this book and to the Editors of *Text + Kritik, Forum for Modern Language Studies* and *New German Studies* where portions of this study first appeared. I should also like to thank Hamish Ritchie of Sheffield University and Arrigo Subiotto of Birmingham University for their help and advice. To John Reddick of Sidney Sussex College, Cambridge, I owe an especial and long-standing debt which I am particularly glad to acknowledge here.

Michael Butler
Birmingham, July 1976

I

Introduction

In a well-known interview given in the summer of 1961 Max Frisch declared : 'With every new piece of work I have the naïve feeling that now, thank heavens, I am getting to grips with a fundamentally new theme—only to discover sooner or later that everything which does not end in fundamental failure, possesses fundamentally the same theme.'[1] The aim of this book is to examine the truth of Frisch's wry admission as far as his five novels are concerned. The characteristic note of irony in the remark, however, should warn the reader against any hasty assumption that he is faced with a writer of limited scope. Far from arguing that Frisch's novels are narrow or repetitive, I wish to demonstrate that they indeed possess a remarkable thematic unity and that it is precisely through this unity that he has been able to produce a group of novels which constitute a major contribution to European fiction.

An important preoccupation of twentieth-century German literature has been the sense that man has lost his vital centre. Writer after writer has struggled with the problems produced by the collapse not just of traditional values but also of the self, the human personality, which this loss of centricity has induced. Hofmannsthal, Rilke, Kafka, Hesse, Musil. Böll, Grass and Frisch are some of the many writers who have sought in their different ways to throw light on an apparently increasing disintegration of human individuality and who have wrestled with the difficulties of portraying man in fiction that this involves. A poem written at the mid-point of the century by Gottfried Benn, whose roots stretch back to pre-First World War Expressionism, seemed to articulate a widely shared and persistent experience :

> Das ist der Mensch von heute,
> das Innere ein Vakuum,
> die Kontinuität der Persönlichkeit
> wird gewahrt von den Anzügen,
> die bei gutem Stoff zehn Jahre halten.

This is contemporary man,
his centre a vacuum,
continuity of personality
is preserved by clothes
which, if of good quality, last ten years.

The imagery of this poem with its characteristic title, *Fragmente*, remarkably foreshadows Max Frisch's *Mein Name sei Gantenbein* which appeared fourteen years later—a novel in which a fictive narrator tries on 'stories' like clothes in an attempt to capture a sense of identity and restore continuity and substance to a fractured personality. But the sense of lost centricity to which Benn alludes affects, in one way or another, all the characters who people Frisch's narrative world. For they are eccentric individuals in that they are shown as living at odds with an environment which, far from exerting any central stabilising power, has itself a void at its core.[2] The frightening nature of this void is disguised from the apparently centric majority only by habit and the repetitive shape of everyday routine. Frisch's characters, indeed, are embedded —the exception is perhaps the hero of his first novel, *Jürg Reinhart* (1934)—in the well-defined context of a modern bourgeois society which is depicted as deeply flawed. For by the conformity which it demands of its members, the rôles which it expects them to perform, and the pressures to which it subjects them, this society is shown to be indifferent, if not inimical, to the maintenance and development of personal integrity. The linchpin of this social system is marriage, and Frisch uses the institution as a microcosm of the larger community beyond. It is not therefore surprising that marriage—and in particular the problematical nature of its supposed centripetence—is the fundamental experience to which all Frisch's protagonists are exposed.

In this way the picture Frisch draws of mid-century European society—and certain pages of *Stiller* (1954) and *Homo Faber* (1957) suggest that in his view the American way of life is not dissimilar— is given an essentially negative character. Society does not reveal within itself, nor offer to the individual, any viable centric principle. Paradoxically, therefore, those who commit themselves to the system, whilst on the surface appearing satisfied and integrated, are in fact disastrously lacking in wholeness and genuine centricity. The reader of Frisch's narrative fiction is thus presented with not one but two poles of eccentricity—a positive and a negative one. Around the latter are clustered such characters as the Oberst,

Ammann and Hauswirt (*Die Schwierigen*, 1943, revised and re-issued in 1957), Julika, Bohnenblust and Sturzenegger (*Stiller*) and Frantisek Svoboda (*Mein Name sei Gantenbein*). Such men and women live on the surface of life, clinging to facts or ideologies as guarantees of stability. Around the other pole (the one which most clearly attracts Frisch himself) are gathered Jürg Reinhart, Anatol Stiller, Walter Faber and, in the last novel, Felix Enderlin —that is, 'die Schwierigen' who are suddenly brought face to face with the hollowness of everyday life, for whom the 'facts' lose their coherence without warning and who consequently suffer a severe degree of dislocation.[3] In the grey area between the two are to be found those characters like Yvonne and Hortense (*Die Schwierigen*), Rolf and Sibylle (*Stiller*) and Hanna Landsberg (*Homo Faber*) who have experienced a comparable sense of alienation from themselves and society but who have settled for an uninspiring, melancholy compromise.

With the exception of the first novel it cannot be said that Frisch depicts the outcome of his heroes' endeavours to locate a centric principle with any optimism. At best the issue is left open. After the straightforward account of the mature Jürg Reinhart's search for a more integrated existence and his failure to discover it in *Die Schwierigen*, Frisch turned to the examination of one individual's attempt to return to society as a 'new man'. Anatol Stiller is brought to realise that his 'angel' experience, which he felt and hoped would function as a dynamic centre around which he could build a new life, is not strong enough to withstand the pressures of a society which can offer nothing but rôle-playing as an alternative.[4] Not only does society in this way offer Stiller a false centricity, it also refuses to brook autonomous eccentricity within its own gravitational field. The effects of such societal intransigence on personality are illuminated by the case of Walter Faber. The danger of total conformity to current social 'normality' is that there exists no guarantee that society's opiates will remain permanently effective. The protagonist of *Homo Faber* is one individual for whom the narcotic effects of a false centricity wear off. The awareness of his life-long 'negative' mode of eccentricity, however, comes too late to give him much more than a tantalising glimpse of what true centricity might be—indeed, the novel is the record of Faber's struggle against precisely this awareness. Finally, with the fictions of his anonymous narrator in *Mein Name sei Gantenbein* Frisch has presented his most radical exposition to date of this fundamental theme. Marriage and the problem of human transience move to the forefront of an intensely private exploration of personal dislocation and inadequacy.

In this narrative world only the 'Schwierigen' come close to perceiving a centre to which they might relate their lives, but they fall victim to the pressures inherent in the very eccentricity which ensures that they are truly alive at all. For it is not possible, Frisch seems to be saying, to live an integrated life on the periphery. Neither love between man and woman nor any form of transcendental faith (posited only in *Stiller*) is shown as ultimately viable. The one is too difficult to sustain in the face of human rigidity and the hostile nature of time, the other depends, as the Christian theologian would put it, on Grace : that is, it cannot be commanded by the autonomous individual. The paradox is deep and bitter : only the 'positive' eccentric has any chance of achieving 'das wirkliche Leben', but the very condition of his eccentricity militates directly against such wholeness.

*   *   *

That Max Frisch should be attracted to the theme of eccentricity is readily understandable when one particular but important aspect of his Swiss intellectual background is considered. This aspect was both investigated and given a name by the Swiss scholar Karl Schmid in his book *Unbehagen im Kleinstaat* (1963). Schmid's study of five Swiss men of letters (C. F. Meyer, Henri-Frédéric Amiel, Jakob Schaffner, Jacob Burckhardt and Max Frisch) makes clear the existence and nature of a persistent malaise which runs contrary to what is generally—and in Switzerland almost exclusively—held to be the central Swiss literary tradition, exemplified by such writers as Albrecht von Haller, Jeremias Gotthelf, Gottfried Keller and Jean-Henri Pestalozzi. This malaise is shown to have three principal sources : the feeling of living on the periphery of historical developments; an unease at occupying an ill-defined position between the great nations and cultures of Germany, France and Italy; and thirdly, as a consequence, the lack of any opportunity to face and take influential decisions in the world. Thus the 'Kleinstaat' with its historical principle of neutrality is felt by these writers to have no central rôle to play, to be condemned to what Schmid calls 'Schicksalslosigkeit'.[5] The surrender of Jakob Schaffner to the temptations of the Third Reich can be seen as an example of the disorientation brought about by such a loss of social, political and human relevance. On the other hand, Frisch's work, despite or because of its pessimistic features, is testimony to the creative possibilities inherent in an eccentricity which is recognised, defined and explored in a positive way.

Another writer whom Schmid could equally have chosen for his argument, and one who deeply influenced the younger Frisch, is Albin Zollinger. Zollinger, indeed, has been called the 'key figure in contemporary Swiss German literature',[6] and it is he who expresses in his novels more than most this feeling of 'Unbehagen im Kleinstaat', particularly acute during the fateful years that saw the Depression, the Spanish Civil War and the rise and initial success of National Socialism. Zollinger's novels, which all appeared during this period, depict protagonists who are 'difficult' in Frisch's sense of the term, 'Sonderlinge' who stand out from their parochial and not infrequently hostile environment by virtue of their troubled scepticism and unwillingness or inability to accept their society's myths, conventions and norms. Most are thinly disguised self-portraits, uneasy primary school teachers like the would-be writer Wendel Bach (*Der halbe Mensch*, 1929), isolated or exiled painters, poets and sculptors like Urban von Tscharner (*Die große Unruhe*, 1937), Martin Byland and Martin Stapfer (*Pfannenstiel*, 1940, and its sequel *Bohnenblust*, 1941).[7] In varying degrees all these heroes suffer from a sense of dislocation and alienation from their fellow countrymen which is compounded by a radical self-doubt. All are highly critical of Swiss complacency and feel that their ideas and passions are greeted by their compatriots with a blank, uncomprehending silence—giving them the impression they are talking 'into cotton wool'.[8] the fear that unites them is summed up by the sculptor Martin Stapfer who is tormented by the vision of a 'toneless death in sterility', a parasitic, provincial existence on the 'periphery of history'.[9] It is not difficult to see in Zollinger's eccentrics prototypes for Frisch's own characters, but it must be said that nowhere does Zollinger achieve the subtlety, depth and unity of Frisch's narrative fiction. As Frisch himself put it in his belated obituary of the older writer : 'Albin Zollinger was in the situation of an emigrant who never emigrated ... Zollinger had no other hinterland but the country in which he lived, and it proved too small to be a productive environment in itself, a country which has lacked a history for too long to yield a true model of the world.'[10]

*   *   *

In a speech accepting the Büchner Prize in 1958 Frisch declared his own solidarity with all those literary figures, from Georg

Büchner himself to twentieth-century contemporaries, who are linked by 'das Emigrantische'. But this solidarity has its roots in a very different world from the one Zollinger left so abruptly in 1941 : 'The notion of emigration which unites us is not expressed in the fact that we neither can nor wish to speak for our mother countries, but that we feel our homes—whether we change them or not—to be merely temporary ones in the world of today.'[11] The physical and moral devastation of Hitler's War, the use of the atomic bomb and the permanent threat of an ultimate, all-embracing holocaust have underlined to a degree hardly imaginable by Zollinger and earlier writers, not only the savage consequences of human disintegration and lost centricity, but also the fact that the eccentric dilemma, the sense of personal and intellectual homelessness, is not simply a Swiss problem but a universal malaise. It is this which has enabled Frisch in his novels and dramas to attain the international relevance which was denied Albin Zollinger.

Ironically, the very marginality, 'Schicksalslosigkeit', which obsessed C. F. Meyer, Amiel and others, can be said to have contributed to Switzerland's defence against the encircling Axis powers during the Second World War. At the same time, although isolated and cut off from the great events in the outside world, a writer like Frisch found himself face to face with an extraordinary paradox : whilst the comprehensive nature of the mid-century upheaval left Switzerland the only corner of Europe unscathed, it made him simultaneously aware of the depths of his roots in the wider culture of Germany. The year 1945, it is true, did not represent for him 'das Jahr Null' in quite the same way as it did for many writers living in or returning to a shattered Germany. Neither was there the same need for Frisch to share in the linguistic 'Kahlschlag' which such writers as Weyrauch, Eich, Andersch and Hans Werner Richter felt was necessary to oppose the aesthetic pretensions of older writers and in particular to eradicate the poisonous undergrowth nurtured by Goebbels' Propaganda Ministry which had threatened to suffocate the German language itself.[12] Nevertheless, Frisch did feel a deep sense of personal involvement in the German catastrophe, an involvement which found immediate expression in his second play, *Nun singen sie wieder* (1945), and many pages of his *Tagebuch* 1946–1949 (1950)—despite the fact that he was not burdened directly with the guilt of a recent and appalling past. Furthermore, Frisch certainly *is* heir to a specific German language scepticism which arose at the beginning of the century—most urgently and interestingly in the peripheral capitals of Prague and Vienna—and which gained powerful impetus from the impact of National Socialist ideology upon the use of language. With Frisch it is not so much the feeling that certain words and phrases, distorted and manipulated by the Nazis, have become unusable, as that language in its literary form has in itself always possessed an element of intractable strangeness. For Max Frisch, as indeed for all Swiss Germans, there exists a basic tension between *Schriftdeutsch* and everyday speech.[13] In a sense, therefore, some aspects at least of that linguistic alienation felt by many of the immediate post-war generation of writers in Germany have long been familiar to Swiss German writers who have chosen not to write in their native dialect. And this fact may help to explain Frisch's own early fascination with the problematic nature of language.

It was, of course, a moment of intense irony for a Swiss German writer to look across the border from his self-conscious position as a 'Verschonter'[14] on the periphery of a rich and dominant literary tradition and to observe that tradition's apparent collapse. It is thus not surprising that Frisch's novels are among the first in the post-war period to raise such significant issues as the problem of identity and to explore the negative and positive tensions which exist in the search for centricity in a shifting, pluralistic world. Despite obvious differences, it is not difficult to see the close relationship of Frisch's eccentrics to such figures as Keetenheuve in Koeppen's *Das Treibhaus* (1953), Oskar Matzerath, Joachim Mahlke and Eddi Amsel in Grass's 'Danzig Trilogy' (1959–63), Hans Schnier in Böll's *Ansichten eines Clowns* (1963) or Leni, the heroine of *Gruppenbild mit Dame* (1971). These novels show, like those of Frisch, the disintegrating effects on human personality and relationships of a social reality which is essentially lacking in health and wholeness. Furthermore, in Frisch's mature fiction narrative continuity itself is disrupted in order to render this reality confusingly opaque and to prevent the reader from assembling simple social and biographical data into comfortable patterns in which to imprison his protagonists. It is this quality of opacity that offers points of contact with such novels as Uwe Johnson's *Mutmaßungen über Jakob* (1959) and *Das dritte Buch über Achim* (1961), Hildesheimer's *Tynset* (1965) or Peter Bichsel's *Die Jahreszeiten* (1967). These authors all reject or modify traditional narrative assumptions, share a common interest in abstaining from reassuring statements about external reality and leave their characters' personalities fluid and hypothetical. The novels of Max Frisch, written over a time-span of thirty years, form an impressive body of fiction in their own right; they can also be seen as central to the contemporary German language novel as it has developed since the end of the Second World War.

II

Jürg Reinhart

In a short autobiographical sketch inserted into his *Tagebuch 1946–1949* Frisch records the result of his first journey abroad and his subsequent experiences in Eastern Europe, Dalmatia and Constantinople as 'a first, all too youthful novel' (II 587). Circumstantial evidence points to the identity of this work: *Jürg Reinhart—eine sommerliche Schicksalsfahrt.* Despite Frisch's own oblique admission of the novel's immaturity, *Jürg Reinhart* is still of some interest in that it reveals many of the thematic preoccupations of the later novels. It is however true that little in the book anticipates the complexity of *Die Schwierigen*, the unique power of *Stiller* or the sensitive handling of character in *Homo Faber*. Nor is there more than the faintest hint of that quality of irony which transfigures all three later novels, but most subtly, perhaps, *Mein Name sei Gantenbein*. The novel, in fact, is a straightforward account—in the tradition of the *Bildungsroman*—of the central character's progress from a hesitant and self-conscious adolescence to the threshold of manhood via confrontation with love, suffering and death. The name Frisch gives to his eponymous hero immediately indicates the author's debt to Gottfried Keller whose *Der Grüne Heinrich* Frisch once called 'the best father anyone could have' (*Tagebuch 1946–1949*, II 587). Like Heinrich Lee before him, Jürg has left the narrow confines of his native Zürich to seek wider experience abroad. Although he too has a gift for painting, he is now a tyro writer earning his living as a composer of newspaper articles and short stories. To borrow a phrase Keller applied to his Grüne Heinrich, Jürg is 'a private and solitary individual'. Frisch calls him significantly 'dieser Sonderling' ('*this eccentric*'). It is precisely this quality of apartness, seen also in varying degrees in the other characters of the novel, that links the book most securely with the later narratives. It is a quality that affects not only the character's appraisal of himself, but also vitiates his relationships with others. An investigation of the thematic elements of the novel must therefore proceed from this dual perspective.

The setting provides a pertinent backcloth for the analysis of these relationships: a 'Fremdenhaus' aptly named *Hotel Solitudo* which is run by Frau von Woerlach and her daughter, Inge, impoverished remnants of the Prussian nobility and close cousins to Fontane's similarly placed Poggenpuhls family. It is a place where people come to unburden themselves, to seek momentary relief from their everyday worries. Its attraction is precisely its anonymity; a sense of freedom comes from the knowledge that they can leave before their true selves are discovered. 'For they liked the idea of being heard sympathetically without having to commit themselves, as if they were aware that they themselves were not capable of love' (I 272). Indeed, the capacity for love, the need to extend it and the problem of how to preserve it, can be seen as the basis of all Frisch's writing. Here the wilful obscurity of people's attitudes towards each other is contrasted with the purity and delicacy of the Adriatic spanned by an immensely clear blue sky, the description of which is placed as a *leitmotiv* at key moments in the novel.

Dr Svilos, of all the characters, is the only one native to this environment—and even he is a black sheep with a prison record for surgical negligence. The rest are strangers, displaced aristocrats or lost souls like the Baron and his younger wife who spend their lives in bored and aimless travel. The lack of a valid contact with their environment points to a similar failing in their personal relationships. A possible exception may be found in the friendship between Frau von Woerlach and Frau von Reisner, the guest whose selflessness and personal commitment contrast sharply with her son's unpleasantness. However, this friendship hardly rises in its treatment above the conventional and serves mainly to highlight the younger people's predicament, in particular Inge's loneliness and vain love for Jürg. And it is this latter relationship—the one that leads to the hero's apparent ultimate self-realisation—which forms the core of the novel. In its frustrations and convolutions it epitomises the dominant theme of the existential aloneness of human beings, their lack of a viable centric principle around which they can build their lives, which has occupied Frisch for over thirty years. It is true to say, however, that this state of affairs is only diagnosed with clarity in the later work; for *Jürg*

Reinhart is made to end on a note of optimism which is not unequivocally deducible from the novel's internal logic.

The novel is composed of three unequal sections : the development of the Jürg-Inge relationship, Jürg's further travels together with Inge's collapse and operation, and finally Jürg's return and Inge's death. The Jürg-Inge relationship is continued in the second section by the devices of a long letter written by Jürg to Inge (but not despatched) and an imaginary conversation he conducts with her—thus preventing a too obvious break in the unity of the novel.

Jürg is a twenty-year-old obsessed with the problem of virginity and its effect on his manhood. Women are attracted to him (witness the middle-aged Baronin's comic attempt to seduce him in the opening pages of the book), but Jürg recognises that maturity cannot be attained through lust. Indeed, the whole question of a full sexual relationship fills him with unease. What, he wonders, do women really *feel* when they are loved sexually—'Isn't it a nameless nausea?' (I 296). It is this haunting feeling that prevents him from gaining satisfaction from his love for Hilde, the Hotel maid. Ironically, when they go for a midnight sail, Jürg can find nothing to say (having said it all in his imagination!) and they sit in their boat 'as in a run-down marriage' with Jürg watching the symbolic passage of a sailing ship whose sails are 'full of possibility' (I 282). That this incident is not merely an adolescent contretemps but meant to possess deeper significance can be seen from the abyss image Frisch uses to describe Jürg's state of mind as he gazes at the sea : 'One needed to smash this watery surface, which stretched from infinity to infinity, and leap down—It was as if sitting above an unknown abyss like this was no longer tolerable (I 286). It is clear from his attitude to Hilde that sexual experience for Jürg is merely a symbol for a higher reality of human awareness, and that if indulged in purely on a sensual level it would prove constricting rather than liberating. In fact, he suffers from the traditional Romantic fear that reality once experienced will fall short of his imaginative vision. The dilemma is no less acute for being recognised. Jürg knows that his 'purity' is a barrier cutting him off from the world; he is at once suffocated by his lack of knowledge of life and paralysed by his own refusal to find out in ways that are dishonest. A vague feeling of having 'no talent for living' widens out into a hallucinatory fear 'as if everyone else was a member of a secret conspiracy which excluded him. Sometimes he really believed it. He could not bear this fear much longer, this feeling of being different, of standing on the periphery' (I 297). This 'stance on the periphery' is the dominant characteristic of Jürg's eccentric attitude, and the quotation comes as a climax to Part One where Jürg attempts to throw himself from the Hotel balcony and is thwarted by Inge. The incident is too improbable, both in its motivation and in the level of its literary expression to be convincing, but it serves to emphasise the unreality of Jürg's ideas, his literary approach to life. This dilettante exploitation rather than serious absorption of experience is clearly seen in a story of his Inge finds in a newspaper. Behind the mask of a fictive narrator, Karnickel, he likens himself to a 'slow-worm' which gropes in the future for happiness only to ignore its realisation in the woman at his side. Jürg himself does not draw the correct conclusion from his own irony : he leaves Ragusa and the woman who loves him, Inge.

Leaving Hotel Solitudo, however, does give Jürg the chance to achieve a more objective perspective. In particular, he realises that mere sexual experience will not of itself bring him the desired maturity. He now sees the latter as the result of undergoing some 'great and fundamental experience' or of performing some 'manly deed' in order to dispel the deep sense of inferiority which has clouded his relationships hitherto. His subsequent picaresque adventures on board ship and in the bazaars of Constantinople reveal another and equally important aspect of his character : his naiveté, and thus Jürg fits into a long line of 'holy fools' who pass through a wicked world protected only by their charm and innocence. Inge herself had noted the quality when she called him 'dieser helle und reine Tor' (I 293). The incident on board ship, where he is mistaken for a concert pianist merely by leaning against the grand piano and wearing—as an economy measure—his hair long, is an amusing side-comment on people's snobbish gullibility, and for a moment one sees the theme of image-making and the ironic humour which come to occupy a central place in Frisch's later work. Likewise Jürg's experiences in the hands of the bazaar traders underline his unworldliness and innate sexual modesty. He [himself] feels only too sharply his vulnerability and the threat posed by the outside world : 'If I am pushed around by mature men, passed from hand to hand, as it were, and everyone is able to fashion me to his own image, I will in the end crumble away' (I 303).

In the same letter—written but not sent to Inge—from which the last quotation is taken, Jürg vividly expresses his doubts that he will prove equal to the challenge of life—a challenge which is crystallised in his anxiety about impotence and the debilitating fear which makes him see woman and her sexual needs as a threat to his personality. Thus it is fear of failure that motivates Jürg's search for a central meaning to life and at the same time drives him (as it later will Walter Faber) to the mistaken belief that physical movement, with its illusion of progress, can bring him closer to the elusive centre. Ironically, Jürg's journey comes full circle when he returns to Inge's bedside as she lies dying of cancer. And it is here that he is faced with the 'manly deed' he has sought so long and so far away : Inge's suffering is unendurable and Jürg gives her a fatal dose of morphine. Tormented by doubt as to the justification of his deed, he finally has an extraordinary vision of Inge who urges him to accept what has happened and the responsibility for it : 'You will stand by your deed. You will not deny that you have at last found the way to act, and you will be proud that you have become a man' (I 382). Having won the mother's blessing, too, for what he has done, Jürg can leave Ragusa after his eventful summer full of a unique sense of happiness.

Such fulfilment, on the other hand, is denied Inge. Ten years older than Jürg, she represents the saddening effect of experience, and thus her character reflects none of the childlike innocence one sees in Jürg. She is, however, a proud woman and shares his desire to find a deeper meaning in life beyond the necessarily limited nature of her close relationship with her mother. But her energy is sapped by the psychological pressures exerted by family impoverish-ment, the loss of her fiancé and a loved younger brother in the First World War and her frequent illnesses, all of which she sees as a fatal combination indicating that 'her blood was exhausted and should not be passed on' (I 294). She is oppressed, like Jürg, by the suffocating dullness of everyday routine and looks back with a Goethean turn of phrase to her earlier carefree days in Rome, 'a life free of routine ... That's when one possessed that sense of dying and becoming' (I 255).[1] Here in Ragusa she has no roots, either in the land itself or in other people. Thus when she appears to Jürg in his imagination after her death, she regrets above all the missed opportunities, the eccentricity of her existence, 'without roots that I might have put down in life, which might have bound me to life, childless—' (I 379).

The irony of her life is most clearly seen in the fact that her relationship to Jürg has to remain on an oblique level. He never understands—until that last moment when he returns significantly like 'a sleep-walker'—the love that she offers him. And the episodes in which he comes closest to such an understanding are typically imagined : the long letter he writes to her and does not post, the soliloquy he addresses to her when alone painting at Delphi, and finally the vision of her he conjures up after her death. In fact, on only two occasions are they exposed to a common experience which might have led to mutual awareness : once when Inge prevents Jürg's suicide attempt only to succeed in filling him with shame at yet another 'failure', and secondly when they visit the Dominican Cathedral and Inge points out the painting of the Assumption of the Blessed Virgin. Inge is attracted to the picture because of its unusual earthly quality in contrast to the more ethereal nature of paintings with such a subject : 'Just look at the radiant and happy expression on her face as she gazes upwards. As if she already had knowledge of something she could no longer speak of. Don't you agree? But her mouth is so gentle and marvelling' (I 270). For Inge the painting does not belong in the Cathedral because of its 'fusion of temporal and spiritual'. 'It is a picture of human love.' But once again Jürg is deaf to Inge's meaning, and it is not until after her death when her mother remarks how the disease had spared her face and describes her mouth in identical terms as 'gentle and marvelling' that the full significance of the picture and the extent of Inge's love become apparent to him. The lack of communication between the two is further underlined by Frau von Reisner's well-intentioned removal of a few lines that Jürg had written in the Guest Book for Inge at her request and which the latter looks for in vain shortly before her fateful operation. Jürg had written that he understood those poets 'who carry a knowledge of death in their breast pocket like tomorrow's tram ticket' (I 310), poets with an acute sense of the transient beauty of life. Although the sentiment is unintentionally banal, it is left to death, as the crowning irony, to bring the two to an understanding of each other. Jürg breaks through to his 'manly deed' in killing the woman who loves him, thereby losing the 'purity' which appeared to be crippling his emotional development, and Inge accepts his deed as a gesture of love, a release from pain denied her by everyone else.

If Frau von Woerlach does not show the radical dislocation experienced by Inge and Jürg, this is because she makes less demands on life. Increasing age and the loss of the family fortune have combined to make her accept her fate with controlled resignation. Indeed, the latter calamity is felt paradoxically as a gain, an opportunity to humanise the materialistic tradition of her noble family. For despite a certain nostalgia she has come to perceive the fragile basis of the community of which she was once the centre, a community no longer held together principally by ideals but by a highly developed sense of property. Her proud aloofness as much as her commercial sense makes her warn her daughter against becoming personally involved in the fates of their temporary guests. Experience has taught her to save her energy for the limited security of a warm mother-daughter relationship. If one gets involved with people 'outside', they have only pain to offer. This self-imposed limitation indicates a determined attempt to defend her private sphere against the intrusions of the world. And yet, despite this entrenched attitude towards other people, Frau von Woerlach clings to the concept of individual worth, to the idea of the innate meaningfulness of each individual's life irrespective of any apparent absurdity in the surrounding world. This deeply held conviction is nevertheless shaken by the failure of her daughter's operation and the prolonged suffering the latter has subsequently to endure. The imminent collapse of the centre of her world threatens the very meaning which she explicitly believed life to possess. This ordeal becomes for her the touchstone of her love for Inge : her daughter must be released from her intolerable suffering in order to prove the quality of that love. The meaning of so much pain must lie in the opportunity it presents to demonstrate love by performing an action which is normally profoundly repugnant. For natural, primitive reasons the mother cannot face this deed herself, and everyone else fails her—until Jürg returns from Greece. It is his serenity of mind, attained only through his vision of Inge after her death, that fully restores Frau von Woerlach to her accustomed poise and certainty. She is left at the end of the novel a sombre, lonely figure but with her capacity to hold the tensions of a basically eccentric attitude restored. She accepts the harsh dictates of necessity but remains well aware of the more organic mode of existence which obtained in the past. This is most vividly expressed when Inge's funeral recalls memories of the family tradition on their former estate where all the peasantry took part in her father's obsequies : 'That's how it was at my father's death. No one was a stranger. And they placed him in the ground which had nourished him and them and their families for centuries' (I 363). The nostalgia for roots, for centricity, is clear enough—as it was in her daughter—but Frau von Woerlach is too realistic, and perhaps too fatalistic, a woman to question the disintegration of that society. She accepts her diminished rôle in the world and the fact that the future belongs (so the novel would argue) to Jürg, and in doing so she reveals the wisdom of a sensitively interpreted experience.

Frau Reisner, too, maintains her apartness despite her friendship with her hostess and the Christian charity that leads her to pay secretly for Inge's medical care and operation. As with Frau von Woerlach, widowhood has taught her the meaning of solitude and she is critical of young men like her son, Robert, who think they are men because of their temporary success with young girls, but who are really cowards afraid of loneliness. Yet Frau Reisner remains a shadowy figure in the novel. Though she is a passing, if regular, guest at the *Hotel Solitudo*, her love for Inge is real enough, as is its frustration when she is forced to wait helplessly for Inge's operation to take place. But her characterisation rarely rises above the conventional : the idea of the rôle she has to play is more convincing than its expression. Her son Robert, on the other hand, is intentionally presented as an insubstantial character. His function is to underline by his 'masculinity' and rapid seduction of Hilde the honesty and genuine hesitancy of Jürg. The latter, though tormented by his virginity, is not in the least interested in escaping his problem via mere self-gratification. Such a course would have destroyed the very validity of personal relationships he is intent on discovering. And indeed this is precisely what is illustrated in Robert's self-centredness and lack of scruple. He cannot give love because he is himself emotionally impoverished.

The two doctors, the Slav Svilos and the Austrian Heller, are similarly drawn with their human weaknesses highlighted. To an extent Svilo's mercenary concern for his medical fees is offset by his heroic effort to save Inge during the four and a half hour operation, which causes the foreigner Heller to meditate on the native temperament with its 'healthier, more organic, less reflective' attitude to life. This hint that Svilos might be more integrated than any other character remains however a peripheral comment, as Frisch gives the reader no further insight into Ragusan society. As for Heller himself—as much an outsider as the inhabitants of *Hotel Solitudo*—he is brought to an unpleasant self-discovery : his solicitude for Inge, his fussing about her comfort after what he knows to have been an unsuccessful operation (which he defends to himself as professional *caritas*), hides the real motive : 'He had pretended to himself that this was love, this cowardly, vain egoism that made him dally with the last days of a woman' (I 339). Thus even a minor character contributes his share to the problem of communication, the depiction of the imbalance btween love and egocentricity.

Nevertheless, it has to be admitted that the novel is ultimately unsatisfactory. Despite its many interesting touches, and particularly the successful portrait of Frau von Woerlach, there are evident, undigested borrowings from older writers such as Goethe, Keller, Fontane and Thomas Mann. But above all the solution of Jürg Reinhart's central problem is too facile and comes with too flimsy a preparation to be entirely credible. It posits an optimism that does not spring logically and clearly from the novel's structure. It can be seen, too, that the devices in Part Two which are meant to keep the Jürg-Inge relationship alive—whilst helping to show the development of Jürg's personality—are in fact arbitrary and unreal. For it is the reader, not Jürg, who witnesses the full extent of Inge's suffering which is meant to be a maturing process for Jürg. His arrival—especially as Frisch tries to convey a sense of inner certainty through the old image of sleep-walking—is thus given an unfortunate aura of melodrama. Occasionally the quality of the writing adds to the reader's unease : far too often it is strained and prone to purple passages which come close to bathos.[2] Nor are some of the ideas free from banality, and the central preoccupation of Part One, Jürg's obsessive sexual modesty and his tendency to emotionalism, strike today's reader as faintly comic. There is an element of shock in the euthanasia theme—no doubt even stronger in the 1930s—but its final link with Jürg's maturation must be declared tenuous. The novel is at its strongest in the straightforward depiction of relationships, but a weakness for melodrama and the 'important statement' betrays the youthfulness of the author.

Despite such criticisms, however, it is fascinating to see the tentative exploration of themes which, in a more intricate form, are to become the unmistakable hallmark of Frisch's mature fiction: the eccentricity of his characters' stance, their sense of personal dislocation, the fundamentally centric nature of the man/woman nexus and the early beginnings of the 'graven image' theme, seen in Jürg's struggle with his sense of what he is and what he thinks others see him as. They undergo a further intensification in Frisch's second novel, *Die Schwierigen*, in which we meet an older Jürg Reinhart in a wider and more complex context.

III

Die Schwierigen

I INTRODUCTION

Frisch was clearly disappointed at the lukewarm reception accorded to his first novel,[1] and this may have accounted for the delay of almost a decade before the appearance of his second, *J'adore ce qui me brûle oder Die Schwierigen* in 1943.[2] The first edition had as its opening section a chapter entitled 'Reinhart/oder die Jugend' which in fact was a version of the earlier novel, condensed to a third of the original text. Frisch is on record as stating that this opening section was provided—against his own inclination—at the behest of his publisher and after the novel had been completed.[3] It is not surprising, therefore, that when he decided to reissue the novel in 1957 with the reversed title, *Die Schwierigen oder j'adore ce qui me brûle*, Frisch should obey his earlier instinct and suppress the first section which he had always regarded with some reserve. It is thus justifiable to take the 1957 text as the basis for this chapter.

The reversal of the title, though an obvious and simple device to distinguish the two editions, can be seen to have a further significance : by taking the emphasis away from the idiosyncratic gallicism and placing it more squarely on 'Die Schwierigen', Frisch indicates where the real tensions of the novel lie. His main characters have difficulty in fitting into society, in finding suitable rôles with which they can identify. And as society is made up of a complex system of personal relationships, checks and balances, it is the problem of such relationships that is in the forefront. In this novel—in contrast to *Jürg Reinhart*—these are seen more clearly, and therefore more convincingly, in their *social* context.

The greater complexity of this work enables us to isolate and contrast a number of essential themes, the discussion of which can best illustrate the problematic nature of Frisch's characters and the critique of society which it implies. These themes can be subsumed under three main headings : (a) the problem of marriage, (b) the problem of the Artist in Society, and (c) the search for 'das wirkliche Leben'. However, these problems are not mutually exclusive but all three closely interwoven. For marriage, perhaps more than any other institution, is the one which most tightly links men and women to the social system, and if the artist is aware of his relationship to society as a problematic one—and it is argued here that *all* Frisch's protagonists can be seen as eccentric figures in their society—then the question of marriage is likely to be a central preoccupation. It naturally follows that the concept of 'das wirkliche Leben' in this novel can only be explored in relation to these two central areas.

2 Marriage : the radical dilemma

The central relationships in the novel—leaving aside for the moment the imposing figure of the Oberst—consist of three marriages in the conventional sense of the word (Yvonne/Hinkelmann, Yvonne/Hauswirt, Hortense/Ammann) and one (Yvonne/Reinhart) which is a marriage in essence. In addition there is the Reinhart/Hortense relationship which founders principally on the question of marriage. These must be looked at in turn to establish the full complexity of Frisch's presentation.

Yvonne/Hinkelmann

In many ways it is Yvonne—and not as one might expect, Jürg Reinhart, the leading figure—who has the deepest experience of what marriage can be. She moves from an utterly dead relationship with Hinkelmann via a brief but intense passion with Reinhart to the limited security of a dull, routine union with Hauswirt. It is a journey whose emotional cost can only be met by a conscious sacrifice of some of that vital spontaneity which made her set out in the first place. She is an unusual person. Characterised from the beginning as an ugly duckling—her mother, a beauty herself, had no compunction in sorrowfully telling her daughter from an early age how unattractive she was—she was made well aware of her status as an unwanted child. Her background and its values are neatly sketched in the opening paragraph of the novel, where the ironic tone gives an immediate indication of Frisch's critical stance. In this smalltown society marriage is seen as an expedient means to a blatantly economic end : the production of factory chimneys rather than love or children. Yvonne's father—the epitome of the

resourceful entrepreneur—did not hesitate to remove his family to
Greece in response to economic pressures, and it is in that country
that we first meet Yvonne—a young girl without roots, her very
existence undermined by her upbringing, her disproportionate
forehead symbolising her oddness and feeling of insecurity. Within
the restricted circle of *émigrés* that (for her) form 'society', Yvonne
stands out by virtue of a quality of nervous energy. It is a world
characterised by narrow inward-lookingness. In fact, these Swiss
expatriates invite French and German inhabitants of the town into
their circle only as 'leavening'—there is no mention of Greeks.

The man Yvonne marries, on the other hand, she sees in contrast
to herself as 'so much taller, so much healthier, so much stronger
. . . a fair-haired rock of a man, whose confident and naïve assur-
ance almost crushed her' (I 397). This assessment of her husband
—and it is fair to say that it is one shared by all who know him—
proves disastrously mistaken, her feeling of oppression only too
premonitory. Despite her unique qualities of sensitivity and awareness, however, it is clear that Yvonne enters this first marriage very
much in the tradition of her family—Hinkelmann is a successful
scholar, like herself, 'of good family background'—love plays no
rôle in her decision. The warning signals are present from the
beginning : Hinkelmann is so incapable of attuning himself to
others' feelings that he can experience his first meeting with
Yvonne as 'an unforgettable evening' whilst she registered it as
merely 'boring'. It is ironic that such a gifted archaeologist should
be dead to his immediate personal surroundings, a dangerous one-
sidedness which is revealed whenever he discusses his work with
enthusiasm; his descriptions never contain people, whether they
be his archaeological colleagues or local peasants. The result is
that despite his descriptive powers Yvonne sees before her not the
splendours of classical antiquity but 'a lunar landscape, airless, not
a fish or a bird, not a shepherd or a single living goat' (I 395). In
this way the contrast between the two is highlighted : Yvonne is
'a woman permanently endangered' (I 391), whilst Hinkelmann,
nine years older and apparently secure in the respect accorded to
him as an up-and-coming scholar, possesses 'a sort of unshakeable
self-confidence, a fearless trust that nothing in the world could go
wrong for him (I 394). What life there is in this marriage is therefore
associated with 'danger'[4] but basically it is shown as empty and conventional. Indeed both partners lack any centric principle that could
give their relationship meaning. Hinkelmann flees the implications
of a deep personal union because of a fundamental immaturity,

and Yvonne drifts through life aware of its rootlessness but lacking any external impetus for changing its pattern.

Two events, however, combine to give her the necessary energy to break out of a deadening routine : she discovers she is pregnant and she meets Jürg Reinhart. The fact of pregnancy forces her to reassess the nature of her relationship with Hinkelmann. Since her marriage she has tacitly accepted 'the rôle of a missing mother' (I 401), but suddenly she is struck by the quasi-incestuous contact she has with her husband : 'One cannot have a child by one's son' (I 402). Their marriage, she realises, was based not on a mutual tension of personality in which both partners could accept each other's being, but on pity for Hinkelmann which she had managed to disguise from herself by thinking of herself purely in the terms set by her own parents. Her marriage has been based on a lie. During the painful days that follow Yvonne's decision to leave him, a terrible truth dawns on Hinkelmann : his marriage has reached a state—perhaps it had been like it from the beginning— where it has ceased to have any spontaneous life at all; everything repeats itself, conversations, silences, arguments. And it is precisely the stifling quality of 'Wiederholung' 'repetition' which is the ultimate threat to human relationships, a theme that comes to assume a central significance in Frisch's work.

As it transpires, Yvonne correctly judges the rigidity of Hinkelmann's character, its essential lack of mobility and response to points outside itself. His 'health' and rock-like appearance are illusory : he is ego-centric in the fullest sense of the term, and he falls victim to the fact that no one has the ultimate strength to hold a world together around a self-dominated core. Since life can only have meaning by reference to others, the disintegration of the periphery will automatically lead to the destruction of the core: there opens up before Hinkelmann 'an abyss, horror in face of another, darker existence' (I 411), an existence which has been invaded by the frightening forces of the unpredictable. It is true that he vaguely realises that he would have to pass through a hitherto unimaginable degree of loneliness to regain human contact, but the insight comes too late and persists too briefly to defeat his upbringing and counter the crippling sense of the correct demeanour to be expected from a scholar and minister's son. His death is typical of his life : he simply disappears 'as if he had never been' (I 416). Hinkelmann's guilt lies in his rigidity, his inability to appreciate and foster the unpredictable as a safeguard against the deadening weight of habit. Much as Walter Faber is later to do, he uses habit as a defence mechanism against the dangers inherent in genuine living; but disastrously this also involves the thrusting of a petrifying image on those around him, a systematic stultifying of life's possibilities. It is precisely the latter that Jürg Reinhart represents, and it is no coincidence that he appears on the scene at a crisis point in Yvonne's life.

From the outset Reinhart is seen as a 'Sonderling', an ill-defined threat to the orderliness and circumscribed patterns of life which the Swiss business community has evolved for itself in Athens. He not only ignores their conventions, but he is the first person to look at Yvonne as an individual in her own right. He is also the first to ask her what she really is—and the effect is startling : the simple question is enough to banish momentarily the whole, unreal world in which she lives. Reinhart brings her face to face with the problem that gnaws away at her mind : the knowledge of lost opportunities and the relentless destructive power of time : 'She smoked a cigarette and in the moment of time it took to tap off the ash, she aged a whole number of years (I 392).[5] It is this confrontation—together with the awareness that her pregnancy must inevitably destroy the basis of her relationship with Hinkelmann—that gives her the strength to break out of a false world. Frisch records this in a sharp and apposite image : Yvonne is aboard the ship taking her away from Athens when she faints and is helped to a seat by Reinhart who appears on the same ship; her limp figure is described as 'a little ridiculous like a puppet with its strings severed' (I 408).[6] The threads of her old existence gave her 'life' only in the sense that a wooden puppet has 'life'. Yvonne has now to discover and harness energy from within herself in order to live in the world. Her reaction to Reinhart, who at this point can be seen as a symbol of a life full of possibilities, unpredictable, free and exciting, is one therefore of understandable fear, but coupled with a vision of rejuvenation, the possibility of a new start beyond that 'restriktive Ordnung' represented by Hinkelmann.

Yvonne/Reinhart

The decision to leave Hinkelmann and return to Switzerland, however, does not mean an immediate entry into a fuller, more authentic existence. Indeed, for some years Yvonne lives in a sort of limbo. Frisch describes the old house in which she has a flat as possessing 'an atmosphere of neglect reminiscent of Sleeping Beauty's castle' and contrasts it sharply with the 'neatness and clarity' (I 417) that characterises the flat itself. Yvonne is thus shown in an ironic relationship to her environment. Indeed it is as much this sense of dislocation as her series of unsatisfactory personal attachments that underlines her own awareness of being an impostor when all her visitors admire her self-sufficiency and apparent independence. The irony is acute, for they look upon her as 'a secure axis in all the confusion' (I 427); they use her for their temporary needs, look upon her as a 'guardian angel', totally unaware of their self-centredness and the fact that Yvonne herself is suffering, is lost and bewildered, needs *them* behind her careful façade of polished hospitality.

Typical of the false relationships in which she finds herself is that with the lawyer[7], a married man with two strapping sons, who fulfils a deep need to enliven the dull regularity of a respectable bourgeois life with illicit adventures of a harmless sort. That the man himself is corrupted by this mental masturbation is made clear enough : he rationalises his own impotence by convincing himself that Yvonne is a repressed lesbian. Two episodes, however, point to the fact that Yvonne *herself* is avoiding commitment, deliberately closing herself to experience : her friendship with the young doctor and more significantly with her violin pupil, Merline. The former is presented as a genuine friend, but a man who cannot take the initiative, who will not force the issue. Thus the friendship lasts for several years but develops no further than the 'Du'. The relationship takes on the sexless unreality of a fairy tale. And the demand Yvonne makes on him is similarly significant : 'the present without a future' (I 421). It is the same fear she expressed on meeting Reinhart on board the ship taking her away from her dead past. The future is the unknown, the realm of total possibility and she has not the courage to accept its uncertainties. On the only occasion the doctor instinctively moves to kiss her, she reacts with a spasm of fear, and the moment—the possibility of emotional commitment—is past before the doctor is ever really aware of what has frightened her. One has to remember that this is not the coyness of a young girl, but the response of a mature woman.

The relationship with Merline, on the other hand, is considerably more ambivalent. As with Hinkelmann, Yvonne finds herself involved in a maternal game as the young girl responds to a warmth that she does not receive from her own mother. From the outset Yvonne is clearly aware of the falsity of this situation, and yet Merline fills a gap in Yvonne's life. She sees in her an image of her own unloved self. Sexual ambivalence gives the tone to this quasi-narcissistic relationship. For Merline, the friendship with Yvonne is an adequate mother substitute whilst she sorts out her feelings for her boy-friend, Keller, but for Yvonne it is decidedly more. At the same time, the irony of the situation, of which she is only too well aware, undermines her; she feels herself more and more cut off from life, a victim of the creeping paralysis of boredom. The emptiness at the centre of her life, the lack of an integrating principle, expands into an experience of radical dislocation :

Im Badezimmer erschrickt sie vor der Spiegelung in den Plättchen, so fremd ist ihr der eigene Leib, als dorre er ab, ohne Lebensfreude mehr, ohne Wurzel in irgendeiner nährenden Hoffnung ... (I 430)

In the bathroom she steps back in horror before her reflection in the tiles, so alien has her own body become to her, as if it were withering away, with no pleasure in life, without roots in some nourishing hope ...

The child she has aborted could have given her that sense of relatedness she needs, might have injected meaning into a hollow existence, but it is now too late : the possibility has become a spectre to haunt her whenever she sees a mother with her child, a growing accusation levelled at her own inadequacies.

It is significant that Merline's engagement, which effectively concludes this episode in Yvonne's life, is announced at a moment of obvious eroticism : the girl blurts out her news whilst the older woman is rubbing her down after a bath. Once again Yvonne is brought to realise that human relationships cannot be played at but must, to bear life, demand total commitment. Her love for Merline, though genuine in itself, is in fact a half-hearted attempt to escape the responsibilities of an adult relationship. The reappearance of Reinhart at this junction thus represents a definitive challenge.

The relationship with Reinhart—it is specifically called on two occasions a 'marriage'—begins in March and is over in the autumn. It thus covers, perhaps rather obviously, a natural time-span of birth, growth and decay. And just as all organic life contains within itself the seeds of its own destruction, the nascent love between the two is characterised on the one hand for Yvonne by a secret feeling of fear at the revival of a hope long since buried, but more significantly on Reinhart's side by a penchant for uncertainty, by a dream-like attitude towards reality. It is this insouciance, this inability to *listen* to the other's fears, that ultimately helps to destroy their life together.

However, Yvonne is in too vulnerable a position to heed such warning signs. Reinhart represents for her the last chance to find a meaning in life outside herself, and she willingly surrenders to his enthusiasm and ideas. Indeed it is Reinhart's youth, with its attractive mixture of romantic melancholy and vigorous optimism, that underlines for her the failures of her past life, its pointlessness and waste. Despite her concomitant fear of experience Yvonne responds instinctively to Reinhart's views when he talks of the destructive nature of time as a 'slow gentle terror' and defines the poles of his life as a painter as 'work and atonement'. Work teaches him to be happy in solitary independence and grants him a freedom of spirit which alone can enable him to avoid the pettiness of routine ties, whereas repentance is the inevitable result of the sudden attacks of melancholia brought on by too much conscious straining after deep personal relationships, which can in fact restrict the other's freedom and individuality. Once a man sees that life is not what it appears on the surface to be, that there is no framework on which to hang his life other than that which he creates for himself, there is no going back, 'no forgetting behind false consolations' (I 435). Reinhart is very close to that existentialist self-awareness, characterised by moral anguish, which opposes the state of passivity, where life is unreflective and vitiated by the temptations of bad faith. To live authentically we must welcome 'das Ewig-Unsichere, das unser Leben in der Schwebe hält wie eine glühende Kugel' (I 435; *'that everlasting uncertainty which holds our lives in the balance like a glowing sphere'*). It was precisely 'das Ewig-Unsichere' that Yvonne chose when she left Hinkelmann and turned her back on a life of mere appearances. The courage of that decision is now to be tested again. Their growing intimacy is signalled by important changes in their private lives : Reinhart leaves his mother's house and begins to live in his studio; Yvonne gives up her job when her importunate employer, Hauswirt, proposes marriage. At the same time their happiness is gradually undermined for the reader by subtle pointers : for example, the scythe heard but not yet seen as it threatens the tall grass of the meadow in which lovers could hide (I 445); Yvonne's pleasure at Reinhart buying his paints—'smiling like a mother at her son'— the full import of which can only be appreciated when the reader recalls her relationship with Hinkelmann and the rôle of the Child symbol in Yvonne's life; Reinhart's impulsive attempt to impress

Yvonne with a display of worldliness when offering Hortense drawing lessons; and—perhaps most important of all—his strange inability to respond to Yvonne's need of sympathy when she finally screws up enough courage to tell him of her past.

The ambivalence of Reinhart's attitude is thus no surprise. In the midst of his happiness with Yvonne he still subordinates their love to his work and sees their evenings together as an almost irresistible temptation to waste valuable working time. His *mauvaise foi*, however, is not one-sided: Yvonne, too, is guilty of it—but this is not revealed until an event that she has secretly dreaded for years finally occurs: the exhaustion of her parental inheritance. With the radical change in the economic basis of her life comes an equally fundamental change in her attitude to her 'marriage' with Reinhart. Or rather the real motivation for her actions comes to the surface.

The crisis comes at the beginning of their autumn holiday in the Ticino over the question of accepting Hauswirt's offer of 300 francs. Characteristically, Reinhart proposes to take the money, seeming to be only vaguely aware that Yvonne looks on it as a test of whether Reinhart will shoulder the responsibility of providing for her. The breakdown of communication is mutual: Yvonne cannot understand why he does not perceive her sense of shame and deep-seated anxiety, whilst Reinhart cannot grasp her sudden obsession with bourgeois appearances and financial security. But it is Yvonne who is principally affected by the gossiping villagers and the priest who considers it his duty to warn his flock against 'certain people', and it is she who is deeply wounded by the indignity of the crazy cart-ride through the village which ends, predictably, with them both flat on their backs in the village square. Moreover, Reinhart betrays a marked insensitivity and selfishness which is pinpointed by the incident with the cart. He had found it in order to fetch Yvonne's trunk from the station, but it is made quite clear that what is passed off as help for Yvonne is in reality a way of filling up his own time which hangs heavy on his hands. The growing falsity of their relationship is thus matched by Reinhart's own increasing doubt of his capacity as an artist. In this way both approach the crisis of their lives simultaneously—Reinhart as a painter, Yvonne as a woman. Frisch delineates the situation brilliantly: Yvonne sits as a model for Reinhart, and as he paints, fascinated by the problems of creating a 'Bildnis' of his wife, she admits to herself her true motivation: 'She could have lived by his side forever, Yvonne thought silently, happily dreaming the time away, if he hadn't woken in her the desire for a child, irrevocable and urgent, aware as she was of her age' (I 466 f.). The fear of the passage of time is linked to the fear 'that she had missed out on what all the others had, what all the others described as the highest of life's possessions'. Thus her emotions are coloured both by envy of others and the pressures of society; the child has become an obsession that in the end transcends even her love for Reinhart.

In this situation Reinhart could only be cast in the rôle of 'protector' and provider of economic security. In her unhappiness Yvonne falls into the cardinal error of making a graven image of what a husband should be. And as Reinhart shows no inclination to fill this rôle, she leaves him with the identical abruptness with which she abandoned Hinkelmann. Indeed, she uses the same cold, firm words to both men, when, baffled, they come to her : 'Explanations can make no difference' (I 471, and see 402). It is significant that both men operate largely on a linguistic or intellectual plane which is, in a sense, the mark of their inadequacy, their deep-rooted egoism, whereas Yvonne works on a much deeper intuitive level where mood, feelings and atmosphere are the guidelines. Thus Reinhart can perceive that something is wrong—he is, of course, a much more sensitive individual than Hinkelmann—but he is unable to penetrate the surface calm, 'die tödliche Maske der Ruhe' (I 469), and reach the real woman beneath. That he is aware that Yvonne *is* wearing a mask is an insight which comes too late to save the marriage : he fails to see the letter accepting Hauswirt's money as Yvonne's secret test and posts it.

When he next sees her after a desperate and vain search of the village and environs—when once her mind is made up, Yvonne demonstrates a streak of ruthlessness in her abrupt and unexplained departure from the Ticino—it is in Zürich and he finds 'Yvonne the lady, upright and neatly combed, without a wrinkle in her face, lips lightly touched with red, Yvonne the lady granting a short interview' (I 471). She has fled back to the rôle she knows best. The mask is in place, the puppet's strings renewed. Ironically, Yvonne's experience has come full circle : she has decided to marry Hauswirt for economic security. She thus returns to the life she knew with her family and with Hinkelmann. Furthermore, the incest motif, noted in her marriage with Hinkelmann, is again hinted at : in a dream she sees her father and Hauswirt as men out of an identical mould. It is a fundamental defeat as Frisch makes plain in the final words of Chapter Two : 'She trod the very path she would never forgive her mother for having trodden : she married the man who could give her security and feel proud to be able to offer her everything a sober person could desire' (I 480). Like her mother, and indeed like her friend Merline, she chooses the bourgeois values of money and property, where happiness is defined solely by economic factors. Such security is not of itself to be scorned, but it is here clearly linked to a refusal of the greater risks—'das Ewig-Unsichere'—inherent in trying to live an authentic life. Ultimately, Yvonne loses faith in Reinhart because he will not respond to her conventional demands, her conventional view of what mariage should be. Faced with his inadequacies, and unable to control her own, she flees from her problems into a past she has already once condemned. This decision must be put down to a failure of nerve, a failure to hold within herself the tensions produced on the one hand by society and its normative expectations, and on the other by her need to find full expression for her personality.

Although in the last analysis Yvonne is alone responsible for what she makes of her life, Reinhart cannot be absolved from his share in the failure of their marriage. From the very beginning he demonstrated a lack of commitment. He was not prepared—any more than Yvonne was—to take the risk of total involvement. To that extent he is guilty of holding to principles in theory without recognising (or accepting) their practical consequences. Thus he recovers from his loss relatively quickly, and produces in the conversation with his client, Ammann, also recently jilted, a string of plausible rationalisations, for example : 'Every woman who is not oppressed by her lover in the end suffers from the fear of her own superiority—the fear that her lover is not a real man' (I 478). This is the reason why Princess Turandot executed her would-be lovers —out of sheer disappointment at their lack of virility and defiance —and explains the sub-title of the chapter : 'Turandot oder das Heimweh nach der Gewalt'.

However, although Reinhart is rationalising his own failure (and that of Ammann too), his remarks are relevant beyond their ironic framework in relation to Yvonne. She does seem to express the need for a masterful protector who is successful and 'conspicuously male', and this is clearly associated with her fear of freedom. As Reinhart puts it, in words quite familiar to contemporary ears :

Befreiung der Frau, es war ein Männergedanke. Am Ende zeigt es sich als die größte Vergewaltigung der Frau, die einzige, die

sie wirklich verletzte, weil man sie mit Zielen krönte, die nicht
ihre waren, nicht ihre sind : man tat ihr die Gewalt an, sie von
der Gewalt zu befreien, die ihre natürliche Sehnsucht ist—und
die Ehen gingen in Massen zugrunde . . . (I 479)

*Women's liberation was a male idea. In the end it can be shown
to be the greatest violation of woman, the only violation to really
injure her because she has been given a crown of achievements
which were not and are not her own: to free her from violence,
which is her natural desire, she had to be violated—and
marriages broke up in their thousands.*

He notes with some perception the outcome of this liberation of
woman : fear of their new state, fear of being alone and unprotected
and 'a longing for violence which is her deepest fulfilment and
secret victory' (I 480). Nevertheless, Reinhart is aware that his
theorising with its pretentious and vague Freudian undertones,
whilst containing an element of truth, is also a dubious attempt to
cast himself in a more nobly sensitive rôle than he actually played.
He breaks off suddenly, non-plussed, in mid-tirade. He is honest
enough to realise that such generalisations cannot be sustained
from his limited experience, that in a word they are *literary*. Thus
unlike Yvonne, he does not retreat, but attempts to learn from defeat.
He recognises that personal relationships can only take on a central
and integrating influence in proportion to the degree of self-
commitment. With Hortense he tries to act for the first time
according to this insight. Before this second major relationship is
examined, however, Yvonne's final essay in marriage must be
discussed.

Yvonne/Hauswirt

By the amount of attention he devotes to them Frisch makes
clear which of Yvonne's relationships is the most important. However, the conciseness with which he treats the Yvonne/Hauswirt
marriage does both it and the novel a disservice. The lack of
definition at this point contributes an air of unreality to the situation which is further compounded by the weakness of the
characterisation of Hauswirt himself. Whereas Yvonne is seen as a
major and in some ways the most interesting figure in the novel,
and one whose physical presence and human foibles are skilfully
realised, Hauswirt is presented initially as a caricature of the
hard-headed, money-conscious businessman, complete with a
working-class employee for a mistress. His offer to pay for Yvonne's

holiday in the Ticino is shown, not as an example of disinterested generosity towards a former secretary, but as a crude attempt to purchase her affections. (Hence Yvonne's deliberate use of her letter of acceptance as a symbolic test of Reinhart's love.) Unsurprisingly, therefore, when Yvonne does finally respond to Hauswirt's overtures, he behaves in a stereotyped fashion, enquiring after the rent when invited for tea and discussing the need of woman for man in terms of the market place. Indeed the man/woman nexus appeals to him precisely by virtue of its perfect economic balance : 'It's not everywhere, he opined, that one finds this refreshing balance between supply and demand' (I 473).

It is all the more astonishing in view of such remarks that Hauswirt should later discover more human traits within himself, presumably due to the influence of his marriage. Thus at the crisis of his life, when he discovers that Yvonne has used, and is using, him as the secure financial basis for her life and that of her son, who is not even his, he nevertheless decides to stand by her and accept the situation and his own diminished rôle. Such a rapid reversal would have been difficult enough to delineate in full focus; as it is Frisch fails to bring the character alive—even his physical attributes are left shadowy and conventional. Yet in one sense, the vagueness of Hauswirt's characterisation might have been justified : as a reflection of the *unreality* of his relationship with Yvonne. Unfortunately, by keeping predominantly to an ostensibly objective third person narrative technique instead of permitting the reader to see Hauswirt only through Yvonne's eyes, Frisch has confused the nature of the compromise she arrives at. As the text stands there is a puzzling ambiguity at the heart of the evaluation of this marriage. For Yvonne the position is clear : she has the financial security she craves—a luxurious home with lift, maid, garden and view over the lake—and she enjoys them for what they are without self-deception. Indeed, she is very well aware that she is not integrated into her environment, 'that she does not belong in this place' (I 550). She cultivates her garden with a Voltairean sense of irony. Like Candide, she has cut her losses and settled for what she takes to be possible with its very real limitations. That this is no idyllic solution, with wisdom and serenity as rewards for a life of struggle, is as true for her as it is for Voltaire's hero. The wheel has turned full circle : just as Reinhart was responsible for awakening her originally to a new life, so he is the indirect cause of her retreat from it. The paradox repeats itself : people seek her out as they did when she lived alone, to confide in

her and ask her advice, deceived by her aura of stability. She plays
the rôle demanded of her with a skilful exhibition of *sang-froid*
whilst inwardly retaining her independence of thought :

> Es ist zum Kotzen, denkt Yvonne, und die Leute fühlen sich
> verstanden, bringen Blumen, sind erlöst, sind dankbar, Gott
> weiß warum, sie sind so glücklich über ihr eigenes Dankbarsein.
> (I 550 f.)

> *It makes you sick, thought Yvonne. People feel themselves
> understood, bring flowers, feel released, are grateful. Heaven
> knows why, they are so happy over their own gratitude.*

Yet the very vehemence of the expression 'zum Kotzen' gives some
indication of the strain to which this duplicity exposes her. (We
see here, indeed, one of the first indications in Frisch's fiction of
self-conscious rôle-playing as a possible way of coming to terms
ironically with the pressures of life in society. The complexities of
the irony inherent in such an obviously eccentric stance will form
the core of the later novels.)

If at the end of the novel Yvonne does seem to attain a level
of serenity, it is at the cost of withdrawing totally from normal
areas of human affection and experience. With the substitution of
'respect' for 'love', her view of marriage is reduced to a quasi-
mechanistic life-process with herself and her biological needs at its
centre unrelated to other human beings. That Hauswirt tacitly
accepts this oddly sterile equanimity—or at least makes no effort
to disturb it despite the humiliating implications it contains for
himself and his self-esteem—contradicts the man's personality as it
has been hitherto revealed. Frisch seems to indicate that Hauswirt
is broken, or at least fatalistically resigned, despite Yvonne's feeling
'a novel and irresistible respect' for him. His depiction of their
subsequent life together thus appears to contain an undertone of
irony : 'The evenings they spent together in front of the fire were
often very long . . . he sat and read, he drank his glass of wine, and
Yvonne smoked; sometimes she played patience—as she was doing
the evening she heard of Reinhart's death—her marriage now was
absolutely secure' (I 597). There is little indeed to disturb this
marriage of compromise. The images Frisch chooses depict a
toneless, living death. The man and woman appear to have become
as insensitised as two statues of grey stone.[8]

Reinhart/Hortense

A similar pessimism of outlook can be deduced from Reinhart's experience as it is developed in the novel. For this attempt at 'the great adventure', as he calls marriage in its socially accepted sense, ends in failure before it has begun. Yet, as in his encounter with Yvonne, the blame cannot be attributed wholly to one person. Hortense, and more importantly, behind her the rigid demands of society, represented by her father the Colonel, add their quota to the pressures that bring about Rheinhart's sense of personal waste and, ultimately, his death.

This relationship, begun as a joke, turns slowly into the final test of Reinhart's integrity. Through it he comes into contact with a world whose apparent solidity crushes the last fragments of his self-confidence. Whilst with Yvonne, Reinhart was able to treat his drawing-pupil Hortense and her pre-occupations with a certain detachment, free from envy. The collapse of that relationship forces him to re-examine his life as an independent artist, unconcerned with the daily round which is the lot of the majority. His subsequent decision to give up art and seek what he now considers to be a more central rôle in society is the turning point of his life. It is marked by a sudden awareness of how he has underrated the importance of economic stability. To an amazed Hortense he confesses that hitherto he has never managed to grasp the reality of life: 'What am I then? A man of thirty who can barely earn his living. Half your life gone, for heaven's sake, half your life! ... When will the real life begin, life which is meaningful and fundamental?' (I 497)[9]. It is deeply ironic that Hortense and Reinhart should meet again at this precise moment, for Hortense is feeling increasingly stifled by her background and family. She is horrified at Reinhart's decision, recalling her memories of a year ago, the objects in his studio and the smell of oil paint which was for her the 'quintessence of distant blue skies and freedom', the promise of that 'Ewig-Unsichere, das unser Leben in der Schwebe hält wie eine glühende Kugel'. She, of course, is seeking all that Reinhart has now turned his back on. The two are fleeing in diametrically opposite directions, and because of this they are condemned never to have any real contact with one another.

Hortense is well aware of the dangers inherent in establishing her own identity—she is associated directly with the motto 'J'adore ce qui me brûle' (I 491)—but she is convinced that in her present surroundings she will not achieve the spiritual re-birth that she longs for. It is this longing which colours her relationship with Reinhart and finally makes her refuse his offer of marriage, which he now sees entirely in conventional terms as an obligation to something higher and more mysterious than the individual. In view of such contradictory attitudes it is hardly surprising that their relationship is equally characterised by bad faith. To speak in the language of a later Frisch, neither is willing to give up the image each has made of the other. The result is disastrous for both Reinhart and Hortense. Life for him loses all its exciting unpredictability, whilst Hortense grows more and more confused.

Unlike Reinhart, however, Hortense *is* linked to her environment sufficiently to feel its strong attraction beyond the intellectual level. For despite his rigidity, she does admire her father. During one of his homilies in particular she feels the temptation of the security he offers her in contrast to Reinhart. But at that precise moment— and the incident echoes a similar one when Yvonne turned to Hauswirt—the familiar incest motif occurs to underline Frisch's implied social criticism : 'If only there were a man for her like her father, Hortense mused as she walked by his side, but a flush of shame obscured the thought' (I 506). That Hortense feels shame indicates that she is aware of the trap such security offers, and it is to her credit that she fights for the right to live her own life, however confused her ideas might be. Nevertheless, the mounting tensions between Hortense and her family are inevitably transmitted to Reinhart. Already the idea of a conventional marriage—felt as a passport into society—had exposed him to social pressures which drive him to attempt to trace his family tree. This in turn leads inexorably to the meeting with Hortense's father and his discovery of his bastardy. Before this encounter—which effectively puts an end to their relationship—a startling incident occurs which is paradigmatic for Reinhart and his problematic stance in the world. The night before his critical interview with the Oberst Reinhart spends walking in the woods. He comes across a man and woman copulating in the undergrowth : 'As if compelled, he watched the couple, holding his breath; a couple entangled in the ecstasy of sex . . . Reinhart stood barefoot, his shoes in his hand' (I 543). Reinhart's eccentricity is clear : he stands at the edge of life, the outsider gazing, humble but impotent, at a world from which he is excluded.

The element of desperation which colours Reinhart's actions and words after this incident is enough to alert Hortense to the impossibility of their relationship. For the first time she sees Reinhart as he really is—'a conglomeration of painful defects, suspect in all he does or omits to do'. She realises that he has given up the search for a personal integrating principle in favour of a more parasitic stance : 'He demanded from her what he could not offer himself. Having taken from her the support of her family, he was now looking for just such support from her for himself' (I 548). The insight is decisive. Lacking a fruitful social framework for their love, it has no way of realising itself. A familiar image returns —'Side by side, they had been wearing masks for each other' (I 549). The real face peers out too late.

Hortense/Ammann

Of the final marriage relationship in the novel little needs to be said. Hortense, like Yvonne before her, succumbs to social pressures and makes an acceptable match : the architect Ammann. (The character is an obvious forerunner of Sturzenegger in *Stiller*.) Ammann, like Hinkelmann and Hauswirt, comes from a world where marriages are made according to economic principles. A creature of convention, he is first seen sitting for his portrait which is to be presented to his fiancée (the Lieutenant's uniform and even the colour of the book he is holding have been regulated by his family!), 'an extraordinarily unfree person, cramped by sheer good manners' (I 542). And yet it is precisely such a man who is shown as ultimately 'successful' in professional and family terms. Only Reinhart when painting his portrait is able to detect the man's inner fear, the insecurity beneath the bland exterior. Social criticism in the novel is continually revealed in this oblique fashion. Hortense herself has no illusions about a marriage she contracts principally as an act of revenge against Reinhart. Whilst outwardly conforming to the social norms of her class, she maintains from the outset her mental reservations. Nevertheless, it is part of Frisch's artistic integrity that he avoids stark black and white divisions in the novel. Hortense *does* come to appreciate Ammann's qualities as much as his undoubted limitations. Although she never abandons her vision of a deeper, fuller life, as the final crucial meeting with Reinhart in his rôle as Anton, the gardener, will show, she has realised that life is not possible outside the social framework she has inherited. There can be no dramatic breakthrough—each generation must make its humanising modifications to the existing structure, however insignificant the change may appear to be. Amidst the pessimism and resignation that colour the final pages of the novel, Hortense alone (Ammann has faded away) stands as a gleam of hope.

3 'Bürger' and 'Künstler' : the malfunctioning dialectic

In choosing the 'Bürger/Künstler' ('bourgeois/artist') topos Frisch
is clearly looking backwards at a long and well-established tradition in German literature. And it must be admitted that his
handling of the theme is at times hardly very original. His formulation of the problem, for example, relies heavily on Keller and
particularly Thomas Mann, whose ambivalence and sense of irony
he shares. In one respect, however, Frisch's novel scores a signal
success : the figure of the Oberst. Although the presentation of
this man and his social milieu borrows much from *Buddenbrooks*,
Frisch nevertheless achieves through subtle shifts of linguistic tone
a unique and impressive character.

It is from the Oberst's collection of art objects that the sub-
title of the novel—'J'adore ce qui me brûle'—originates, for it is the
motto on a medallion he had once brought back from his travels
in Provence. Significantly, the Oberst himself has never known
what to make of the strange motto (in contrast to his own daughter),
for

> Er schätzte das Sichere, das Ordentliche, das Eindeutige, und
> die Gefahr (the medallion depicts a negro crouched ambiguously
> over a flame) war nicht da, damit man sich daran berauschte,
> Gefahr war das Böse, sie durfte nicht genossen, sie sollte über-
> wunden, vom Leibe gehalten, durch tapfere Vorsicht und
> männliche Haltung aus der Welt geschafft werden. Aus der
> Welt, das heißt : aus dem Staat, aus der Familie, aus dem eigenen
> persönlichen Leben. (I 481)

> *He valued what was reliable, orderly, unambiguous. Danger did
> not exist to intoxicate the senses, danger was evil and had to be
> overcome not enjoyed; danger had to be kept at arms' length,
> eradicated from the world by far-sighted courage and manly
> composure. From the world meant from the State, from the
> Family, from one's personal life.*

In this diminuendo there is something typically Swiss, a reminis-
cence of an earlier *Biedermeier* attitude. The Oberst's life is centred
on an equally ideological concept of 'honour' : 'Honour for him
was something absolute, beyond our judgement, credible naturally
only in the bourgeois form of his own class'. Here the adverb
'naturally' sounds a first critical note which is immediately confirmed by a neat insight into the Oberst's psychology : 'In the

prime of life, he was in no way willing to have his daughter (even if she wasn't his son and heir) play a silly trick on him'. In the midst of an account of the man's qualities the parenthesis points to the hubris and double standards of the Swiss bourgeoisie, and links the Oberst and the society he represents to the cruder personalities of Yvonne's parents and their economically motivated marriage.

Nevertheless, Frisch's artistic (and emotional) integrity allows the Oberst honesty of purpose : this is no façade consciously exploited to further oppressive ends; he works hard with no thought of personal gain in the interests of his native town and what he understands as a proud historical tradition. 'In short he was a member of the upper bourgeoisie, a world which has much to be said for it and which needs to be taken as seriously as any other human sphere, although like many others, including that of the artist—it considers itself to be the real, natural, indeed the only authoritative world' (I 482). Here is expressed the dangerous complacency that allows both bourgeois and artist to make absolute claims for their way of life, claims which lead to hermetic isolation and mutual impoverishment. The reader is made aware of the missing central ground where bourgeois and artist might have met in common respect. It is important, however, when thinking of Reinhart's personal disaster, to notice that the Oberst's world, too, appears to be in decline : in the face of a problematic future he turns increasingly to the past. It is small wonder that his daughter, Hortense, experiences a typical summer Sunday after church on her father's estate, 'discussing faraway wars over black coffee in relaxed comfort', as 'a prison' (I 482 f.).[10]

Reinhart's approach towards this tight, self-sufficient circle is recognised immediately as a threat, and the Oberst exerts typical authoritarian pressures on his daughter to stop the relationship. We are shown, however, Hortense beginning to think for herself, developing her own individuality and thus coming more and more into conflict with her parents' world. She is initially attracted by opposites—'J'adore ce qui me brûle'—attracted by the same dangers to which Yvonne exposed herself by leaving Hinkelmann. Frisch is nevertheless careful not to depict Reinhart's world as an obviously *real* alternative, but one which merely appears to offer undefined excitement and possibilities. The juxtaposition of these two worlds is thus not presented melodramatically but ironically : for whilst Reinhart has not the confidence ultimately (nor indeed, it would appear, the necessary talent) to make the life of an artist a valid alternative to bourgeois society, Hortense herself never in fact rejects her father and his standards outright. Indeed, the relationship between Hortense and the Oberst—the basic affection beneath the mutual incomprehension—is one of the best observed in the novel. The fragility of the latter's world, however, is strikingly symbolised by the 'Zunfthaus' episode.

During an inspection of the reconstruction work on the ancient building with her father, the floor beneath Hortense collapses and she is buried under falling débris. Hortense is rescued from the ruins not by her father but by a 'stranger' in a white coat, or so it appears to her in a semi-conscious state : 'The stranger took her bereft of clothes in his arms : Let's see now how to get over the river, said the stranger in his white cloak. Beyond him rose a town out of the mist, every bridge seemed destroyed' (I 492). The meaning of this erotic 'dream' is clear : if she is to become a free individual she must leave behind a world endeavouring to shore up the ruins of the past and follow the promptings of a youthful longing in companionship with Reinhart. That in her dazed state she confuses the workman with Reinhart is confirmed by similar white-knight-in-armour imagery used to mark her return to the painter after six months' convalescence.

It is at this critical moment that the Oberst, aware of her decision, subjects her to the full pressure of the social tradition in which she has been brought up, and brings into sharp focus the fundamental antimony between his view of the world and Reinhart's. Hortense's father takes his stand on a rigid concept of breeding. He admits that 'at all levels of society there are beings who are fit and useful, even splendid and valuable' (I 503), but his language makes it quite clear that society takes precedence over the individual and that such qualities depend on the individual recognising and accepting his position in society without wishing to change it. The Oberst therefore represents the classic reactionary posture. He produces a revealing parallel in the art of dog-breeding : every breed has its points, only the mongrel—'der Bastard'— is rejected. 'Men have an innate need to preserve their racial purity, a need which is all the more strongly developed in the sturdier, healthier, purer individual—that's just the way things are' (I 503). This simplistic doctrine is for the Oberst indisputable : he never questions his bald assertion that this 'need to preserve racial purity' is 'innate'—despite the fact that he has to expend so much energy defending what is supposed to be an innate need against his own flesh and blood. The Oberst does admit with a chilling magnanimity that 'bastards of all types and all social levels' can reach pinnacles of achievement, yet—and here we see the full complacency of the man and the society he represents—the bastard indicates a dead end :

> Er hat vollauf das Recht zum Dasein, er bereichert die Welt vielleicht um Entscheidendes; was seine Art von Größe ausmacht, seine Art von sittlicher Verpflichtung, der sich keiner entzieht, das ist, daß er sich als Ausnahme und Einmaligkeit weiß, daß ihm das Recht auf weitere Fortpflanzung in hohem Masse fehlt. (I 504).

He has an absolute right to exist, he may make a decisive contribution to the world; but the nature of his greatness, the nature for him of that moral obligation which no one can escape, is determined by the knowledge that he is a unique exception, that he has lost to a large degree the right to further propagation.

Through the Oberst's words appears again and again that bourgeois ideology which Max Weber has characterised as the 'Protestant Ethic' : immense advantages of upbringing and education have to be paid for by the fulfillment of social duties and hard work (which will in turn justify future temporal reward); even the harshest of social laws must be accepted as 'natural' and beyond our limited understanding. The tasks one sets oneself must be taken up and completed by one's children, for natural human weakness will prevent total efficiency :

> Man arbeitet, wenn auch nicht als großer Feldherr und Staatsmann, immerhin für sein Vaterland. Man wacht und waltet über ein bescheidenes Stück eigener Erde. Man hat eine Frau, man hat Kinder, die es fortsetzen werden. (I 505).

One works—even if not in the capacity of a great general and statesman—for one's country. One watches over and rules a modest piece of land. One has a wife, and children who will continue the work.

With the blindness of his class the Oberst does not realise—or at least deign to mention—that such an existence, such a stability, depends in the last analysis on a working class which will have no chance to develop such continuity of tradition or to acquire 'ein bescheidenes Stück Erde'—not to mention the splendid estate which the Oberst in fact owns. Only Reinhart experiences the reality behind the Oberst's rhetoric : that life for most people is 'wage-slavery'. In this way Frisch laconically underlines the cliché-

ridden nature of the Oberst's homily, and at the same time he indicates a certain lack of inner certainty in the man himself : the
world he has just described belongs clearly—even in Switzerland—
to the past, and almost as if the Oberst himself sensed the anachron-
istic nature of his position, he suddenly falls silent in the middle of
his admonition—'he had lost the thread'.

The deeply conservative nature of the Obert's concept of society
is fully brought out when he resumes the argument and includes,
in a veiled form, the truth about Reinhart's origins. Society for
him is a system of interlocking duties and restraints whereby the
individual is subordinated to the whole. What is important is
'moral backbone', 'self-denial', 'the awareness of duties beyond the
self', above all 'discipline'. Such concepts however are developed
by an élite to preserve its own position, no matter how much the
Oberst would see them as innate and natural. It is indeed significant
that throughout this exposition of the bourgeois ethic there is no
mention of God or any transcendental justification; the matter is
purely one of *social* organisation, and individuals with a more
flexible and pragmatic life-style, typified by the artist, must be kept
at bay.[11]

The oblique revelation of Reinhart's birth involves the Oberst
in a neat sketch of his own father whose management of his estate
is shown as having been both paternalistic and authoritarian. His
employees are depicted as having been happy, simple people only
too glad to transfer their worries and responsibilities to the 'master'.
Hortense's grandfather was, like his son, a man with a deep sense
of honour, and when his children's governess—significantly a
German not a Swiss!—was made pregnant by the local butcher's
boy, he found the fact incomprehensible, not because he was a
prude with a narrow view of morality, but because he could not
understand the lapse in good taste. The rigidity of the dominant
social code is once again apparent : the crime is as much one of
betraying one's class and one's breeding as simply an act of sexual
immorality. The child of this union (i.e. Jürg Reinhart) is today,
the Oberst admits, 'a young man who is making his way in life in
quite a respectable manner . . . despite the fact he is an artist'. The
distaste inherent in this last phrase cannot be disguised by the
Oberst's subsequent gloss that even an artist can become 'ein
Mensch' : 'Different destiny, different attitude to life. Who has the
right ring? Perhaps there are many different ways of becoming a
man, but each of us has only one' (I 511).

The sudden magnanimity, with its arch reference to the tolerance exemplified in Lessing's *Nathan der Weise*, is hardly deceptive. The Oberst acknowledges the superficial attractiveness of the artist's way of life but in his last words he draws the contrast between society and the 'Sonderling', sharply and irrevocably rejecting the dialectic that might have produced a viable synthesis. In the last analysis the artist's rootlessness, his freedom from social obligations and familial tradition, are irreconcilable with the forces of stability which can only be found in class continuity. The oberst's mistake— and the reason why he fails to convince Hortense—lies in his thinking that he and his class are and can be independent of all others : the economic advantages he enjoys and which enable *him* to realise his potentiality as a human being necessarily imply the diminishing of others' possibilities. What this means for this society's attitude to the artist, Reinhart perceives early in the novel whilst working on Ammann's commissioned portrait : society will admire his talent, may even envy his 'gypsy-like' freedom, but fundament- ally it will mistrust and despise the artist as 'eine Schrulle der Natur' ('*Nature's eccentric*'), tolerate him merely as 'a sort of court jester' to help the bourgeoisie fill up its leisure hours.[12] The Oberst's concept of society thus boils down to an acknowledgement of (bourgeois) tradition and its normative demands on contemporary life, together with the embracing of class prejudices to shore up the power structure. For the Oberst is obsessed with keeping his 'race' pure, that is to say, with making sure that his children marry their social peers and thus ensure the propagation of the ideals and traditions which he sees as a sort of categorical imperative from the past. (One could also point out that, though the Oberst never mentions it, 'suitable' marriages also have the advantage of keeping economic power in traditional hands.)

In this connection it is significant that the word complex 'gesund/ Gesundheit/das Gesunde' ('healthy, health, the healthy') runs like a *leitmotiv* through the novel—another patent debt to Thomas Mann. In practically all cases the references are to people who *belong* to society, that is to the bourgeoisie. Characters described as 'gesund' are Hinkelmann, the Doctor who visits Yvonne, Merline, Ammann, his son, Peter, Hortense, her godmother Gerda, and the latter's two children. The mixture on this list, and in particular Hinkelmann's presence on it, indicates the degree of irony with which Frisch invests the term. The absolute quality indicated by the Oberst is relativised even within his own class. Most of the references, however, are clearly linked with the safe, unadventurous lives these characters lead. Their health appears to involve an emotional impoverishment—indeed, in the case of Hinkelmann, such impoverishment paradoxically proves fatal. Its value is seen at best expressed in lives led in an uncomplicated and naïve way. But it is possible to live in this way only by turning a blind eye to reality and retreating behind well-defended class barriers. This is, in a sense, what Hortense does in marrying Ammann. And, significantly, it is Reinhart who describes her as 'healthy', once in contrast to Yvonne, ('a woman permanently endangered'), and later after his defeat by, and capitulation to, the pressures of society. The term is thus shot through with irony, a point which it is important to make when Reinhart's final position and fate are discussed.

The abyss separating 'Künstler' and 'Bürger' in the novel is thus shown as an unbridgeable one. From one point of view Reinhart can be seen by his artist friends as a 'failure', an 'apostate', from the other he and his fellow artists are 'braggarts with no future, with no significance in a greater whole' (I 522). The two worlds are rarely allowed to coincide or react creatively on one another. In an important sense, of course, the bourgeois/artist clash is not a genuine one in the way that, say, Goethe depicted it in *Torquato Tasso* or Thomas Mann in his early fiction. For Reinhart is *not* a dedicated, nor even (apparently) a very good artist. He certainly lacks the confidence and persistence that are required, as much as talent, to pursue such a calling successfully even from a purely egocentric viewpoint. In this respect he is closer to the dilettante, Christian Buddenbrook. What he undoubtedly is, however, is an Individual. It is perhaps more accurate in this context to speak of a clash between Society and the Individual. Frisch has taken a traditional and well-worn topos as a starting-point for discussion of a more generalised problem. Thus Reinhart exemplifies the title of the novel : he is a 'Schwieriger', a man who cannot fit into any of the categories society offers and who experiences the reality it represents as increasingly problematical. Because society is shown as incapable of absorbing such individuals creatively, Jürg Reinhart is condemned to remain 'ein halber Mensch', a close relative of that earlier group of confused eccentrics—the heroes of Albin Zollinger's pre-war novels.[13]

4   THE SEARCH FOR 'DAS WIRKLICHE LEBEN'

If the theme of *Die Schwierigen* can be said to be 'the self-realisation of the individual',[14] the search for 'das wirkliche Leben' is the central factor in this process. From this point of view Reinhart can be seen as the pivotal figure in the novel rather than Yvonne. For his search is at once the most intense and the most self-destructive. The preoccupations of the other characters are primarily seen in relation to his ideals and his failure. The crisis point for Reinhart comes, as already noted, with the abrupt realisation that he is thirty years old, when he is forced to admit that the insouciance of youth must give way to a more sober assessment of what has been achieved and what neglected.[15] This abrupt confrontation with the pressure of time is a permanent preoccupation with Frisch and it is always accompanied by the painful awareness that youthful confidence about the imminent onset of a 'real, meaningful life' has proved deceptive. Unhappily for Reinhart, this sudden insight, common enough it must be conceded, goes hand in hand with an equally abrupt loss of self-confidence. The search for an integrating centric principle, the key to 'das wirkliche Leben', is thus embarked on in an atmosphere of panic. In this unhelpful frame of mind Reinhart seizes on the concept of marriage as the way to put down roots in 'a larger, more valid form of life' (I 498). Marriage he now sees as the great adventure which might offer at a stroke the longed-for sense of permanent achievement. Marriage, i.e. the possibility of creating a lasting bond between a man and a woman, is the central problem for all Frisch's characters. Reinhart's mistake is to confuse this fundamental relationship with its conventional expression in society, as if it were some direct passport to 'acceptance'. Thus the more he looks upon the institution as an escape from his essentially solipsistic dilemma, the more he falls prey to the taboos and norms currently held by such exemplars of society as the Oberst. Under such strains the consciousness of his own worth disintegrates with increasing rapidity. Art, he now confides to the woman he takes erroneously to be his mother—an ironic situation—'is a matter for a complete man, and that I have never been' (I 531). At the same time the empty experience of working in an office, together with his capacity for sensitive observation, tell him that this world, too, is not what it appears to the outsider to be. The process of conforming to it would entail ignoring the ubiquitous fear he sees in those around him and which they hide from themselves behind a mask of poise and maturity.

The dichotomy at the heart of Reinhart's confusion lies in the fact that he wants the impossible : the defeat of time. Like so many of Frisch's characters, he seeks relationships 'without a past, without a future, without fear' (I 513), and sees everyday routine as a curse: an endless repetition of triviality. Nevertheless the temptation to accept society's rules, and thus evade the tensions of his eccentric stance, drives him to the conventional, but fatal interview with Hortense's father. This interview can be seen in a paradoxical way as Reinhart's initiation into society. From its impressive representative he learns the truth about his family and, by implication, his due place in the system. But far from it giving him insight into 'ein wirkliches Leben', this accelerates his downward path. Society's judgement is merely confirmed when he takes lodgings, unrecognised, in his own father's house—an ironic version of the theme of the Prodigal Son—discovers his unwitting incest with his half-sister and former model, Jenny, and ultimately fails in a ludicrous attempt to shoot his father. Even negative distinction is denied him.

Hortense proves to be Reinhart's final chance to enter into a creative relationship with life, for only another's love could have saved him, as he points out prophetically to Hortense in their last conversation before they leave each other: 'That another human being believes in us and gives us back our faith in ourselves when we have lost it—that, I thought would be love, the miracle of love, grace, inexplicable like the drawing near of an angel...' (I 545).[16] Instead his life has become one of resignation and withdrawal. To the emptiness of the world around him he has attempted to reply with a stoic silence. Once this refuge of pseudo-rustic simplicity crumbles, suicide becomes the inevitable alternative, and this throws an ironic light on the final section of the book. By fleeing into the rôle of Anton, the gardener, Reinhart tries to hide the nature of his failure behind decadent social theories of predestination. It is in this sense that the chapter 'Anton der Diener, oder das Wirkliche Leben' is to be understood and the long discussion between 'Anton' and an older, wiser Hortense interpreted.

This discussion reveals the extent of the gulf which has continued to widen between them over the years, and at the same time underlines the pessimism of Frisch's outlook. Whereas Hortense has kept alive her belief that at least Reinhart had found 'a more real life far away' (I 585), and with this compensatory trust, her own faith in the realisation of such a possibility, Reinhart has given up the struggle and taken over to an alarming degree the ideology of the Oberst—a fact which Hortense herself notes. Thus Reinhart now sees fulfilment as a human being in terms of a rigidly stratified choice. A man, he argues, can either use his inherited gifts to make a single and magnificent mark in life, regardless of the consequences (this he had hoped to do himself), or he can settle for bourgeois marriage and a healthy existence, passing on his values intact to later generations. The third and only other possibility is to recognise that he has inherited a life so fundamentally flawed that his only recourse is to end it himself. That such acquired beliefs have little relation to any integrated social reality is clear from the sober picture of bourgeois marriage that Frisch actually gives, not least Hortense's own. Everything she says in this conversation indicates that she is not fulfilled as a person. Indeed, when one sees Ammann betraying the rigidity of his class, for example, in his authoritarian treatment of his daughter, one grasps one of the reasons why. Similarly, Yvonne, whilst materially secure in her marriage to Hauswirt, never emerges from her spiritual isolation. Hortense, for her part, immediately recognises the stultifying stubborness that Reinhart is exhibiting. Far from being the key to 'a real meaningful life', she points out, 'any inflexible adherence to a momentary insight can only lead to more mistakes' (I 588). But her words are spoken too late. Reinhart's neurosis has progressed too far; his thinking has grown so muddled in his solitude that he can even interpret his death wish in terms of a kind of 'noble mission', aimed at not increasing the world's stock of 'Halblinge'. That Reinhart is unaware that he *has* a son, and indeed that his son is courting Hortense's own daughter, only adds to the intensity of Frisch's irony.

In one respect, however, Reinhart puts his finger on a fundamental truth. He sees that happiness is connected with *instinctive* living. It is the power of *reflection* that ultimately makes life problematical. A naïve individual experiences a sense of continuity, his identity, in an uncomplicated way. (It is exactly this 'naive identity' that Mann's Tonio Kröger so admired in the shape of Inge and Hans). However such a concept of a naïve, instinctive life of grace is a dream, as Heinrich von Kleist recognised over 150 years ago.[17] There is no going back once one has reached a certain stage of intellectual and emotional development, and the hankering after 'lost innocence' can easily turn into a destructive nostalgia. As Colin Wilson points out in his study of the Outsider: 'The Outsider's chief desire is to *cease to be an Outsider*. He cannot cease to be an Outsider simply to become an ordinary bourgeois; that would be a way back . . . His problem is *how to go forward*.'[18] Jürg Reinhart attempts to find the way back, and it costs him his life, for he sacrifices in so doing any sense of personal uniqueness. His death is significantly accompanied by comic, not to say, grotesque elements. Whilst he lies dead on the floor of his bedroom, a drunken party goes on below : the image is one of life, in its crudest and greediest terms, mocking his pretensions. Indeed, the book closes with the final image of Reinhart's wig falling from his head as he is placed in his coffin—frightening the maids, but trivialising the event.

The black humour of this last image hints, perhaps faintly, at a possible way forward, but for the characters in this novel it is too late. For none of them attains human fulfilment, and what stability is achieved in the bourgeois field, is seen in terms of resignation, renunciation, limitation. The two children, Hanswalter and Annemarie, serve only to intensify the pessimistic vision of an endless, absurd repetition. Hanswalter, indeed, already shows signs of his father's dissatisfied yearnings and Annemarie her mother's rebelliousness against restrictions.[19] Thus in a phrase which is repeated like a refrain in the book 'Everything repeats itself, nothing comes back to us, summers pass, years are nothing . . .' (I 559, 593, 599). We are victims of time, part of the transience of all things. 'Das wirkliche Leben' remains an object of longing; the greyness of everyday routine is dominant. This profound dissatisfaction with everyday reality, however, can at least be seen as an awareness of the rich potentiality of human nature, and in *Stiller* Frisch throws a more searching light on the constraints that restrict an individual's attempt at a radical personal transformation.

IV

Stiller

I INTRODUCTION

With the publication in 1954 of *Stiller* Max Frisch established a claim to major status in the history of the novel in post-war Germany and Switzerland. Hitherto respected, like his fellow countryman Dürrenmatt, as a leading dramatist in the German-speaking world, Frisch suddenly produced a narrative work of unsuspected depth and fascination. Although his powers as a novelist had been refined and intensified since the earlier novels by the composition of his *Tagebuch 1946–1949*, this was the first occasion they had been put to the test in a sustained narrative. Typical reviews welcomed the book as 'one of the best German language novels of our time' and as Frisch's 'first masterpiece',[1] and since its appearance *Stiller* indeed has attracted a large number of commentators. The novel has been discussed variously and cogently as an examination of the 'problematic and tragic nature of marriage', as an 'artist-novel in an age of reproduction' and as an exposition of Kierkegaard's existentialism.[2] Faced with such widely divergent interpretations (and each has its specific strengths as well as weaknesses), the reader must look for a common denominator that will allow each emphasis its due weight. For to grant any one view exclusivity would be to impoverish a very rich structure. This common denominator—the creative principle which joins the disparate parts and themes of the book together—is *irony*.

It is only in the ironic mode that *Stiller* achieves its unity as a novel, for practically every page reveals an essential ambivalence that Anatol Stiller himself characterises : 'Jedes Wort ist falsch und wahr, das ist das Wesen des Wortes' (III 525; *'Every word is false and true, that is the nature of words' 133*).[3] Viewed thus, the 'Postscript by the Public Prosecutor', for example, cease to be a *Formbruch*[4] and becomes a kind of 'Eighth Notebook' giving a final but none the less subjective perspective to the story of Anatol Stiller. Other ironic features of the novel are similarly striking.

The most obvious and the most complex, of course, is the device of 'Mr White' writing about Stiller as a third person; it enables Frisch to achieve a high degree of ambiguity which means that no account can be taken at its face value but each is relativised by the others. Furthermore an essential paradox is contained in the idea of Stiller as the centre of the other characters' world, a 'prisoner' to whom the 'free' come to tell the important stories of their lives. Ironic, too, is the contrast between the freedom Stiller appears to secure in prison and the constraints to which he falls victim once he is released. The many parodistic literary associations and the fact that Stiller's defence counsel proves hostile and the prosecuting counsel sympathetic are examples of the mode in minor key.

An interpretation of the novel, therefore, will actively involve the reader's experience to a high degree. He must play a *creative* rôle in piecing the evidence together and coming to his own conclusion. His own experience and view of life will lead him to give more credence, now to this character, now to that. Frisch himself has declared in his *Tagebuch 1946–1949* that the principle enjoyment in reading is that 'the reader above all discovers the richness of his own thoughts' (II 446 f). The truth itself is inexpressible in words—a sceptical attitude towards language Frisch shares with many twentieth-century German writers—but it can perhaps be located in the tension between what is said and what is meant: 'One makes statements which never express our true experience which remains inexpressible; such statements can only circumscribe the truth as closely and accurately as possible; reality, the inexpressible, emerges at best as the tension between our statements' (II 379). It is this scepticism which has led Frisch to prefer the fragment form, the 'sketch', as an expression of mistrust of premature 'wholeness', of formal perfection which cannot correspond to his experience of an essentially fragmented world. Stiller's concern is the same : he relates his fragmentary stories in an attempt to escape the finished image ('Bildnis') other people are intent on fixing upon him.

2 STILLER'S STORIES : THEIR FUNCTION AND NATURE

Stiller's response to his defence counsel's demand that he write down 'the plain, unvarnished truth' (III 362, 9) is entirely in tune with the Diary entry quoted above. Stiller begins to tell stories as a method of approaching, obliquely and tentatively, the expression of his unique experience. At the same time he is aware—in the third sentence of the novel—of the danger he is in, although his attitude at this early stage is one of defensive humour : 'For experience has taught me that without whisky I'm not myself, I'm open to all sorts of good influences and liable to play the part they want me to play, although it's not me at all' (III 361, 9). Indeed, the novel's opening exclamation—'I'm not Stiller!'— coupled with the breathless hypotaxis of this sentence (it covers fourteen lines of text), underlines the fragile nature and the tensions of the position Stiller is trying to hold. The stories he tells constitute an effort to preserve intact the vision of a new self and to forestall society's desire to recapture its fixed image of its 'lost' citizen.

The stories vary a good deal both in their length and in their importance. Although they are ultimately meant for his defence counsel, Dr Bohnenblust, the actual audience varies from Bohnenblust himself to Knobel (who receives the bulk of the tales), and from Julika to Rolf, the holder of the State's brief. Two appear to be written primarily for himself (i.e. the first version of 'Isidor' and the final version of the Florence story). They occur predominantly in the first Notebook, in which Stiller's attempt to escape his identity still seems possible,[5] and finally in the third Notebook after which they cease. And they cease for the good reason that their essential function—the gradual revelation of Stiller's personality culminating in the 'experience with his angel'—is taken over by the stories the *others* tell *him* and the increasingly painful self-analysis this forces upon White/Stiller until the two identities are, legally at least, synthesised.

That the stories consist of a gradual revelation of true experience can be seen if their nature is examined. They progress from the relatively lighthearted story of the murder of the 'hair-oil gangster' Schmitz, via the apeces of the Isidor, Rip van Winkle and Jim White episodes, to the bitter honesty of the real story of Florence the mulatto girl. In other words, the actual relation of the stories slowly turns against the narrator's intention of establishing beyond doubt his identity as Mr White. This ironic movement can already be seen in the changing character of the stories Stiller tells to Knobel and Bohnenblust. In both cases they start boldly and colourfully (Knobel : the Schmitz murder—the daring escape from the burning sawmill with Florence and the murder of her husband, Joe; Bohnenblust : life on a corrupt minister's hacienda in Mexico —work on the tobacco plantation and the volcanic eruption at Paracutin), become slowly more sober (Knobel : the brief episode

of Helen with its disappointing anti-climax but thereby more con-
vincing than the fanciful version apparently given to Bohnenblust;
Bohnenblust : the story of Little Grey with its oblique reference to
Stiller's abortive suicide attempt), and end on a note of deep
seriousness (Knobel : Jim White in the Carlsbad Cavern;
Bohnenblust : Rip van Winkle).

None of the stories is pure invention for its own sake. The
Schmitz murder, for example, proves to be motivated by Stiller's
resentment against a real life 'Schmitz' who refused to pay Stiller
for a commissioned bust; the hacienda tale fits into a growing
polemic against Switzerland, the very vehemence of which ironically
underlines the Swissness and sense of involvement of this would-be
'American of German origin'; and the volcano story, with its
obvious psychological connotations of sexual potency, contrasts with
the banality of the Helen fragment and so indicates the tension
between the two identities, Mr White and his *Doppelgänger* Herr
Stiller. Four stories, however, require specific discussion as illustra-
tions of Stiller's eccentricity and in view of their significance as
part of what has been correctly called his 'disguised self-analysis' :
those of Isidor, Rip van Winkle, Jim White and Florence.[6]

Isidor

The function of the Isidor tale is clearly to serve as a warning.
Stiller first rehearses it to himself in preparation for Julikas' first
visit, as an oblique signal of the danger she courts if she persists
in seeing him as her 'lost' husband. Isidor is a respectable bourgeois
chemist who lives with five children in 'bester Ordnung', troubled
only by his wife's propensity for nagging questions. The sudden
break for freedom this eventually causes and the ensuing absence
of seven years point to the link with Anatol Stiller. Isidor seeks
the exciting possibilities of the desert with the Foreign Legion (a
detail borrowed from Knobel's statistic that three hundred Swiss
men a year escape to the Legion 'when it gets on their nerves
here'[7]) which is to 'make a man of him'. It is Mr White's hope,
too, that he has left behind him his impotence and sense of
inferiority. The significance of the parable for Julika's situation
lies in the negative response of Isidor's wife when he returns. To
his immediate sexual advance she replies only with plaintive
questions. Habit proves too strong—she has not understood the
reasons for Isidor's abrupt flight. The result is catastrophic on both
sides : Isidor—in an action clearly symbolic of sexual frustration

—draws his revolver and fires three shots 'into the soft, still un-touched cake decorated with sugar icing' (III 396, *36*). His re-appearance a year later is of even shorter duration. Encountering the inevitable question as to his whereabouts, Isidor promptly abandons his family for good, leaving his wife to seek for herself a life of convention and 'Ordnung' ('so important for the growing children') via divorce and a safe second marriage to the inevitable lawyer.

The version Stiller gives to Julika is deliberately and significantly altered : the five children are omitted and the shooting climax is replaced by Isidor revealing stigmata—an image borrowed from a premonitory dream Stiller has had of this confrontation with Julika :

> Sehe von außen durchs Fenster, wie ein jüngerer Mann, vermut-lich der Verschollene, zwischen den Kaffeehaus-Tischlein geht, die flachen Hände erhoben, um die hellroten Flecken zu zeigen, und sozusagen mit Stigma hausiert, was ihm niemand abnimmt, Peinlichkeit, ich selbst stehe draußen, wie gesagt, neben mir die Dame aus Paris, deren Gesicht ich nicht kenne; mit der etwas höhnischen Erklärung, jener Stigma-Hausierer sei ihr Mann, zeigt sie mir ebenfalls ihre Hände : ebenfalls mit zwei hellroten Wundmalen, wobei es offenbar, nur soviel ahne ich, zwischen den beiden darum geht, wer das Kreuz ist und wer der Gekreu-zigte, all dies unausgesprochen; die Leute an den Kaffeehaus-Tischlein mit der Illustrierten. (III 415)

> *I am looking outside through a window at a youngish man, probably the missing man, walking between the café tables and raising his outspread hands in order to display the bright red patches, hawking his stigmata, so to speak, which no one buys from him; embarrassment; I myself am standing outside, as I said, with the lady from Paris, whose face I don't know and who is explaining rather scornfully that the stigma-hawker is her husband, she also shows me her hands—also bearing two bright red scars. It is obvious, this much I can guess, that the point is to show who is the cross and who the crucified, though none of this is put into words; the people at the café tables are reading magazines. (54)*

The picture of a vigorous, active Isidor has been transformed into one of a passive sufferer. The virile warning has changed into mute pleading. (The ambiguous question of guilt, clear enough in the dream, finds no expression in Stiller's account to Julika—which fits in with his generally defensive posture.) Julika unhappily does not take the story seriously and subsequently falls into the very trap of reproachful questioning that drove Isidor away forever. That her attitude provokes a physical attack—a frustrated outburst of violence—is both a measure of Mr White's desperation and of his involvement with this woman.

The dream itself, disclosed in full only later in the Notebook, is a microcosm of the novel's basic themes : the stigmata touch on the existential nature of Stiller's dilemma; the image of refracted identity symbolises Stiller/White's eccentric stance; society, embarrassed, prefers to ignore the man's importunate suffering in favour of the less demanding, secondhand world of the 'Illustrierte'; Julika herself reveals identical wounds which intensifies the ambiguity of the whole. Most revealing of all is the fact that Julika is only given Stiller's side of the dream and is thus expected to react solely to Stiller's image of himself. The later recording of the dream in full (it is entered pointedly immediately after the Little Grey episode) is part of the slow accumulation of evidence, tentative and fragmentary, that constitutes Stiller's complex journey of self-discovery.

Rip van Winkle

The story of Rip van Winkle, as adapted by Stiller, is that of the archetypal eccentric. Incapable of conforming to society's norms, which do not grant him any sense of identity, Rip is faced with a central conflict between his dreams and external reality. The immediate motivation for the story is Stiller's final attempt to get through to his industrious, but obtuse defence counsel. It appears shortly after Stiller's recognition of his fundamental fear of 'repetition' and is thematically linked to it.

The telling of the *Märchen* shows significant divergencies from the original tale by Washington Irving. Irving's hen-pecked Rip was a genial character whose meekness of spirit brought him universal popularity. His return from his twenty-year sleep in the mountains was indeed marked by a momentary crisis of identity when confronted with his son—an exact counterpart of himself twenty years younger. But the story ends happily with Rip resuming his former life in his daughter's house, enjoying great favour with the rising generation and becoming with his 'story' an accepted part of the community tradition. Stiller's version, whilst following the general outline of the original, is given features which can subsequently be seen to point to the identity of the narrator with his hero: for example, Rip's bad conscience, his need to appear 'manly', his gun which does not fire (a clear echo of Stiller's cowardice on the river Tajo), the endless task of setting up skittles (Irving's Rip had merely to supply the players with drink), and most important of all, his decision not to reveal himself to his daughter, but to live on as 'a stranger in an alien world'. Like Stiller, this Rip inhabits a hostile environment, far removed from Irving's nineteenth-century idyll, and one intent on maintaining its own image of the man. The repetitive setting up of the skittles is a symbol of the repeated, futile attempts Stiller had made in the past, and is still making via his 'stories', to achieve an identity of his own creation. The others will not accept either Rip or Stiller on his evaluation, and thus their response on returning to the world is identical: they deny their past and with it their old personalities. For Rip this means accepting the rôle of an eccentric standing on the edge of society; for Stiller it is the beginning of a struggle for a new identity.

James Larkins White and the labyrinth

This story in the third Notebook marks a change from parable to extended metaphor, as indeed it marks a stage in Stiller's developing self-awareness. The change is further underlined by a shift of narrative view-point from the third to the first person. At the end of the first Notebook Stiller is already fully conscious of the specific problem he faces: 'How can anyone prove who they really are? I can't. Do I know myself who I am? That is the terrifying discovery I have made while under arrest: I have no words for my reality!' (III 436, 67). The Jim White story, however, comes closer to expressing Stiller's existential crisis than any of the previous ones.[8] It is also the first story that Stiller unequivocally declares to be an imaginative construct and not the literal truth about his experience. When Knobel asks him directly if he is Jim White, his reply mystifies the prison warder but hardly the attentive reader: 'Not exactly! But you see, my experience was precisely the same—precisely' (III 521).

The image of the labyrinth is of venerable antiquity, and indeed Stiller's specific reference to Ariadne (III 511) indicates its pedigree. But there is no Minotaur in the depths of this labyrinth; there is rather a confrontation—no less intimidating—with the *self*. For the descent of the historical Jim White into the Carlsbad Caverns in 1901 stands as a convenient metaphor for the narrator's descent into the deepest layers of his consciousness. The motivation for this descent is as significant as White's frame of mind : boredom with a repetitive life-style and the desire to locate a more compelling reality (the 'search for water') drive him down into the cavern. To search for a new source of vitality he has to risk the descent into himself. The unsatisfactory nature of surface reality explains the temptation of the labyrinth : it holds out the promise of an end to the uncertainty of mere appearances. But what in fact the cavern symbolises is the treacherous comfort of *solipsism* (the ultimate logic of which is suicide), and the spuriousness of this temptation is indicated by the human skeleton Stiller/White stumbles across. In a sense, flight from everyday routine is a flight from time, the impossibility of which Stiller has to learn. For time, in fact, is not suspended in this strange underworld; permanence is only an illusion. As Stiller/White progresses through the layers of consciousness, past the petrified 'Arsenal der Metaphern', he comes to a final cavern where no vestige of rock is visible. Stalagmites and stalactites have combined to form a veritable jungle of marble, but one which over the aeons cannot avoid the shifts and changes of an implacable transience. It is this discovery, together with the warning of the skeleton (which he has difficulty in not seeing as his own), which drives Stiller/White back to the surface and real life. But after such an experience it is not possible to return to dull routine, flight from which had led to the discovery of the labyrinth in the first place. The solution is sought in the death of that part of himself which is so securely anchored in his previous life, i.e. the biographical reality called 'Stiller'. The struggle that results from this attempt at separation is begun, Stiller/White suggests, by his better self, but won ambiguously by 'the stronger man'.[9] Significantly however, Jim White also suffers a cut forehead underground. The pointer to the mark of Cain indicates that a solution involving the total denial of a part of oneself will be frustrated as was the murderer of Abel. It is this detail which sets up an ironic tension between the meaning of the story and Stiller/White's confidence that the 'missing man', i.e. the historical Jim White's companion (but by extension the other self he has jettisoned), will not return. James Larkins White, as the surname suggests, is the *tabula rasa* Stiller hopes he has created for himself in preparation for his return to Europe.

The mulatto girl called Florence

The first version of Stiller's relationship with Florence is presented as being told to Knobel in the first Notebook immediately after an entry which indicates his growing sense of panic and encirclement : 'I'm not their Stiller. What do they want with me? I'm an unfortunate, insignificant, unimportant person with no life behind him, none at all. Why am I lying to them? Just so they should leave me my emptiness, my insignificance, my reality; it's no good running away, and what they are offering me is flight, not freedom, flight into a rôle. Why don't they stop it?' (III 401, *41*). Stiller has also just been informed that Julika has fixed the date of her first visit, convinced in her own mind that she knows her husband better than he does himself. It is not surprising, therefore, that this first version is a blood-curdling adventure story involving the rescue of Florence from a blazing sawmill and the swift murder of her importunate husband. The flight of fantasy is neither boasting to impress the gullible Knobel, nor the wishful thinking of a man with an inferiority complex—it is too lurid for that, and in any case Stiller is perfectly well aware of who he is speaking to and who he is writing for. The story is rather a further example of defensive irony : Stiller is trying to protect himself from the encroachment of the people around him by an exercise in veiled self-mockery.

The fact that this subterfuge fails is one of the bitter pills that Stiller has to swallow in prison. For during the process of inventing his stories and keeping a record of his conversations with others he begins to suspect that he is not going to get through to people who have no sense of the ambiguity of experience, who are not out of phase with surface reality. 'Stories' for such people are either true or false according to fixed categories of thought (factuality, congruence, probability)—multivalence of meaning is simply not recognised. People are not open to the uniqueness of another's feelings and perceptions; there is 'no terra incognita nowadays', since 'We live in an age of reproduction. Most of what makes up our personal picture of the world we have never seen with our own eyes—or rather we've seen it with our own eyes, but not on the spot : our knowledge comes to us from a distance, we are televiewers, telehearers, teleknowers' (III 535, *140*). In this pessimistic frame of mind Stiller records (towards the end of the third Notebook), with an air of despair, the 'true' story of his relationship with a mulatto girl called Florence. With its note of sober realism it effectively concludes Stiller's stories and thus this particular experiment in communication.

The final version of the Florence story underscores the same point as the Isidor and Rip van Winkle tales : Stiller's eccentricity.

His stance is once again firmly on the periphery. The centre is held by the graceful beauty of Florence whose dancing is of such natural fluency that it makes Stiller feel a cripple within his own body. There is an echo of Rousseau's 'noble savage' in the passage describing the dance and the circle of admiring spectators which serves to emphasise Stiller's malaise in the New World. He is an outsider (he watches his Negro neighbours preparing for a garden barbecue from behind his curtains; he feels a 'Fremdling' amidst the congregation of the Negro church), and yet at the same time he is aware that the Negroes themselves are outsiders trying to ape white society and only succeed in creating a petit-bourgeois caricature. Stiller's eccentricity is therefore doubly underlined : he fits neither into his own society, in Europe and America, nor into this outside group trying to imitate it. But for once the experience is, as it were, objectivised, and he can see clearly his own predicament —an insight characteristically inserted in parenthesis :

(Ach, diese Sehnsucht, weiß zu sein, und diese Sehnsucht, glattes Haar zu haben, und diese lebenslängliche Bemühung, anders zu sein, als man erschaffen ist, diese große Schwierigkeit, sich selbst einmal anzunehmen, ich kannte sie und sah nur eine eigene Not einmal von außen, sah die Absurdität unserer Sehnsucht, anders sein zu wollen, als man ist!) (III 542)

(Oh, this yearning to be white, this yearning to have straight hair, this lifelong striving to be different from the way one is created, this great difficulty in accepting oneself, I knew it and saw only my own predicament from outside, saw the absurdity of our yearning to be different from what we are!) (147)

This is a decisive, if momentary, insight, and it is linked with Stiller's fears regarding his own potency. Set against the warm but challenging sexuality of Florence is the feline obduracy of the cat, Little Grey. The battle with 'the delicately elegant beast' clearly echoes Stiller's marriage to Julika, and can be seen in general as a symbol of Stiller's unsatisfactory relationships with women. Certainly Little Grey is seen by Stiller himself as the harbinger of that central crisis which was to culminate in his attempted suicide.[10]

The nature and function of Stiller's stories—and the four elaborated here are paradigmatic for the rest—are thus clear : they constitute, to a lesser or greater degree, an imaginative exploration of the narrator's past experience and present attitudes, an attempt to make himself understood in a situation in which linguistic communication has become problematical. The recurring motifs of flight and return, eccentricity and personal inadequacy, intensified by the pressures of society, are sufficient to link the narrator and his invention at a level deeper than the apparent surface incongruities. Ironically, they cannot be said to fulfil their principal aim. For the people surrounding Stiller cling to their original image of him by refusing to acknowledge the rules by which he plays. Nevertheless, the stories do help Stiller himself to take the first hesitant steps towards a more honest delineation of his personal dilemma.

3 SWITZERLAND : THE TEMPTATION OF SOCIAL CONFORMITY

It is clear that Stiller's outward eccentricity, at least, could have been immediately cancelled by his simply assuming the identity of the missing sculptor. The Smyrnov spy affair would have been quickly cleared up, and after payment of fines relating to non-payment of 'government tax, military tax, old age and dependants' insurance contributions' and a due portion of legal costs (the ultimate total comes to a punctilious 9,361.05 Swiss francs), Stiller would have been free to resume an acceptable rôle as a Swiss citizen. Such a solution, however, Stiller shuns until the very last moment, and his sustained polemic against Switzerland and the Swiss, whilst revealing the strain he is under, produces some of the best comic pages in the novel. It underlines Stiller's non-conformism and the antagonism it arouses perhaps more clearly than his stories did, just as the fury of his outbursts, going far beyond a sense of grievance at wrongful imprisonment, points to a particular feeling of involvement in this country and its people.

Karl Schmid has remarked that the basic characteristic of Swiss national thinking is 'the small group. The small, embryonic, cell-like community of few people who are dependent on each other.'[11] It is precisely this sense of organic community that Stiller has lost and to which Dr Bohnenblust and the society he represents refuse to readmit him on the highly individualistic terms Stiller proposes. What they offer him instead is social conformity, a safe, comfortable return to the centre in exchange for his abandoning his irritating rôle of critical outsider. For such individualism is suspect and always problematical : 'Anything which has no reference to the realistic centre of the community spirit, which cannot be linked to the dominant idea of the small, rooted group, leaves no lasting trace behind it. The Swiss mind is seriously not prepared to deviate from this centre. Such deviance occurs when the *individual* is made the focal point of thinking.'[12] Thus Stiller's conflict with Swiss society emerges from his increasingly deteriorating relationship with his defence counsel who, ironically, sees it as his task to present the case of the community against the individual he is appointed to defend. Bohnenblust becomes a convenient vehicle for conveying the clichés in which Swiss society thinks of itself. For example, he is smugly convinced that justice reigns supreme in his country, that no reasonable person could deny its 'spiritual grandeur' or fail to admire that universal self-sufficiency that only Stiller appears to find oppressive. Bohnenblust's myopia and general complacency bring him very close to Gottfried Keller's nineteenth-century Seldwyla and Dürrenmatt's more sinister Güllen—not to mention Frisch's own Andorra.

Indeed many of the themes running through Stiller's bitter diatribe have been constant factors in Frisch's work since 1945. In the plays, and particularly in the *Tagebuch 1946–1949*, he subjects post-war Swiss society to a rigorous examination, a process which he has continued into the 1970s with an ironic dissection of the national myth, *Wilhelm Tell für die Schule* (1971), and further reminiscences of his military service, *Dienstbüchlein* (1974).[13] In this wider context Bohnenblust's favourite defence of his country, which consists of an almost ritualistic recital of impressive historical facts and personages, can be seen as an echo of what Frisch has dubbed 'culture as moral schizophrenia'.[14] What interests Frisch (and Stiller) is the *contemporary* relevance of Switzerland and Swiss culture. Far from accepting Bohnenblust's assertion that the Swiss possess spiritual grandeur, Stiller sees their lack of self-questioning, their refusal to admit that Switzerland could be anything else but 'a stronghold of peace, freedom and human rights',[15] as a demonstration of their essential *unfreedom*. What freedom and independence Switzerland does enjoy, he argues, are due simply to its historical insignificance in the modern world. Restricted to the periphery of the international stage the Swiss concern for liberty is expressed in an overriding desire for 'Ordnung'. (Dürrenmatt notes wrily in his review of the novel that in Stiller's diary 'the prison comes out well ... the prison is in order'.[16]) Stiller learns this at first hand : 'They want to drive me crazy, merely so that they can make a citizen of me and have everything in order' (III 690, 272). For a Swiss citizen who refuses to acknowledge his Swissness poses a threat to ruling preconceptions—and it is a fact of some significance that the bulk of the novel turns on the authorities' attempts to condemn Stiller to be himself, and therefore a Swiss, whilst the Smyrnov affair remains firmly in the background. In short, Bohnenblust demands that Stiller should conform. Acceptance of the status quo is the price he must pay for freedom. The effect on personality of such dearly bought 'freedom' is shown in extreme form in the character of the architect, Sturzenegger.[17] Sturzenegger is presented as the achetypal conformist. Stiller, for his part, immediately senses this man's bad faith, the automatic behaviour patterns of the man who has sold out. This is the alternative Stiller is being offered by his defence counsel : a retreat into the past, where habit will dull all memories of what might have been and remove all necessity for painful choices. It is a chance—indeed a temptation—for Stiller to become, like his former friend Sturzenegger, 'a puppet on the invisible strings of habit' (III 591). Thus his criticisms of Swiss architecture addressed to Sturzenegger stem directly out of his present situation.[18] By renouncing creative initiative and bold experimentation, Sturzenegger (and Swiss society) has retreated from the problems posed by modern life, has accepted the safe, ordinary compromises which can only lead to the withering away of imagination. Just as society demands that Stiller give up his attempt (misguided though it may be) to achieve a new identity as Mr White, which unsettles the social order, so in its architecture it turns its back on the exciting possibilities and risks inherent in trying something new. Stiller is right to desire change (though his method may be wrong), but the architects of Zürich are totally unaware of the *need* for change; unaware that they think and feel differently, they do not perceive the need to build differently : Zürich's new buildings are erected on the same scale as the mediaeval *Altstadt* despite the fact that the social circumstances which might once have given the *Altstadt* its harmony no longer exist. Such timidity is repeated in contemporary Swiss literature—at least as far as can be judged from the selection presented by official organisations to the prison library!—as Stiller remarks : 'Most, and probably the best, stories carry the reader off to a country idyll; peasant life seems the last refuge of introspection.'[19]

Nothing underlines Stiller's eccentricity in terms of Swiss society so clearly as the nature of the fear felt by both parties. Stiller is afraid of suffocating normality, of habit which restricts growth and change; society fears the reverse. The irony is not lost on Stiller who reads in his fellow countrymen's faces 'their fear of the future, their fear of one day being poor, their fear of life, their fear of dying without life insurance, and finally their fear that the world might change, their absolutely panic fear of spiritual audacity' (III 548, *151* f.). Stiller is only too aware that freedom is problematical, that it is a question of moral strength. What he sees about him is a society, rigid in its self-righteousness, which has refused to believe that freedom requires any effort at all.[20] Bohnenblust and Sturzenegger offer him a false *bonhomie*, a 'cheerful resignation' (III 590), a substitute for reality. Yet both these men are shown at the centre, whilst Stiller is at the periphery. The clearest expression of this paradox is Bohnenblust's astonishing tirade in the climactic scene in Stiller's studio. Over four and a half pages the defence counsel pours out every cliché for which he stands in a speech that notably recalls that of Lucky in Beckett's *Waiting for Godot*:

Ich solle doch Vernunft annehmen... also Kopf hoch und heraus mit dem Geständnis... Ehe als sittliche Aufgabe und nicht als Vergnügen... Wurzeln braucht der Mensch... nicht alles von der bösen Seite sehen... niemand kann aus seiner Haut heraus, eine positivere Haltung meinerseits vonnöten... heutzutage genug Nihilismus in der Welt... das Ewig-Weibliche zieht uns hinan... heutzutage genug Intellektualismus in dieser Welt, nicht immer denken und zweifeln... Kopf hoch und hoffen... alles andere ist Schall und Rauch... Ordnung muß sein... aber Opfer vonnöten... ein bißchen Glaube an Gott unerläßlich, Zerstörung der wahren Werte durch die Hast unseres modernen Verkehrs, ferner durch Kino und Sport... vor allem aber durch Kommunismus... Familie als Keimzelle des Volkes ... die Freiheit ist ein köstliches Gut, kurzum, die Schweiz noch immer ein ideales Land... Pietät am Platze... Halt in der Gemeinschaft... (III 716 ff.)

I should come to my senses... so chin up and out with the confession... marriage a moral obligation, not a pleasure... man needs roots... mustn't always look on the black side... nobody can change his skin, a more positive attitude called for on my part... enough nihilism in the world today... the eternal feminine draws us upward... enough intellectualism in the world today, mustn't always be thinking and doubting... chin up and hope... everything else but noise and smoke... we must have order... but sacrifice needed... a little trust in the Almighty indispensable, destruction of true values by the speed

*of modern traffic, also by the cinema and sport ... but above all
by communism ... family the germ-cell of the nation ... liberty
is something to be valued, in short, Switzerland is still an ideal
country ... a spot of piety required ... a stake in the community
... (298 ff.)*

And so on. Like Lucky's speech, the fragments of truth and cliché
are so distorted as to become comic and barely recognisable, and
like Lucky's speech, Bohnenblust's 'eloquence' is a *tour de force* of
parody, a rich catalogue of beliefs ill-considered but fervidly held.

It is true, of course, that the pages devoted to Stiller's polemic
against Switzerland, whilst being a source of much of the novel's
humour, are not subject to the corrective objectivity that informs
the rest of the book, and that occasionally they verge on caricature.
But this does not necessarily detract from the portrayal of the
basic temptation facing Stiller: the false centricity of social
conformity. The issue is first shown, as it were, in black and white,
only later to be more subtly presented in ambiguous shades of grey.
An examination of this later configuration must await an analysis
of Rolf's rôle in the novel and the specific nature of the solution
he offers to Stiller.

4 MARRIAGE : THE ELUSIVE CENTRIC PRINCIPLE

As has already been seen, the relationship between man and woman
is of fundamental importance for Frisch. It is the central preoccupation of much of his dramatic work and all his novels, including his most recent work, *Montauk* (1975). Marriage, as the
expression of this relationship at its deepest level, is the institution
to which Frisch's characters look in their search for a centric
principle to give coherence and purpose to their lives. Thus Stiller's
marriage to Julika becomes for him 'dieser letzte Prüfstein' (III
752; *'this ultimate touchstone'*, 334) against which he can measure
his sense of identity. His love for her and his failure to break
through to a true, creative relationship with her, however, combine
to produce a second, and this time fatal, débâcle. The stages in this
process are charted from three distinct points of view : from the
past, i.e. Julika's account of her marriage as related directly to
Stiller (or indirectly to him via Bohnenblust), an account which is
further relativised by passing through 'Mr White's mind; from the
present, i.e. Stiller's own record of his reassessment of Julika which
is contemporaneous with the Diary itself; and finally, from Rolf's

account in his Postscript of their attempt to renew their marriage in Glion.

As Karl-Heinz Braun pointed out in an early study of the novel, not only is it the case that the subjective statements in the odd-numbered Notebooks are contrasted with, and mutually influenced by, the 'Protokoll' character of the even ones, but the device of 'Mr White', in particular, enables Frisch to give subjective truth an aura of objectivity.[21] Thus Mr White gains the freedom to listen with detachment to Julika's story and to venture critical analyses of her character, of Stiller's and of their life together. These analyses show a considerable insight into the weaknesses of *both* partners which helps to strengthen their authenticity. For instance, Mr White points to the fear of personal inadequacy that acts as a bond between Julika and Stiller : she is afraid of not being a complete woman, whilst Stiller has persistent worries about his virility. His cowardice at the river Tajo during the Spanish Civil War, for example, is related by Mr White to a decidedly feminine reticence and a hypersensitivity which earns Stiller the dubious label of 'eine männliche Mimose'. Thus the sexual tension between them is seen to be expressed on the one hand by frigidity and on the other by impotence. It is reflected, too, in Julika's attitude to the ballet which reveals a basic narcissism, illustrated most clearly by her voluptuous pleasure on stage where she is the centre of attraction yet untouchable—protected by the music which was like 'a spell cast round Julika whom everyone could watch but no one touch' (III 478).[22] Stiller, on the other hand, feels his impotence, highlighted by the Tajo episode, merely confirmed by his comparative failure as a sculptor and as a bread-winner. Thus a sexual imbalance vitiates their marriage from the outset and indeed was heralded by a stray remark from Julika on their wedding night which burnt itself into Stiller's consciousness. The remark itself is never revealed but it is clearly related to Julika's intense distaste for the sexual act. From that moment Stiller felt himself to be 'a greasy, sweaty, stinking fisherman with a crystal water-fairy' (III, 449, *80*)—a physical malaise from which he never seems to recover.[23] The result of this sterile situation—Julika's delicate health and career put children out of the question, and Stiller has to accept the dog Foxli as a substitute—is a mutual retreat from self-commitment : Julika withdraws further into her dancing with its concomitant need for care and protection, whilst Stiller succumbs to an increasingly unrestrained egocentricity.

The insistence on Stiller's egocentricity is one example of Mr

White's careful attempt at neutrality. This is seen at its most convincing in the delineation of the crisis at Davos. Whilst Stiller suffers a severe emotional collapse—significantly ending with his head pressed into Julika's lap in a position that mocks post-coital satisfaction—Julika remains aloof, faintly worried about people seeing them in such a ridiculous posture and idly wondering whether her husband's histrionics remind her more of Goethe's Clavigo or Schiller's Mortimer. Mr White records the episode through Julika's eyes. Thus we see how she finds it impossible to take Stiller seriously : she treats him like a child ('Now, now— you're a poor little chap!')—a favourite defence mechanism of Julika's to avoid adult contact. At the same time Mr White resists total condemnation of Julika for her insensitivity by consistently ironising Stiller's position : 'When he noticed his eyes were filling with tears Stiller buried his head in her lap, clung with both arms to Julika, who suddenly, as was to be expected, saw the open landscape in front of her'; 'Stiller had hands like claws, and Julika naturally found it funny, even embarrassing, that he was clutching at her buttocks'; 'He even tried (ridiculous though it sounds) to bite into her lap, to bite like a dog, but because of her thick corduroy skirt he couldn't manage it' (III 474, *104*). The effect of such tragi-comic juxtapositions is to relativise both points of view and underline vividly the isolation of these two people, imprisoned in their separate worlds.

In the Davos sanatorium Julika is given a chance to clarify her dilemma with the help of the young Jesuit seminarist who visits her bedside. With him she feels safe, for he treats her as he would a nun, or rather as 'ein Neutrum'. From him she hears the familiar Frisch exegesis of the commandment 'Thou shalt not make unto thee any graven image'. At the safe time the Jesuit perceptively points out her 'infantile innocence' and makes explicit her permanent and destructive belief that she was always the victim and never the initiator of pain in her marriage. It is significant that Julika takes from the seminarist only what appeals to her (and can be used against Stiller) and evades the accurate shafts he aims at her own guilt by taking shelter behind a defensive wall of banter. This superficiality prevents her from expounding the 'Bildnis' theme with any conviction on Stiller's final visit to the sanatorium. Because she has not applied the lesson to *herself*, the truths she utters have a hollow ring, easily detected by her husband ('Where did you get all that from?').[24] Julika cannot, or will not give up her 'Bildnis' of Stiller ('Whoever told you to talk such awful

nonsense, my good Stiller, that's not you speaking!'), for this would
involve an honest self-analysis. This evasion in turn prevents Stiller
from doing likewise ('If I hadn't made you my test ('Bewährungsprobe'), the idea of fettering me with your ill-health would never
have occurred to you'). It is Stiller's grave mistake to use another
human being as a 'Bewährungsprobe', but Julika's never to grasp
the seriousness and extent of her husband's anguish.

The brief affair with Sibylle, a woman of normal sexual appetite,
serves only to emphasise Stiller's difficulty in building a valid relationship with a woman. Sibylle's own motivation, however, does
not help the situation. Frustrated by her own husband's fixed image
of *her*, she attempts to break out and give him what she considers
a long overdue shock. But in doing so she accepts a romanticised
image of Stiller. She is attracted by 'the magic of the provisional'
which she detects in the atmosphere of Stiller's studio and which is
such a contrast to the solid, bourgeois order of her own environment. It is not therefore surprising that the real Stiller proves disappointing. It is apparent from the opening episode of their affair,
where Stiller enacts the phases of a bull-fight—with himself as the
bull and Sibylle as the matador!—that Stiller's inferiority complex,
his fear of impotence, will undermine this relationship, too. Sibylle
has not the strength—or rather her own needs are too paramount—
to hold the affair in balance. She finds herself in the dominating
rôle but unable to break through Stiller's egocentricity. She aborts
Stiller's child secretly and subsequently develops a fatal motherly
attitude towards him.[25] The result is that Sibylle changes from one
fixed image to another : initially attracted to Stiller in the excitingly
anonymous atmosphere of a *Fasching* masked ball, she now—
echoing Julika—denies him the possibility of change : 'I don't
believe you will ever change, not even in your outward life' (III
647, 232). As Frisch remarked in his *Tagebuch 1946–1949* (II 370
and 374), this wilful rigidity is the antithesis of love.

In many ways the most telling perspective through which we see
Stiller's marriage is that which is contemporaneous with the Diary
itself. The alienating device of having Mr White write of Stiller
in the third person not only enables Stiller to be objective about
past mistakes, but also to see Julika afresh, indeed as a different
woman altogether. It may well be a hopeless undertaking to deny
the past its existence in this way, but at least one can argue that
Stiller's attitude, in the circumstances, is more fruitful than Julika's.
He notes, for example, that Julika's plucked eyebrows lend her
face 'a slightly masklike appearance, as though perpetually miming

surprise' (III 407, 47) and that only when he can shake her momentarily from her fixed idea that a marriage had genuinely existed between them—Julika is quite incapable of distinguishing between an existential and a historical truth—does her face come to life : 'Her face, partially unmasked by quiet dismay and more beautiful than before, making one think that contact must be possible, contact in the realm of truth' (III 410, 50).

The renewal of this relationship (recorded in the odd-numbered Notebooks) goes hand in hand with Stiller's struggle and marks its critical moments. Thus in the earlier Notebooks the possibility of a 'meeting in the realm of truth' looks bright. But as Stiller is slowly worn down by the pressures surrounding him, the 'second' marriage begins to take on all the signs of an appalling repetition of all the old mistakes. Julika once again assumes the dimensions of a 'Bewährungsprobe', and in the seventh and last Notebook Stiller acknowledges the fate he has tried so hard to escape : 'Either we smash ourselves to pieces on one another, or we succeed in loving each other' (III 688, 270). In the last desperate effort to maintain his rôle of Mr White intact Stiller is forced to admit defeat in the face of Julika's impassive superiority : she watches his attempt to destroy his old studio, and with it his old identity, with a devastating equanimity. The tragedy of the situation is that by clinging to her own image of Stiller, Julika forces him to take up again *his* old image of *her*. That is to say, he sees in her once again—and despite the evidence—the hope of a centric principle on which to build his life, another chance to give 'the vacuum that binds us together' (III 689, 271) a meaningful shape and content. The result is described from the third and last perspective : Rolf's account of their life in Territet and Glion.

The mistake has been frequently made of accepting this final viewpoint, if not as a throwback to the nineteenth century tradition of the omniscient narrator, at least as that of a neutral, unprejudiced observer.[26] On the contrary, the ultimate irony of the novel is to be found in what is actually the highly *subjective* viewpoint of the public prosecutor's Postscript. For example, Rolf's sympathy for Julika is made very clear, although it is equally obvious that he does not get to know her well. Indeed, his reactions to her frequently recall Stiller's own; he notes her lack of self-awareness and the difficulty of detecting her real feelings : 'In all likelihood she had no inkling how little of herself she communicated' (III 742, 324); her laughter, too, 'was pure mimicry, and as a matter of fact, when I look back, I can't remember this woman laughing in any other way' (III 745, *327*); and when after her seizure, of which Stiller knows nothing, she reappears freshly made-up, Rolf, too, has the distinct impression of seeing a totally different person. Yet despite this insight into the very real difficulties with which Stiller was faced in his relationship with Julika, Rolf's judgement of where the fault principally lay is firm, and only the ultimate crisis brings him to a realisation (too often overlooked) of his own limited viewpoint, his own personal inadequacy—a confession to which we will have to return later.

In general, however, Rolf does give an accurate account of the disintegration of Stiller's second and final attempt to achieve balance through marriage. Their eccentricity as a couple—they live initially in a hotel amidst 'outsiders and solitaries', or, as Stiller puts it laconically, as a 'couple of Swiss inland emigrants'—is matched by their increasing isolation as people. Detached from the outside world, they grow ever more detached from each other, and the roots of this second failure are clearly traceable to experiences before their retreat into this ironic country idyll. Julika complains to Rolf when he at last gets round to paying them a visit : 'How can I change? I am as I am. Why does Stiller always want to change me?' (III 748, *330*). Here we can see, on the one hand, Julika's fatal blindness to the need for a new start based on the awareness of personal deficiencies, and on the other, Stiller's Promethean hybris in thinking that he could change another human being single-handed and to a design of his own fashioning—in Rolf's words : 'You set yourself up as her saviour ... You wanted her to be your creation' (III 765, *346*). The two positions are too entrenched for love to stand a chance. Inevitably Julika and Stiller repeat their 'first' marriage. Their inability to communicate with one another leads Julika to hide the seriousness of her illness from Stiller for six months, and when the illness does break out, with fatal consequences, this in turn convinces Stiller that he alone was responsible for her death. The centric principle cannot be found, but Stiller is unable to forget the glimpse he once had of it. He has invested so much energy in its pursuit that he feels he has gone beyond the point of no return :

Warum ich zurückgekommen bin?!... Wenn du ein halbes Leben lang vor einer Tür gestanden und geklopft hast, Herrgott nochmal, erfolglos wie ich vor dieser Frau, vollkommen erfolglos, Herrgott nochmal—und dann geh du weiter! Vergiß sie, so eine Tür, die dich zehn Jahre versäumt hat!... was heißt da schon Liebe? Ich habe sie nicht vergessen können. Das ist alles... Weil's einen Punkt gibt, wo sich das Aufgeben nicht mehr lohnt. (III 768)

Why did I come back?... When you've stood half a lifetime knocking at a door, great God, unsuccessfully as I stood before this woman, absolutely without success, great God—then see if you can pass on! See if you can forget a door like that, after wasting ten years knocking at it!... Where does love come into it? I couldn't forget her. That's all... Because there comes a point where it simply isn't worth while giving up. (349)

Given the fact that society has condemned him to be Stiller, unwilling to allow a transformation in its sphere, and that Stiller himself has not found the inner strength to achieve a personal transformation in defiance of society, and that Julika never seems to be aware there is a struggle going on at all, it is not surprising that Stiller slips back into a corrosive egocentricity.

Further evidence for a more tempered view of Stiller's failure can be adduced from the prose sketch *Schinz*, published four years before the novel in Frisch's *Tagebuch 1946–1949* (II 723–49), and from the radio play, *Rip van Winkle* (1953). In the former, which is clearly the germ for the later novel, Schinz is seen in a favourable light, despite his failure to escape from a society depicted as powerful and repressively benevolent. More significant, however, is the sympathetic delineation of Anatol Wadel's dilemma in *Rip van Winkle*.[27] Not only is the Julika of the radio play a predominantly negative figure, but the public prosecutor himself appears very much more in harmony with the 'Sonderling' Wadel (=Stiller), whom he is supposed to prosecute, than with the demands of a hostile society. For example, the young Jesuit seminarist's ideas, learnt parrot-fashion and fundamentally misunderstood by Julika in the novel, are here put into the public prosecutor's mouth : 'We make an image of a man and won't let him out of this image. We know that's the man he was, and it doesn't matter what happens to him, we will not tolerate him changing. Indeed, you can see that his own wife won't tolerate it; she wants him just as he was and thinks this is love... You really should read the tale of Rip van Winkle. I can't explain it any better. A man awakes to his real self, but we—' (III 834). The negative rôle played by society and its destructive effect on the individual is central to the play's theme. Naturally, parallels between these works should be drawn with care. It is obvious, for example, that in the novel the rôle of public prosecutor has become much more ambivalent, if not socially conformist, and Julika's character has been given greater depth and complexity. Yet *Schinz* and the radio play do provide useful indicators to the development of Frisch's intentions in the novel, and *Rip van Winkle*, in particular, throws much light on the specific nature of Stiller's self-alienation and the process of self-acceptance which constitutes the essential dynamic of the novel and which now must be analysed in order to understand fully the reasons for the collapse of marriage as an integrating principle.

5 'SELF-ALIENATION' AND 'SELF-ACCEPTANCE': THE SEARCH FOR
SYNTHESIS

The pattern and substance of Stiller's spiritual odyssey can be traced via a number of highly subjective reflections which occur exclusively in the odd-numbered Notebooks and which bring them into dialectical relationship with the more objective material of the even-numbered ones. Not surprisingly, these observations, some philosophical musings, others more like cries of despair, are most numerous in the final Notebook, in which the struggle to fuse the identities of Mr White and Anatol Stiller into a viable synthesis is apparently successful. However, the deeply serious nature of Stiller's mental journey is plain enough in the very first Notebook. Alongside the humour and comic incidents, and thus relativising them, Frisch has placed specific pointers to Stiller's existential crisis.

It is clear from the Diary that the characteristically excessive demands Stiller makes on himself began with his decision to fight in Spain. He admits to Sibylle, for example, that his motivation was anything other than a desire to combat fascism. Unnerved by a favourable review of his work as a sculptor, he was actually running away from the sudden expectations aroused in the world around him. The explosion of the Spanish Civil War merely offered a convenient and convincing escape route from what he felt to be constructing social pressures. Thus Stiller fits into a long line of Frisch heroes who feel oppressed by the image others make of them. In each case, however, the desire to flee such definition leads to a grave overestimation of their inner resources. For Stiller the moment of truth comes when he is overpowered without a struggle by enemy soldiers at the river Tajo. His love for Anja, his Polish girl-friend, forces him to conceal his real behaviour (abject cowardice) and begin living a lie. Once back home, the deception deepens and he allows his failure of courage to be interpreted as humanitarianism, and in this way he becomes a prisoner of his friends' and acquaintances' view of himself—ironically, the very fate he had fled from in the first place. The enervating bad conscience which this engenders vitiates his relationships with both Julika and Sibylle and is correctly diagnosed by Stiller himself as 'the beginning of all evil, as a curse, an ill-omen' (III 492, *117*). As Rolf remarks, such self-deception stultifies life and leads inexorably to a loss of identity—a move away from the living core of true experience into a barren isolation.

The most intense experience of self-alienation suffered by Stiller is his non-relationship with Florence and his subsequent suicide attempt. As we have seen, the latter is indeed the existential basis for Stiller's assumption of the *tabula rasa* identity of Mr White. Paradoxically, he experienced it as a mysterious re-birth, a moment of terror when all time stopped, 'ein Sturz, der auch wieder keiner ist, ein Zustand vollkommener Ohnmacht bei vollkommenem Wachsein, nur die Zeit ist weg' (III 726; *a falling that was actually no falling, a state of total powerlessness accompanied by total wakefulness, only time had disappeared, 306*).[28] This encounter with death Stiller calls his 'meeting with his angel'.[29] It is the ground bass against which he henceforth measures his life's rhythm, the guarantee that the past (and with it the continuity of his previous identity) has been expunged. Yet however true this experience is *existentially,* it proves incapable of standing up to the practical test of Stiller's return to Switzerland. As he discovers, it is just not possible to destroy one's past as if one were the only person concerned, for it is part of the past of many other people who have a vested interest in not having *their* lives challenged in this way. Only his brother, Wilfried, and to a lesser extent Rolf, who had never met Stiller before, are prepared to be at all flexible in their relationship with the 'new' Stiller—all the others insist on him accepting his past and thus indirectly confirming their own experience and identities. It is Stiller's mistake to think that he can solve the problem of time by simply avoiding it. As Frisch put it in his *Tagebuch 1946–1949*: 'We are the past, even when we cast it off, no less than the present—Time does not transform us. It merely unfolds us' (II 361). A genuine transformation, in other words, must subsume the past, not destroy it. It is a question of creating a new synthesis out of the totality of experience. It is not given to human beings—as Kürmann, the protagonist of *Biografie* (1967), discovers—to start afresh with the slate wiped clean. Nevertheless, Stiller's struggle is not shown as a ridiculous one. It is true that he requires society to change if he is to benefit, and that this insistence resembles the intransigence of Molière's great eccentric, Alceste in *Le Misanthrope*. But Molière's society was self-confident and stable, where Frisch's is depicted as problematical and insecure. Thus the nature of Alceste's eccentricity is unequivocally comic, whilst that of Stiller is deeply ambiguous. Alceste affords amusement to his environment, but Stiller poses a threat to his. In both cases society wins, but in *Stiller* the victory is presented as a highly dubious one in which a man is grimly and unceremoniously driven back into himself. If one accepts the close affinity between the radio play *Rip van Winkle* and the novel, one may agree with Frisch's description of this essentially negative process which he appends as a motto to the play : 'This is the sketch of a man who had no life, because he forced himself to be what other people wanted him to be. And one day, as he awoke out of this nightmare, lo ! people knew his name, a respected name, and they would not allow anyone to live without a name. They clapped him in prison, they condemned him to be what he had been and would not tolerate his transformation.' Society cannot accept Stiller's transformation, partly because its own existence is based on historic continuity, which such a metamorphosis would deny, but partly also because it is in the nature of Stiller's 'angel experience' that it cannot be expressed in direct social terms at all. Stiller is thus faced with two interrelated problems : on the one hand, he cannot find the *language* in which to express his experience of renewal ('I have no language for my reality'), on the other, he cannot locate the centric principle—in this context akin to religious faith—which will guarantee the genuineness of his experience in the face of eventual opposition. It is arguable that some such faith, indeed, would have obviated the desperate need to convince the outside world of his new identity altogether.

From the outset Stiller is aware that his inarticulateness is associated with the dangerous nature of words, the way they tend to obscure rather than clarify meaning. The more he attempts to pin down his 'angel' in language, for example, the more insubstantial and unconvincing the experience seems to become. This problem goes to the heart of Stiller's dilemma, a dilemma of which he is acutely conscious even as he is spinning out adventurous tales for the gullible Knobel :

Man kann alles erzählen, nur nicht sein wirkliches Leben;—diese Unmöglichkeit ist es, was uns verurteilt zu bleiben, wie unsere Gefährten uns sehen und spiegeln, sie, die vorgeben, mich zu kennen, sie, die sich als meine Freunde bezeichnen und nimmer gestatten, daß ich mich wandle, und jedes Wunder (was ich nicht erzählen kann, das Unaussprechliche, was ich nicht beweisen kann) zuschanden machen—nur um sagen zu können : 'Ich kenne dich.' (III 416)

You can put anything into words, except your real life. It is this impossibility that condemns us to remain as our companions see and mirror us, those who claim to know me, those who call themselves my friends, and never allow me to change, and discredit every miracle (which I cannot put into words, the inexpressible, which I cannot prove)—simply so that they can say: 'I know you'. (55)

Momentarily, however, Stiller is hopeful that the people surrounding him will accept the words he writes—his 'Geflunker'—and leave him to himself. For the alternative they offer him is an escape into rôle-playing which would mean re-establishing a continuous identity, and in his eyes, falling victim to repetition. That this repetition has little to do with Kierkegaard's religious category is clear. Whereas the Danish theologian saw repetition as God's will and the ultimate meaning of life,[30] Stiller uses the term for deadening habit, the sterilisation of experience.

Nevertheless, Stiller does grasp the irony of the paradox before him : on the one hand—to quote Frisch's words in an analogous context—'Everything we write down at this time is basically nothing but a desperate defence mounted at the permanent cost of truth' (*Tagebuch 1946–1949*, II 376); on the other, Stiller realises that language is his only connection with reality :

Schreiben ist nicht Kommunikation mit Lesern, auch nicht Kommunikation mit sich selbst, sondern Kommunikation mit dem Unaussprechlichen. Je genauer man sich auszusprechen vermöchte, um so reiner erschiene das Unaussprechliche, das heißt die Wirklichkeit, die den Schreiber bedrängt und bewegt. (III 677)

Writing is not communication with readers, not even communication with oneself, but communication with the inexpressible. The more exactly one succeeds in expressing oneself, the more clearly

appears the inexpressible, that is, the reality which oppresses and
moves the writer. (260)

He seems to acknowledge that the ultimate goal must be a self-
sufficient silence, a region from which misunderstandings are
banished : 'We possess language in order to become mute. He who is
silent is not dumb. He who is silent hasn't even an inkling who he
is not.' In this context Stiller's relationship with his brother,
Wilfried, is significant. For Wilfried reveals himself as the only
totally disinterested figure in the book. He does not force his image
of Stiller on to Mr White, rather does he exercise admirable tolerance and flexibility. There is not a trace of ambivalence in his
behaviour—which makes Stiller describe him as 'a man of natural
existence, not a man of expression' (III 674, 258). Wilfried's serenity,
indeed, makes Stiller feel garrulous even when he is silent, and this
self-sufficiency fundamentally confuses him. For he is suddenly
aware that although Wilfried takes it for granted that he is the missing sculptor, the fact does not upset him, because Wilfried—unlike
Bohnenblust, Julika and the rest—still allows his brother the possibility of change. He is motivated by an affection and respect for
the individuality of the other. Stiller's brother, however, offers only
a fleeting glimpse of what personal relationships could be, for he is,
and remains, a minor character in the novel.

At one other point Stiller touches on the idea that 'das wirkliche
Leben' is one of silence. Faced by Bohnenblust with an album of
photographs, Stiller tries to define what reality means to him and
puts his finger on the central philosophical problem of the book:
'It is difficult to say what makes a life a real life. I call it reality,
but what does that mean? You could also say it depends on a
person being identical with himself' (III 417, 56). A 'real life' will
leave a deposit 'in the shape of something alive, not merely in a
photograph album yellow with age' :

> Ablagerung ist auch nur ein Wort, ich weiß, und vielleicht reden
> wir überhaupt nur von Dingen, die wir vermissen, nicht begreifen,
> Gott ist eine Ablagerung! Er ist die Summe wirklichen Lebens,
> oder wenigstens scheint es mir manchmal so. Ist das Wort eine
> Ablagerung? Vielleicht ist das Leben, das wirkliche, einfach
> stumm... (III 418)

> *Deposit is only a word, I know, and perhaps we are talking all*
> *the time about things that elude us, things we can't grasp. God is*
> *a deposit! He is the sum of real life, or at least that's how it*

sometimes seems to me. Is language a deposit? Perhaps life, real
life, is simply mute ... (56 f.)

Bohnenblust is deaf to such admittedly vague gropings towards
solutions. Mr White will not accept the identity of Stiller because
Stiller's life has left no 'deposit in the shape of something alive',
and it was therefore not properly a life at all. Language is thus a
critical matter for Stiller, for it is the only instrument—and one of
questionable efficacy—he has for defending his 'angel-experience'
before other people.

Even more crucial, however, is the related crisis of *faith*. It is
clear that faith in God might have provided Stiller with the centric
principle he needed so much, might have enabled him to accept
himself with all his limitations, secure in the knowledge of his own
uniqueness and value. His failure to acquire this faith undermines
his qualified acceptance of the court's verdict and throws an ironic
light on those pages of the novel which derive from Kierkegaard.

Stiller knows from the start of his imprisonment that escape is
impossible, that somehow he must find the strength to hold and
control the tensions of a paradoxical position. In fact, the only
feasible solution is to adopt the strategy of accepting his past failures
outwardly at society's evaluation and inwardly of clinging to the
truth of his 'angel':

Heute wieder sehr klar: das Versagen in unserem Leben läßt
sich nicht begraben, und solange ich's versuche, komme ich aus
dem Versagen nicht heraus, es gibt keine Flucht. Aber das
Verwirrende: die andern halten es für selbstverständlich, daß
ich ein anderes Leben nicht vorzuweisen habe, und also halten
sie, was ich auf mich nehme, für mein Leben. Es ist aber nie mein
Leben gewesen! Nur insofern ich weiß, daß es nie mein Leben
gewesen ist, kann ich es annehmen: als mein Versagen. Das
heißt, man müßte imstande sein, ohne Trotz durch ihre
Verwechselung hindurchzugehen, eine Rolle spielend, ohne daß
ich mich selber je damit verwechsle, dazu aber müßte ich einen
festen Punkt haben—(III 589 f.)

Today it was perfectly clear once more that we cannot bury the
failure in our lives, and so long as I try I shall never get out of
the failure, there is no escape. But the bewildering thing is, other
people take it for granted that I have no other life to produce,
and so they consider what I take upon myself to be my life.
But it was never my life! And I know that only in so far as it

*was never my life can I take it upon myself—as my failure.
This means one must be capable of passing without defiance
through their confusion of identities, playing a part without ever
confusing oneself with the part; but for this I must have a fixed
point.' (186)*

This entry in the fifth Notebook is the key passage for understanding Stiller's struggle as recorded in his Diary. It indicates that the Kierkegaard motto which Frisch fixes to the novel applies only to its first Part. For the seven Notebooks constitute the struggle for himself, just the 'angel-experience' corresponds to the awakening in Stiller of 'the passion for freedom'. Hans Mayer is surely correct when he argues that the motto is not the key to the whole book, but rather stands in an ironic relationship to it.[31] The irony, indeed, goes very deep. For the one insight Stiller never attains is that he is most wholly *himself*, a unique and fascinating individual, during and because of the actual *composition* of his prison diary. In this way he struggles for the possession of his true self 'as for his happiness, and *that is his happiness*' (Kierkegaard motto, my italics).

As we have seen, Julika and marriage fail to provide Stiller with 'einen festen Punkt'. In an interesting study of alienation and experience R. D. Laing has remarked : 'If our experience is destroyed, our behaviour will be destructive. If our experience is destroyed, we have lost our own selves.'[32] This is precisely the situation Julika brings about in refusing to accept that her husband has changed. Her rigidity, together with society's, results in Stiller's self-conscious attempt to destroy his studio. In this impasse, faith in—to use Rolf's circumlocution—'the certitude of an absolute authority beyond human interpretation' (III 670, *254*) is the only remedy. Stiller, however, never achieves this certainty because, in Kierkegaard's terms, he does not experience despair deeply enough. He knows this perfectly well : 'I am not sufficiently without hope, or, as believers say, not submissive enough' (III 690, *272*). In fact, he lays down conditions *before* accepting God, and this bad faith effectively keeps God out of his life, leaving behind 'dieses schwarze Loch' (III 601; *'this black hole'*, *188*), an abyss of uncertainty. Kierkegaard's answer is to take the risk of leaping into the abyss and thus into the open arms of God. But for this, absolute resignation is necessary, a complete and unconditional surrender to God. There is no concrete evidence that Stiller is ever ready to risk such a leap which he acknowledges himself to be 'the step into freedom ... a tremendous step, a step with which we leave behind everything that has previously seemed like solid ground' (III 548, *152*). Rather does he adopt a strategy of inward withdrawal : 'My angel keep me on the alert' (III 729, *309*). His acceptance of the court's decision remains at best a neutral rather than a positive one.

What in effect Stiller tries to do is to take faith in God as a kind of hypothesis in the hope that ensuing experience, underpinned by his 'angel', will prove its validity. Disastrously, he puts the cart before the horse : there is no other way to faith than the surrender to the absolute with nothing tangible to grasp. Thus his attitude to repentance, which Kierkegaard—in orthodox fashion—regards as the true route to God and reality, is ambivalent; he fails to break through to the 'ethical' plane and remains on the 'aesthetic' one. For as Kierkegaard says, 'When a man lives aesthetically his mood is always eccentric because he has his centre in the periphery. Personality has its centre within itself, and he who has not his self is eccentric.'[33] Failing to locate 'a fixed point' either within himself or outside, Stiller falls back into a *passive* waiting for a miracle to transform him and ends, predictably, in solipsism. In such circumstances it is not surprising that he falls victim to his dreaded repetition and collapses into a second 'Selbstüberforderung'. For Stiller is faced with a permanent paradox : existential truth contradicts biographical truth. A synthesis of the two could only have been achieved in a religious context.[34] An alternative would be to discover a viable strategy to hold the tensions between these two poles and live out the contradiction. For this course Stiller's soul lacks, in Kierkegaard's phrase, 'the elasticity of irony'.[35] His life instead becomes a parody of the artist/hermit on the periphery of society in a faintly ludicrous 'country idyll'.

6   ROLF : THE AMBIVALENCE OF 'ORDNUNG'

It is tempting to accept the 'Postscript of the Public Prosecutor' as a quasi-judicial summing-up, an objective assessment of Stiller's life after his release from prison. Such a reading would have the merit of tidying up loose ends and leaving the reader with the satisfying feeling of a 'case history' suitably completed. But to do so would seem to imply a narrative omniscience which is expressly denied Stiller, and the loss of which has proved a hallmark of serious fiction in the twentieth century. Rolf himself certainly makes no such claims. On his inability to help Stiller after his release he remarks revealingly : 'I probably wasn't sufficiently capable of putting myself in his place' (III 737, *320*). And later, at the moment of greatest crisis in the early hours of Easter Sunday, he is forced to admit : 'I stood there helpless. I felt my lack of any official authority, for whatever I might have said remained merely my own personal opinion (III 772 f., *353*).[36] Furthermore, his own life, as it is reflected in Stiller's Notebooks is far too problematical. An examination of the rôle he plays as prosecuting counsel in Stiller's case—which inevitably relativises his stature in the Postscript— suggests that it makes more sense to see Part Two of the novel as a kind of 'Eighth Notebook', itself characterised by an ingrained subjectivity.

The reader is struck by one dominant characteristic in Rolf's personality : his lucidity. As befits a lawyer, his ideas—whether on marriage or life—are well-ordered, economically and fluently expressed. They contrast sharply with Stiller's more tentative and disorganised utterances. Indeed, the suspicion arises at times that Rolf's views are a little too pat, a little too reasonable. Sibylle certainly finds his lectures on marriage unhelpfully academic, not to say smug. More remarkable, however, is Rolf's apparent need to tell the story of his marriage to Stiller. (Stiller himself had quickly noted this : 'My immediate impression was that this man has some confession to make to me', III 383, *25*.) The sense of urgency and the desire to be exact, that can be felt in his account, indicate that Rolf is intent on something more complex than simply trying to help Stiller, by analogy, to grasp the meaning of 'Selbstüber-forderung'. Indeed, as the investigation wears on, Stiller finds himself in the ironic position of *judge* between Rolf's account and Sibylle's of their marriage, just as he—as Mr White—found himself the 'Protokollführer' of Julika's story of *her* marriage.

A comparison of the two accounts–remembering that Rolf and Sybille have been together for some years since the crisis which forms the substance of their stories–reveals interesting discrepancies. For example, it would appear that Rolf suppresses moments of undignified behaviour : Sibylle records an incident of frustrated anger in which Rolf hurls a coffee cup at the wall; Rolf in his version depicts himself as coldly aloof and mentions no coffee cup. In particular, in view of the time-gap, the two separate accounts of Sibylle's visit to Rolf's office are illuminating. Rolf's version shows a man, secure in his belief that he is right, calm, superior but objective and fair; Sibylle, on the other hand, depicts herself as the injured party, forced to go to Pontresina because of her husband's insensitivity. Neither account is without some insight, but fundamentally both reveal a breakdown in communication. For example,

Sibylle records an important conversation on marriage during this interview that Rolf does not even mention. It is just as likely, of course, that the conversation never actually took place, but represents Sibylle's thoughts which she genuinely believes she expressed in words. But that is not the issue. What *is* important is that these two irreconcilable accounts represent their current views of an important part of their common past at a time when they are reunited and have been so (apparently harmoniously) for some years. Such evidence inevitably undermines Rolf's implied claim that he and Sibylle have attained a creative, if belated, marital stability. And indeed, the Sibylle we see in the Postscript is a strangely shadowy figure. Even her name is mentioned only twice throughout Rolf's statement. (Oddly, a puzzled Rolf remarks at one point on the fact that Stiller seems to be avoiding uttering it—perhaps he takes his cue from Rolf who refers to Sibylle practically throughout his narrative simply as 'meine Frau'.) The result is to give the impression of a sensible accommodation with few demands made on either side, rather than a warm, living relationship. This 'answer' to the problem of marriage has been adumbrated before : Yvonne and Hauswirt in *Die Schwierigen.*

One further discrepancy must be noted : Rolf's strange story of 'the parcel of flesh-pink cloth'. From many incidents in the novel it is clear that the Rolf-Sibylle marriage is a parallel to that of Stiller and Julika. Rolf certainly believes that, at one time, he was guilty like Stiller of making excessive demands on himself. Thus the story of the 'parcel of flesh-pink cloth', with its labyrinthine motif, is presented as a rough equivalent to the metaphorical expression of Stiller's experience in the Carlsbad Cavern story. Rolf himself explains the symbolic meaning of the parcel and describes two negative ways of dealing with it :

Die meisten von uns haben so ein Paket mit fleischfarbenem Stoff, nämlich Gefühle, die sie von ihrem intellektuellen Niveau aus nicht wahrhaben wollen. Es gibt zwei Auswege, die zu nichts führen; wir töten unsere primitiven und also unwürdigen Gefühle ab, soweit als möglich, auf die Gefahr hin, daß dadurch das Gefühlsleben überhaupt abgetötet wird, oder wir geben unseren unwürdigen Gefühlen einfach einen anderen Namen. Wir lügen sie um. (III 668)

Most of us have a parcel of flesh-pink cloth—namely our feelings—that on an intellectual level we would like to ignore. There are two ways out of the difficulty which lead nowhere:

either we kill our primitive and therefore unworthy feelings, as far as we can, at the risk of killing our emotional life altogether, or we simply give our unworthy feelings another name. We transform them by lies. (252)

And with customary clarity he indicates the inevitable consequences : self-alienation. This has obvious reference to Stiller's predicament, but what is easily overlooked as one reads Rolf's calm and measured exposition is its applicability to his own situation. For nowhere in the novel does Rolf give us the *positive* answer to the problem of the 'parcel of flesh-pink cloth'. When Stiller enquires about its fate, he is told that Rolf simply threw it down a train lavatory!

What we do get from Rolf, however, is an expression of the religious dimension, without which self-acceptance appears difficult, if not impossible. The trouble is that there is no conclusive evidence either that the religious experience means anything more to Rolf than academic discussion of 'eine absolute Instanz' or 'eine absolute Realität'. He avoids, as Stiller is quick to note, the word 'God' and indeed any direct confrontation with Christianity. Despite the ideas he borrows from Kierkegaard, he declares revealingly : 'I was never an expert on Kierkegaard' (III 737, *319*). And the failure to get to grips with the essential Christian aspect of this religious thinker partly explains the lack of conviction his words carry. His vague answer, for instance, to Stiller's desperate plight as he waits for news of Julika's operation—'To be quite practical: you must learn to pray for one another' (III 772, *353*)—may be called anything but 'practical'. When Rolf talks of 'self-knowledge' as a first, indispensable step on the way to freedom that can only be found in faith, we suspect that he too has not got beyond this initial movement and thus shares the melancholy of Kierkegaard's 'aesthetic' man—a man who may have given up his own false rôle-playing but who has not yet found a creative alternative.

It may therefore be more accurate to see Rolf not as a man who has successfully come through the crisis of his life, but as one who has side-stepped it by retreating into an 'Ordnung' structured by convention—not a free man, but a conformist. As a symbol of convention he can be seen as eminently reasonable; for after all, convention makes life in society tolerable—it is, in C. G. Jung's words, 'a collective necessity'. At the same time, not accepting society's conventions in favour of developing one's personality, as Stiller tries to do, is 'an unpopular undertaking, a deviation that is highly uncongenial to the herd, an eccentricity smelling of the cenobite, as it seems to the outsider. To develop the personality is a gamble, and the tragedy is that the daemon of the inner voice is at once our greatest danger and our indispensable help.'[37] The 'daemon of the inner voice' can readily be identified with Stiller's 'angel', but in his case it led him so far from the corrective forces of society that arrival at a bleak solipsism became inevitable. Rolf, on the other hand, seems to have deliberately turned a deaf ear to the 'inner voice' and chosen instead to come to terms with social 'Ordnung' and all that this imples for the individual. Rather than risk the dangers to which Stiller exposes himself, he has sought shelter behind what he calls self-revealingly 'affairs of social or professional importance' (III 741, *323*). Rolf's outward 'success' counterpoints Stiller's 'failure' and represents for the latter the ultimate temptation to conform—a temptation far more insidious than the crude machinations of his defence counsel. For placed as he is as a counterweight to Bohneblust, Rolf is a man only too aware of the fragility of 'reason' in times of stress : 'I didn't know what to do. I felt myself that my common-sense approach was very shallow' (III 762, *343*). Although he can be taken as a representative of a society which still clings to faith in an order long since emptied of meaning, it is difficult to overlook that attractive, sympathetic element in his character which is plain to Stiller, who sees in him 'a sceptic, who doesn't even believe everything he says himself' (III 383, *24*).

Strangely enough, it is Sibylle who is given an essential insight into the sympathy the two men have for each other. Of her husband and lover she remarks : 'Both of them rolled into one, that would have been ideal!' (III 631, *217*). The echo of Leonore Sanvitale's words in *Torquato Tasso* is not entirely fortuitous.[38] Like Tasso, Stiller is finally 'ship-wrecked', like Tasso, he founders on the rock of society represented by a mature but ambivalent friend; and like Antonio and Tasso, Rolf and Stiller would each have benefited by a more just proportionment of their respective talents.

'Who did violence to whom? On this point much could be said' (Rolf; III 750, *332*). Like so much else in this fascinating novel, our ultimate view of Rolf remains clouded, his rôle ambivalent. We see Stiller from several perspectives, the same is true of Rolf : 'Every word is false and true, that is the nature of words.' The 'Postscript of the Public Prosecutor' must take its place alongside the other seven Notebooks as a fragment of an essentially opaque reality. It thus adds to the authenticity of the novel and shares in that irony of tone which is its unifying principle.

It is Max Frisch's particular *tour de force* in *Stiller* that his chosen form prevents the reader from jumping to conclusions about events and characters. An integral part of the method is the sacrifice of the traditional omniscient narrator. Thus even at the end of the book one cannot be absolutely sure about anything. One cannot, for example, say with the grotesque confidence of Stiller's former friends : 'I know you!' For Frisch 'everything which is complete ceases to accommodate the human spirit'.[39] It is in this sense of posing questions and then leaving them open, of refusing to seize the neat and comfortable answer, however 'real' it might seem to be, that Frisch demonstrates most clearly his gifts as a subtle and humane ironist.

V

Homo Faber

I INTRODUCTION

Having drawn in *Stiller* the portrait of a man intensely aware of a personal eccentricity in a world that has itself lost its centre, in *Homo Faber* Frisch turns the problem through a hundred and eighty degrees. Whereas Anatol Stiller's story begins with the recognition of such a severe dislocation, Walter Faber's ends with it. For fifty years Faber has lived, as it were, at the dead centre of an ostensibly stable world, his rôle circumscribed by precise problems and precise solutions. In fact, Faber's life has been what Stiller feared most: repetition, routine, banality.

If *Stiller* explored the artistic temperament, it was in a sense a logical step for Frisch the architect to proceed to an examination of a technologist who might represent that other sphere of human activity with which the novelist himself has been most closely involved.[1] However, technology as such plays surprisingly little part in the novel. Frisch makes no attempt, for example, to describe its rôle and impact in the modern world, and Hanna's criticisms in the 'Second Stop' are directed strictly *ad hominem*. What the reader is shown instead is a certain attitude of mind rooted in rigid mental categories which Frisch has observed before in other fields of human endeavour—for example, the Law (Bohnenblust), the Army (Ammann), Architecture (Sturzenegger) and Commerce (Hauswirt). Such an attitude enables men to take refuge in practical affairs and neglect the more difficult problems of the spirit. Precisely the process of showing an individual confronted with the disastrous one-sidedness of this type of thinking gives *Homo Faber* its particular shape and interest.

Faber's 'report' is composed at two unexpected moments of inertia (confinement to his hotel room in Caracas and to his sick-room in an Athens hospital) amidst a flux of normally undifferentiated sense impressions. Clearly, the writing of a report can hardly be seen in itself as an unusual activity for a UNESCO engineer, but what is abnormal is the fact that Faber should be turning his scientific training—i.e. in the observation, enumeration and assessment of data—on to *himself*. The tragic loss of his daughter forces him to go over the past and search in it for a pattern—or rather, to deny the existence of a pattern only to create one by the choice of those memories which he deems significant.[2] What the undertaking undoubtedly demonstrates is that his mental attitude and the style and language which reflect it, however suitable for the evaluation of technical problems and achievements, are simply not capable of dealing with the larger imponderables of human behaviour.

During the course of his story Faber becomes—whatever he may himself think—more than a 'typical' engineer or technologist, just as Stiller similarly became more than a 'typical' sculptor and artist. Indeed, it is arguable that if they did not achieve such individuality their stories would not hold the reader as they do. Both are, of course, representative of problems general to life in mid-twentieth-century society, but both wrestle with intensely private concerns. In Faber's case it is his fear of human involvement—'Menschen sind anstrengend' ('*People are a strain*')—a fear he hides behind the system of neat conventions which is technology. For technology provides Faber with an escape route to the periphery of life where he can avoid being sucked into the dangerous vortex—Stiller's 'black hole'—of real experience. This personal, 'technocratic' rigidity strongly recalls that of Bohnenblust—but with one crucial difference : unlike Bohnenblust Faber is struggling against a suspicion, faint but nagging, which he would dearly be rid of, namely that society and his rôle in it are no longer in meaningful conjunction. Bohnenblust never questions surface reality, the apparent stability of the world, but what we read in the opening pages of *Homo Faber* are the words of a man who, however self-confident his motivation, has begun to move in a fateful direction : that of an attempt to assert that life, his life, is congruent, understandable and therefore controllable. With typical Frisch irony he achieves the precise opposite of this. But, paradoxically enough, the very destruction of his preconceptions gives Faber—too late, perhaps—that vision of genuine centricity which can only be gained by the recognition of centrifugal extremes and the consequent necessity to steer a path between them.

In Walter Faber Frisch presents us with an unwitting spiritual brother of Anatol Ludwig Stiller. On this occasion the central character's eccentricity can be traced in three major contexts : (a)

vis-à-vis his environment (Nature), (b) vis-à-vis his personal relationships and (c) vis-à-vis language. An examination of these three
manifestations of dislocation will reveal the book's dynamic: the
ironic revelation of Faber's eccentric attitude to the man himself
against the grain of his ostensibly factual 'report'. This will lead in
turn, via a discussion of the related polarity of 'Ratio' and 'Mystik',
expressed in the extremes of 'chance' and 'fate', to judgement of
how deeply Walter Faber's ultimate recognition of his real self has
penetrated and permeated his thinking and attitude to life.[3]

2   ITINERANCY : THE DISLOCATED ENVIRONMENT

A remarkable feature of *Homo Faber* is the fact that well over half
its pages concern travel of one sort or another. Like a modern
Ahasuerus Walter Faber covers thousands of miles in an apparently
endless criss-crossing of continents. On closer inspection, however,
all this toing and froing reveals one common characteristic:
circularity. And this is caught in a brilliant image towards the end
of the novel : Faber is sitting in Zürich's Café Odéon and drawing
'on the little marble table . . . a spiral, there was a fossilised snail in
the yellow marble' (IV 194, 208). The 'spiral' is an evocative symbol
of Faber's progress in the book. At this moment (it is the second
and final encounter with Professor O.—itself an initial pregnant
with meaning) narrated time and narrative time are moving rapidly
towards their meeting point in the last pages of his hospital diary,
and the connotations of labyrinth and vortex fit perfectly. Held in
the rigidity of marble, the fossilised snail still manages to suggest
movement towards its own centre, just as Faber, held fast in the
deadening routine of a life-time, is nevertheless fast approaching
his real identity.

The account Faber gives of his journeys reveals an inability to
relate to his environment that is closely associated with a similar
emotional dislocation. Moments of stasis, or the slowing down of
tempo, present dangerous challenges to his control of life. Speed
alone keeps him on the track's rim and prevents him slithering
down into the pit. But for this exercise physical fitness is mandatory,
as indeed is the stability of the track. Both fail him at the crucial
moment. First, a stomach cancer disturbs the complacent rhythm
of Faber's life; secondly, the aeroplane taking him to Caracas is
forced down in the Tamaulipas Desert. In other words, Faber is
faced with the sudden disintegration of an apparently efficient
centric principle : *habit*, anchored in the perfection of machinery.

As Samuel Beckett has put it: 'Habit is a compromise effected between the individual and his own environment, or between the individual and his own organic eccentricities, the guarantee of dull inviolability.'[4] Changes in tempo or unexpected breaks in routine 'represent the perilous zones in the life of the individual, dangerous, precarious, painful, mysterious and fertile, when for a moment the boredom of living is replaced by the suffering of being'.[5] The decision to accompany Herbert to the plantation is the outcome of just such a moment of disorientation. A creature of habit succumbs to an inexplicable flash of spontaneity. In a sense the whole novel hinges on the half-reluctant pursuit of the inner self which made Faber's decision possible.

In the complex pattern of Faber's wanderings two major and complementary parabolas can be discerned: firstly, the visit to Joachim in Guatemala and the 'ascent' through Europe with Sabeth to its apex in Akrokorinth, followed by the rapid descent to a fatal conclusion in Athens (='First Stop'), and secondly, its mirror-image: the second visit to Guatemala, a similar climax in Cuba and the return (via a significant detour to Zürich) to apparent eclipse in Athens (='Second Stop'). In each case Faber approaches a more comprehensive understanding of life's inner reality, represented by Sabeth and Cuba respectively, only to swing away to the last moment—once through the death of his daughter, finally through his own. Thus it will be seen that the second cycle thematically repeats the first, but to an intensified degree.

'First Stop'

(a) *Tamaulipas*: The first major journey sequence is introduced by an important hiatus—the emergency landing in the desert. Before this event, it can be justifiably assumed that Faber's journeys were always hermetically sealed off from contact with the localities (and their peoples) in which they take place. Planes, airports, hotels are the reference points in Faber's world, and all have a standardised international flavour, frequently characterised with the slogan THE AMERICAN WAY OF LIFE. Thus his immediate reaction in the desert of Tamaulipas is to underplay the uniqueness of the incident. He mocks Herbert's sense of excitement and attempts to trivialise the experience by continuous, indiscriminate filming of the landscape and natural phenomena. This activity clearly represents a method of neutralising experience by absorbing it safely at second hand and becomes a *leitmotiv* in the novel. Yet even Faber can be caught off guard in that grey area between waking and sleeping and catch a glimpse—immediately blinked away—of personal aridity reflected in the desert around him : 'When I woke up in the morning, looked out of the little window and saw the sand, the nearness of the sand, I took fright for a second, unnecessarily' (IV 26, *30*). Momentary cracks such as this in the façade of blasé worldliness give the clue to Faber's instinctive recoil when he is jolted (or wrenches himself) more radically out of his accustomed 'Ordnung'.

(b) *Campeche – Palenque – Guatemala* : It is the journey into the Guatemala jungle that presents the reader with the most obvious example of Faber's defective relationship to his environment. A man whose profession is to control natural phenomena is confronted with Nature depicted not only as unmistakably hostile but as anything other than controlled. The exoticism which was seen by Stiller in his prison cell as a symbol of untrammelled, exciting possibilities, here launches an assault on the senses. Everywhere 'stench', 'putre-faction', 'slime' coalesce into a minatory, impersonal power against which the regular taking of showers is useless, so that the round of beer-drinking-perspiring-thirst-beer-drinking appears as a vicious circle of pointlessness. Nature's malevolent superabundance not only saps Faber's physical energy, it also threatens to destroy his sense of time. As physical movement gets slower—the difficult terrain and poor communications conspire to make long delays a feature of travel—so Faber gets the day wrong. Time ceases to function as the secure, logical progression of evenly spaced moments—'Suddenly it was midday' (IV 35, *38*). Indeed, within a very short space even sun and moon begin to take on the same slimy appearance.

This landscape is characterised by an oppressive heat which causes Faber, the man of action, to drift into a state of apathy. The final trek to the plantation, therefore, takes on the quality of a progress through an exhausting, nightmarish labyrinth. And it is a labyrinth which is alive for Faber in a peculiarly disgusting way. For the rôle of the male as dominant decision maker in the creative process is superseded by a protean anonymity : 'Wherever you spat it germinated!' (IV 51, *55*). The sexual ambiguity that informs Faber's discomfort serves to underline his growing loss of balance, both on the physical and emotional planes.[6] After the confrontation with Joachim's corpse, this complex dislocation is given its most intensified expression :

. . . Verwesung voller Keime, glitschig wie Vaseline, Tümpel im Morgenrot wie Tümpel von schmutzigem Blut, Monatsblut,

Tümpel voller Molche, nichts als schwarze Köpfe mit zuckenden Schwänzchen wie ein Gewimmel von Spermatozoen, genau so— grauenhaft. (IV 68)

... decay filled with seed, as slippery as vaseline, pools in the red of dawn like pools of filthy blood, menstrual blood, pools of newts, nothing but black heads with jerking tails like a seething mass of spermatozoa, just like that—horrible. (73 f.)

A more thorough refutation of Rousseauistic pathos than Faber's voracious and excrescent nightmare is difficult to imagine. Nature, in this monstrous and extreme guise, claims Herbert as a victim, as it had his brother, leaving Faber to struggle back into the world— only to fall victim to his own 'monstrous' form of extremism.

(c) *New York – Europe – Athens* : The almost overwhelming disgust at the extravagance of Nature and her threatening presence is in stark contrast to the colourlessness of Faber's journey to and through Europe to Athens. The reason is not far to seek : his daughter Sabeth occupies almost his total field of vision. However, this journey shares one characteristic with the other journeys he undertakes : the quasi-suspension of time. Towards the end of the novel, Hanna remarks preceptively on Faber's typical method of avoiding involvement with normal human experience : 'Technology as the knack of eliminating the world as resistance ... of diluting it by speed, so that we don't have to experience it' (IV 169, *182*). Tempo also helps to control time, to divide it up into neat consecutive units. But these journeys are conducted in a far different, leisurely manner. They are, in fact, detours—movements away from the safe course set by habit. They leave Faber open to experiences which he finds difficult to neutralise.

On board the liner sailing to Europe Faber meets the antithesis of the tropical environment of Guatemala : 'We remained in the centre of a circle of glass, as though fixed' (IV 76, *81*). But this is a false centricity and a false security, for the voyage reveals very clearly just how peripheral his existence is compared with the vitality of Sabeth who by virtue of her youth and exuberance is really at the centre of things. Faber, on the contrary, sinks ever more deeply into the passive rôle of observer—and what he sees emphasises over again his separateness from the deepest aspects of human love—its expression in sexual union : 'I tried not to think of the way men and women couple, but the picture sprang unbidden to my mind accompanied by a feeling of amazement and the sudden shock that jerks you out of a doze ... It makes you feel you must be crazy even to have such an idea, positively perverse' (IV 93, 99). Instinct and reason are in permanent conflict in Faber's personality. The former can be horrible, as when he associates it with unbridled, tropical Nature, or occasionally comic when its base appetites are allowed gratification with Ivy—a relationship which is the perfect miniature of Faber's dilemma : the separation of cognition from feeling, the aura of disgust in sexual matters, the triviality of mind, the devaluation of the individual.

Nevertheless, the voyage to Europe (like the trip to the plantation) does constitute a break with habit and thus is part of that gentle spiralling towards the centre, the physical approximation to which is the slow and winding drive through Europe. In the Guatemala jungle Nature was dominant, here she practically disappears. The artistic achievements of European civilisation take her place and form the backcloth to Faber's journey to Greece. Faber fails to relate to these manifestations either, but at least his progress through this particular labyrinth of cities, paintings and sculptures is guided by an Ariadne who acts as a link, however tenuous, with the environment. Yet the virtual disappearance of natural phenomena, together with its replacement by fragments of ancient civilisations, succeeds only in underlining the unnatural relationship that develops between father and daughter. Coupled with the former's slow, but inevitable physical decline, this relationship is captured in a single resonant image : the moon eclipse in Avignon. Fully explicable under normal circumstances to Faber's trained scientific eye, the moon takes on a sinister aspect : 'To look at it was rather oppressive, an enormous mass drifting, or hurtling, through space (IV 124, *131*)—a far cry from his earlier description in the Tamaulipas desert : 'A calculable mass circling round our planet, an example of gravitation, interesting, but in what way an experience?' (IV 24, *27*).

(d) *Akrokorinth – Athens* : In the last phase of the first parabolic movement certain central concepts recur—for example, the symbolic aridity of Tamaulipas ('All around there was nothing but gorse, thistles, olives and waterless land, not a single human being', IV 128, *135*) and the coagulation of time characteristic of Guatemala ('a mile was an eternity'). But before Faber's cherished preconceptions about the predictability, and hence stability, of life are shattered by Sabeth's accident, he and his daughter spend an idyllic night under the moonlit Attic sky.

This experience unites both the prosaic, rational attitude of the one with the playful imagination of the other in a beautiful synthesis. It is suggested by a language game which forces Faber to actually *look* at the landscape and find echoes of it in his way of life. The vocabulary of technology meets the phenomena of Nature in a creative symbiosis. It is remarkable, indeed, that although Faber appears to lose the game overall, several of his similes are more powerful and more original than those of his artistic daughter. A balance between the two ways of comprehending the world is momentarily achieved and symbolised by the sudden eruption of warmth and colour, as Faber for the first time achieves a vibrant relationship with his environment. But it is a synthesis that cannot last. Just when he needs them most, the technical achievements which alone he had found admirable during his trip through Europe —'the way they built their roads and bridges, the new Fiat, the new station in Rome, the new Rapido rail motor, the new Olivetti'— are reduced with savage irony to a 'road of gravelled tar', a donkey cart and a lumbering lorry. Nature retreats into total indifference, leaving Faber to encounter his third and most frightening labyrinth, 'a horrible town, a chaos of tramcars and donkey carts' in which directional signs in Greek complete his disorientation. The subsequent death of Sabeth sends Faber back to the New World like a boomerang.

'Second Stop'

(a) *New York* : Faber's return to New York four days after Sabeth's death is marked initially by an attempt to slip back into the safe groove of habit—he goes to his colleague's 'usual Saturday-night party'. It is a hopeless move. The old environment with its repetitive round of parties and small talk is drained of its anaesthetising protection against reality. The confusion so graphically conveyed by the ludicrous lorry lurching through the maze of Athenian streets has now invaded the deepest level of consciousness —his very identity is threatened. The key to his flat—and former life—has been lost and he hears a stranger's voice at the end of his own telephone : ' "Who are you?" I ask back : "Are you Walter Faber?" ' (IV 164, *176*). This contretemps presented in terms of sterility and empty fellowship skilfully echoes the Tamaulipas episode and is followed, as that was, by a second visit to the plantation, a visit prompted yet again by Faber's tell-tale stomach pains.

(b) *Campeche – Palenque – Guatemala:* It is a feature of the intricate narrative situation of the 'Second Stop' that both the 'report' sections and the 'diary' entries are pithier. For time is running out for the narrator, a fact which he suspects even if he does not openly acknowledge it until the last moments.

His decision to repeat his detour and visit Herbert stems clearly from a desire to test reality. At the station in Campeche he succeeds for a moment in transforming the immediate past into a 'hallucination'. Everything is as if nothing had happened : the clammy air, the stench of fish, Palenque and the Maya ruins. But reality is not so easily defeated; the attempt to wind back the clock like a film does not withstand the very first sign of change : the Rio Usumancinta is in spate. Herbert, too, has changed. He has faded into the environment, as it were, 'like an Indian'. Faber has no alternative but to seek to escape by a route which has stood him well for half a lifetime : he plunges into the technical problems of cleaning and overhauling Herbert's Nash. Whereas on the first journey to Guatemala he was obsessed with the natural environment and the labyrinthine struggle to arrive at all, here Faber directs all his energy to describing his failure to contact Herbert and the painstaking restoration of the car. His technical know-how, however, is revealed as absurdly inappropriate, and their reunion ends in the foolery of Herbert and Faber acting out a game of 'rush-hour traffic in Düsseldorf' before an audience of uncomprehending natives.

(c) *Cuba* : The detour to Cuba lasts four days, and it is the most notably eccentric of all Faber's journeys. This is brought about mainly through his own increased awareness of his situation. This in turn arises from the act of composing his report, the first part of which he completes during his fortnight's confinement to his Caracas hotel immediately prior to his arrival in Havana. Here for the first time Walter Faber manages to get both people and environment into balanced focus for any length of time—and he achieves this by standing *outside and looking on*. Where hitherto in his peregrinations he has been deeply and personally involved, he has either seen Nature or people looming exclusively, or nearly so, in the foreground. Only briefly at Akrokorinth did the two attain precariously balanced proportions—and then Faber was on the *inside*. The irony of Cuba is that everything happens too late. Like Gustav von Aschenbach in Thomas Mann's *Der Tod in Venedig*, Faber sits in his rocking-chair and observes the life around him, a man apart and patently moribund, but one who is suddenly and intensely aware of beauty. But as in Aschenbach's Venice, here too the beauty has perversion at its core. Faber, who has embraced the American way of life, is promptly taken for an American and becomes a target for exploitation by the numerous pimps and prostitutes of Havana.[7]

It is in writing about Havana that one significant half of Faber admits his inner emptiness. (The other—the brain—is busy noting in diary form discussions with Hanna and trying desperately to stave off the final recognition of his true self. The entries are set contrapuntally against the on-going 'report' sections in a dialectic of supreme irony.) With Sabeth dead and time running out, the essential sterility of his life overwhelms him : 'Later like a school-boy, I draw a woman in the hot sand and lie down in this woman, who is nothing but sand, and talk aloud to her' (IV 177, *190*). This ludicrous attempt to recall the night on the beach at Akrokorinth, to raise the dead as it were, as well as his sex, brings him to the painful realisation that he lacks a co-ordinating principle around which to organise his life in any meaningful way. His inability to relate to his environment results finally in a crucial loss of identity, a sensual and temporal disorientation which makes a sharp contrast with the people around him, whom he sees as 'strange animals' precisely because they fit so naturally into their surroundings. In this company he feels—much as did his predecessor in Venice, but without Aschenbach's intellectual penetration—like a living corpse, and in a telling phrase he registers a 'vacuum between the loins' (IV 178, *191*). This is followed by the premonitory attack of impotence with the two prostitutes and the recognition of approach-ing dissolution—'from time to time I shower my body that is leaving me'.

Neverless, Cuba does represent for Faber—as did the brief moment in Akrokorinth—a peak of happiness, that is, a moment suspended outside time where habit is negated and a glimpse of true centricity caught. But precisely because this experience of life is outside time (or so it presents itself to Faber) it cannot take on a life-enhancing shape for him. His belated decision to change his life-style is wishful thinking—a point which is emphasised by the simultaneous composition of his hospital diary which records a good deal of incomprehension in the face of Hanna's probing remarks. In fact, the whole Cuba sequence has the atmosphere of a vivid dream, a tantalising hallucination, but one figured with a firm grasp of realistic detail. But it is all too late. The last word is 'Abschied'.

(d) *Düsseldorf – Zürich – Athens:* In contrast to Faber's previous voyage to Europe, this journey is marked by *haste*. A brief stop in Düsseldorf where he is forced to review on film the key events of the recent past (much as a drowning man is said to see his life flash before his eyes), is followed by a last sentimental visit to Zürich which serves to underline the downward movement of this second parabola. It is here, in his native city, that he meets for the second time that harbinger of Death, Professor O. Professor O., formerly Faber's revered teacher at the Eidgenössische Technische Hochschule, represents for him the acme of the rational spirit; he is a man on whose example he has based his life and work. But like the mysterious, dark figures which dog Gustav Aschenbach's footsteps in Mann's novella, the teacher who gave Faber faith in scientific order and stability himself becomes a recurrent symbol of disintegration and death.

During Faber's final flight from Zürich to Athens the repeated note of parting is struck. The Swiss Alps and lakes pass beneath him but in a region which is receding rapidly from his grasp : 'Everything goes past as though in a film! /The wish to grasp the earth—/ Instead we climb higher and higher' (IV 195, *210*). Yet despite this image of dislocation, he succeeds in holding together in his imagination the tensions represented on the one hand by the aeroplane (symbol of man's drive to solve problems by dynamic technology) and on the other by the natural features of his birthplace (Nature's grandeur as symbol of the mysterious dimension of life). As in Akrokorinth and Cuba, the language controls the experience in a meaningful synthesis. The freshness of vision he here achieves remains unclouded to the end.

This return to Athens and the woman of his youth is in fact the last significant feature of his completed report. From this point on the diary entries take over exclusively. The report has fulfilled its esential function of self-revelation : 'I know everything. Tomorrow they are going to open me up and find out what they already know : that there is nothing they can do any more' (IV 198, *213*). Spiritual insight and physiological fact coincide.

It can be seen from the above analysis that the characteristic shared by the two major journey sequences in the novel is indeed circularity : both start in the New World, move through a point 'at the end of the world, or at least at the end of civilisation' (IV 37, *40 f.*) and end in the cradle of Western humanism, Greece. All Walter Faber's journeys lead backwards—back in time and back into himself. Itinerancy becomes for him—as it did for Jürg

Reinhart and Anatol Stiller—a means of self-discovery. For no matter where their travels take them—Dalmatia, Mexico, America, Guatemala, Greece and, inevitably, Switzerland—the progress of all three is the same : a return to their roots and the source of identity.

3 HANNA AND SABETH : THE IRONIC REPETITION

If itinerancy pointed to a basic imbalance between Faber's view of life and his environment, depicted both in terms of Nature and his own physical decline, an examination of his personal relationships will show that his eccentricity goes very deep indeed.

In a famous essay Albert Camus wrote : 'Un monde qu'on peut expliquer même avec de mauvaises raisons est un monde familier. Mais au contraire, dans un univers soudain privé d'illusions et de lumières, l'homme se sent un étranger.'[8] For fifty years the world has presented a familiar face to Walter Faber, a familiarity anchored in his ability to account satisfactorily for its workings. Essential to this skill is a mechanistic view of human behaviour. Faber's hybris lies, it is plain, in his wilful reduction of human relationships—spontaneity and love—to the artificial realm of mathematical calculation. It is his fate to witness his world suddenly deprived of its comfortable illusions, to come face to face with that 'sentiment de l'absurdité' which Camus traces back to 'ce divorce entre l'homme et sa vie, l'acteur et son décor'.[9]

It is clear that Faber's adjustment to his environment has been based on a devaluation of feeling in favour of 'Ordnung', the manipulable, the predictable. This has necessarily involved a high degree of isolation—indeed, a total refusal of commitment to people—which could only be sustained by a thorough-going egocentricity. In such a situation relationships with other people at any level other than the most casual superficiality will always pose problems, if not outright danger, to the individual's autonomy. This is certainly the case with Ivy despite the fact that her affair with Faber has a hard, metallic quality undiminished by her apparent love for him. Faber himself is well aware of her sado-masochistic need for pain to inject feeling into her life. In her tantrums there is a decidedly mechanical element. The constant veering from extreme to extreme, fashionable visits to the psychiatrist, regular attention to make-up and obsession with triviality, for example, the desire to match the colour of her car with her clothes and lipstick, all suggest that her career as a mannequin has been well chosen. Small wonder that Faber is able to see and treat her as an object and that their sexual unions should be recorded as the effects of undifferentiated impulses. Such behaviour fits neatly into Faber's understanding of cybernetics, as he explains the subject later to Sabeth, when he describes human action as automatic responses to information, reflexes largely independent of the will. But Ivy is a puppet programmed with a predatory instinct— her very name has a threatening, vegetative connotation. It is a grim picture of human isolation that Frisch has Faber unwittingly paint. Behaviour at this level of experience—where attitudes are so rigid—is clearly predictable, but none the less exhausting to control. It is this aspect which differentiates it from that of a machine and forces Faber into periodic withdrawals into himself— 'Menschen sind anstrengend'.

In such an ordered, rationally conceived world the smallest defect can have severe repercussions. And indeed, two such defects —the failure of an aeroplane's engine, a pain in the stomach— render Faber vulnerable to experiences that could not have been predicted, in particular the relationship with Sabeth which finally reveals to Faber that what he had always assumed to be his secure, integrated position in life is in fact the reverse. It is recorded against the backcloth of his old engagement to Hanna, and the two are closely woven into the novel's retrospective structure so as to suggest that the former is an ironic repetition of the latter.

Faber describes three phases of his relationship with Hanna, interpolating the relevant material in various stages in his report:[10] an account of the critical years 1933-6, the reunion immediately prior to Sabeth's death in hospital, and the few days leading up to his own operation for stomach cancer. The first two phases share one common characteristic: bad faith. It is not until the last pages of the novel that either Faber *or* Hanna faces the truth about his or her own self. Faber's guilty rôle in the abortive affair is clear, but Hanna's share in the outcome is an interesting feature of the novel which is frequently overlooked. Her original refusal to marry Faber, her relatively successful professional career and her apparent forthright independence appear to underline her superiority over her former fiancé. But such characteristics do not withstand a careful examination. Indeed it is Hanna herself who admits to Faber that her own life is 'verpfuscht' (IV 139; *'ruined'*, *146*). And it is Hanna who breaks down at the very end of the novel and falls on her knees to ask *Faber's* forgiveness. The truth of the matter is that Hanna's life-style reveals a similar, devastating egocentricity to Faber's. Her late husband, Joachim, for example, must be counted at least partially a victim of it. She is guilty of the same overweening claim to self-sufficiency, the same refusal to commit herself to the dangers of an equal love relationship, for which her daughter is a 'safe' substitute. There is indeed a bitter irony in the fact that Frisch has Hanna produce the same dishonest arguments of political and economic expediency against Joachim's desire for a child, as Faber used against her in 1936 (cf. IV 202 and 105; *217* and *111*). From another point of view, too, Hanna's love for Sabeth can be seen as unnatural as she declares Faber's to be : his incest is matched by her refusal to create a home for Sabeth based on mutual respect and love between male and female, mother and father.

Thus, despite her daughter, Hanna never locates a centric principle which would enable her to lead a fully integrated life. The result is that she falls into an extreme life pattern, different it is true from Faber's, but just as distorting, just as peripheral and ultimately just as sterile. Whilst Faber concentrates on keeping reality at bay through machines and cybernetics, Hanna 'patches up fragments, sticking the past together' (IV 139, *146*); she takes refuge in the culture and mythologies of the past. Both shy away from the pressures of the present—for Faber's career in helping underdeveloped countries and Hanna's dedication to maternal self-sacrifice are both, paradoxically, ways of refusing outward-going and creative personal relationships.

There is thus a double irony at work : just as Sabeth penetrates her father's ordered, encapsulated world and helps to destroy it, so Faber erupts into Hanna's enclosed domesticity and destroys that, too. Faber had been willing to marry Hanna but for the wrong reasons (the fear of being thought anti-semitic); Hanna had wanted her child to confirm her womanliness and independence— neither was motivated by genuine concern for the other. Their punishment for such basic dishonesty is all the more exemplary for being so long delayed. And yet the old and clearly defective relationship appears to have meant more to them than they cared to admit. Their reunion—despite its tragic circumstances—bridges the long gap of twenty years with comparative ease. For neither Faber nor Hanna has filled the intervening years with much meaningful experience; therefore significantly little has changed. In a similar encounter when informed that he had remained unchanged despite the passing years, Brecht's Herr Keuner went pale with shock. This is an *aperçu* which, if it comes at all, is granted to Hanna and Faber only at the last moment. Before that moment occurs they circle each other with small-talk, half questions and withheld answers. With only two questions burning in their minds—paternity and incest—Sabeth's parents (whilst she lies critically ill in hospital) conduct a pathetic ballet of *non sequiturs*:

'Was hast du gehabt mit dem Kind?'
Dabei war sie sehr nervös, ich sah es.
'Wieso keine Kreuzotter?' frage ich.
'Komm,' sagt sie, 'trink deinen Tee!'
'Seit wann trägst du eine Brille?' frage ich—(IV 127)

'How far did you go with the child?'
She was very much on edge, as I could see.
'How do you mean, it wasn't an adder?' I asked.
'Come' she said, 'drink your tea.'
'How long have you been wearing glasses?' I asked—(134)

More than any other factor in the novel the reunion with Hanna brings Faber face to face with the falseness of his life-style which he had dimly begun to suspect under Sabeth's influence. By refusing to commit himself to other people in the past, it becomes progressively more difficult for him to actually see them as whole people at all. With Hanna, the only woman with whom the sexual experience has had any meaning, he becomes at one moment critically and symptomatically disorientated:

Ihre Hand (ich redete sozusagen nur noch zu ihrer Hand) war merkwürdig: klein wie eine Kinderhand, älter als die übrige Hanna, nervös und schlaff, häßlich, eigentlich gar keine Hand, sondern etwas Verstümmeltes, weich und knochig und welk, Wachs mit Sommerprossen, eigentlich nicht häßlich, im Gegenteil, etwas Liebes, aber etwas Fremdes, etwas Entsetzliches, etwas Trauriges, etwas Blindes, ich redete und redete, ich schwieg, ich versuchte mir die Hand Sabeth vorzustellen, aber erfolglos, ich sah nur, was neben dem Aschenbecher auf dem Tisch lag, Menschenfleisch mit Adern unter der Haut, die wie zerknittertes Seidenpapier aussieht, so mürbe und zugleich glänzend. (IV 141)

Her hand (I was, so to speak, talking only to her hand) was remarkable: as small as a child's hand, older than the rest of Hanna, tense and slack, ugly, really not a hand at all, but something maimed, soft and bony and flabby, wax with freckles, not

really ugly, on the contrary, something sweet, but something
alien, something horrible, something sad, something blind,
I talked and talked, I fell silent. I tried to picture Sabeth's hand,
but without success, I could only see what was lying beside the
ash-tray on the table, human flesh with veins under the skin,
which looked like crumpled tissue-paper, so crinkled and at the
same time glistening. (148 f.)

The passage is crucial : emotional dislocation of a severe kind is
here translated into a sensual confusion that is almost surreal. The
movement of this intense distortion is clear : first, the person is
reduced to a part of the whole; second, the part itself becomes
reified, 'like crumpled tissue-paper'.

In a stray remark, ironically about her former husband, the
opportunist Piper, Hanna puts her finger on the nature of their
problem : 'What he had lost was a spontaneous relationship to
reality' (IV 144, *151*). For this is precisely what has made Faber's
and Hanna's behaviour in the past so rigid. It accounts, for instance,
for the *leitmotiv* of blindness that accompanies Faber's progress
through the book. In this connection Hanna's story of her relationship with the blind man, Armin, is significant. The light-hearted
games the old man (a clear forerunner of Theo Gantenbein) and
the schoolgirl played in Munich have their serious side. Hanna
enjoyed the excitement of the older man's experience and attention
but without danger—she possessed the freedom of not being seen :
'The girl had to read to him out of her school books, so that he
could learn it by heart. This was, so to speak, his way of raping her'
(IV 184, *198*). Their plan to visit Greece together never materialises;
the blind man knows that it is only a game. The parallel to Faber
is very clear : the man who 'sees' is 'blind'; the 'game' he plays
turns into bitter reality. On the other hand, Sabeth's warmth and
affection contrast sharply with her mother's self-indulgence. As for
Walter Faber, as long as the topography of his world remains
unchanged, orientation is a simple, if—as with the blind man's
stick—a somewhat remote matter. But once the environment has
changed—through physical sickness or unusual journeys, for
example—he too is a man groping in the dark.

Spontaneity and light are the two qualities that Sabeth brings
into Faber's life. In effect she humanises her father's environment.
What she offers him is a chance to realise the nature of his wasted
years. She *is*, in a sense, the young Hanna, and for a desperate
moment Faber bridges the gap and is thirty once more. But of

course there is ultimately no escape from the tyranny of the past; what Faber experiences momentarily with Sabeth is 'one of those rare miracles of coincidence, when the calendar of facts runs parallel to the calendar of feelings'.[11] He discovers what it is like to live fully in the present. Sabeth is the hint of synthesis that springs from the two polar opposites represented in extreme form by her mother and father.[12] For she not only loves art and respects the mysterious, creative side of human nature, she is also fascinated by Faber's explanations of the ship's engine room (characteristically, her sympathy goes to the stokers who sail the oceans for such long periods of time and who yet see so little of them) and in general shows an intelligent appreciation of his technological elucidations— that is, once Faber has dropped his defensive cynicism. This is in sharp contrast to the student Marcel who irritated Faber 'like all artists who think themselves loftier or more profound beings simply because they didn't know what electricity is' (IV 39, 43), or the Baptist who hides his ignorance (and his own rigidity) behind a mask of facetious condescension. Sabeth thus represents an integrating principle : the power of intuitive feeling to counter-balance the intellect. Whereas Faber and Hanna have become fossilised into opposite poles of behaviour, Sabeth is made credible precisely because she is not innocent and virtuous. There have been at least two other men in this twenty-year-old's life before Faber, and there is no reason to believe that Faber is lying when he writes defensively : 'Anyhow it was the girl who that night . . . came into my room' (IV 125, *131 f.*).

Ultimately, however, it is the denial of time which prevents Faber from comprehending experience in a fruitful way, and it is time which prevents him from making good his mistakes. The message which breaks through at the end of his report is that lost time cannot be regained; the turning he missed at thirty cannot be taken at fifty, as if age were merely a superficial phenomenon. Despite the ambivalence of her own rôle it is Hanna, as we have seen, who points clearly to this error in Faber's attitude which stems from a corrupt view of 'technology as the knack of so arranging the world that we don't have to experience it'. To act as if time were merely a mechanical process of addition which, if need be, can be made to run backwards ('I talked about the watch I had given to the lorry-driver and about time in general; about clocks that were able to make time run backwards', IV 155, *163*) is to ignore the central paradox of life : death. For death alone, rightly understood, can give meaning to life. Faber fails to make the essential distinction between 'time' and 'transience' of which Frisch speaks in his *Tagebuch 1946–1949* : 'Time as what the clocks show and transience as our experience of the fact that our being is constantly confronted by a non-being which we call death . . . Only through an awareness of non-being do we grasp for seconds that we are alive' (II 499 f.). Significantly, the only occasion Faber talks freely about life and death, and then only in generalisations, is at a moment of symbolically stopped time—the moon eclipse in Avignon. For as a technologist, Faber has tried to live without death and has thus embraced Stiller's nightmare : repetition. By ignoring the need to shape life according to the contours which time lays down and which make up the natural cycle of youth, middle and old age, Faber becomes, in Kierkegaard's terms, the 'aesthete' who lives for the moment, as opposed to the 'ethical' man who accepts the responsibility of building continuous relationships.[13]

The 'aesthetic' dislocation in this case is severe. Faber evinces a preference for machines over men; that is, he is guilty of the total devaluation of feeling in favour of mechanical efficiency. It is clear that behind this predilection for the logic and reliability of robots Faber's motive is *fear*—he is afraid of the human body and the shocks it is heir to :

Schlim nur die Zähne. Ich habe sie immer gefürchtet; was man auch dagegen tut : ihre Verwitterung. Überhaupt der ganze Mensch!—als Konstruktion möglich, aber das Material ist verfehlt : Fleisch ist kein Material, sondern ein Fluch. (IV 171)

The only bad thing is my teeth. I have always been afraid of them; no matter what you do you can't stop them decaying. It's the same with the whole human being—the construction is possible, but the material is flawed: flesh is not a material, but a curse. (184)

On the other hand, he admits that only pain brought him near to an understanding of Hanna : 'For one moment alone I understood Hanna—when she hammered my face with her fists beside the deathbed. Since then I have never understood her' (IV 193, 207). Like Büchner's Lenz, Faber has grown so turned in on himself, so dead to the world, that it requires physical pain to keep him in contact with it. In a related sense, of course, it was his stomach pains which turned out to be his original re-entry point into the world of experience and time. Time, however, exacts its revenge on Faber in the 'Second Stop', and this completes the central idea of the book's shape: the 'First Stop' presents Faber's hybris—the attempt to live outside time like the Gods; the 'Second Stop' belongs to nemesis and the accompanying final anagnorisis.

The picture of personal relationships given in the novel is certainly a bleak one. Sabeth is dead, Faber is dying and Hanna is left to eke out a lonely and peripheral existence as a tourist guide—not to mention Ivy abandoned, Joachim dead and Herbert vegetating in an obvious form of eccentricity. Personal relationships are the measure of our humanity: to refuse them or to deform them, is to dehumanise ourselves. But for them to exercise their beneficent influence over us they must be entered into with love and with a sensitive openness to the essential otherness of the partner. For this a well-founded knowledge of oneself is required, and it is Faber's tragedy (and Hanna's) that this knowledge has to be bought at the cost of the life of the one person who helped him discover it and could have helped him to consolidate it. The quality and extent of this knowledge can best be gauged by an investigation of the language in which the discovery is expressed.

4 'WRITING MEANS READING ONE'S SELF': THE PITFALL OF LANGUAGE

If distortion and incongruity are seen as the common feature in Faber's relationship to the environment and to people, it is not surprising to find the same characteristics reflected in his choice and use of language. Faber sets out to compose a factual report on his recent and not-so-recent past in the obvious hope that it will prove his innocence and uphold his view of life as a system of unemotional orderliness in which all phenomena are satisfactorily accounted for. To succeed in this task, his instrument–language–ought to possess the very virtues of sobriety and order which he desires to affirm. It is precisely these virtues, however, that disintegrate under the pressure of Faber's memories as he relives crucial moments of past experience. The fundamental irony of his report lies in that Faber's language *catches him out*, i.e. the discrepancy between what he says and what he thinks he says becomes increasingly evident, until the point is reached when he himself can no longer overlook it. It is in this sense that the novel constitutes the gradual process of unmasking Walter Faber.[14] Language, indeed, is the mask behind which Faber hides his real self (even from himself); and the composition of the report is the unexpected means by which he is made to recognise this fact. The equation can be demonstrated firstly by examining the texture of this 'linguistic mask' and the way it is held in place; secondly, by observing how from time to time the mask slips and eventually disintegrates.

The mask—texture and fixative devices: The most immediate feature of Faber's language is, of course, his vocabulary. It is dominated by jargon, slang and a profusion of foreign words— 'Start', 'Piste', 'Drink', 'Barmann', 'Propeller', 'Observations-Dach', 'Sandwich', 'Lunch', 'Lunchtime', 'Sensation', 'Biscuits' etc., together with specific mention of makes and models: 'Jeep', 'Jockey-Unterhosen', 'Super-Constellation', 'Landrover', 'Nash', 'Martini-Dry', 'Hermes-Baby' and so on. This is the reverse of individualisation; Faber speaks the standardised, impersonal language of a man of the world, 'a man who has both feet on the ground' (IV 47, 51). The effect is to conceal an essential rootlessness behind an aura of *savoir-vivre*, to create a linguistic anonymity inside which Faber feels safe. Similarly, in an attempt to demonstrate the control he has over his life, he enters exact times and dates in his report and pinpoints certain places down to the last detail (Hotel Lacroix in Palenque, Hotel Estia Emborron in Athens, Hotel Henri IV in Avignon, for example). Finally, Faber's constant tendency to abbreviate sentences and omit verbs contributes to the flat conversational tone of large sections of the narrative and reflects directly Faber's desire to draw a veil of innocuousness over events. But besides being a common feature of everyday *speech*, this characteristic also points to Faber's attitude towards *time*. Speed, as we have seen, is a device by means of which he avoids real experience, and the staccato effect of his 'report' is another aspect of it.

Faber's attempt to seek the anonymity of everyday colloquial speech is supported by a number of devices of a repetitive nature. In an analysis of the opening sentences of the novel Hans Geulen has noted the 'Nervosität des Ichs' penetrating the intricate syntax of the long fourth sentence.[15] And in the report Faber himself constantly refers to his 'nervousness' and his 'nerves'. He tries to control this threatened imbalance by the blanket use of the phrase 'wie üblich' ('*as usual*'). By reducing everything to the level of trivial repetition he hopes to defuse the dangers inherent in novel experiences. Two other devices employed continually by Faber are the use of 'beziehungsweise' (occasionally 'betreffend' or 'in Bezug auf') and the phrase 'wie gesagt'. Both occur a great number of times in the narrative, the one to plaster over the insistent fact that much of what Faber is relating as his experience is and remains 'bezie-hungslos', the other to bolster his narrative with a spurious sense of logical progression. Significantly, however, all three linguistic tricks—'wie üblich', 'beziehungsweise', 'wie gesagt'—gradually evaporate, occurring in the 'Second Stop' on only a handful of occasions. This matches exactly the movement of the report away from strident self-justification towards a more positive, more humble self-enquiry. In other words, their disappearance or diminution allows the mask to slip and the real man to peer out.

The mask—incongruities and maladjustments : A commonly noted feature of the novel is the large number of brief sentences inter-spersed—often as isolated paragraphs—throughout its length, which underline important moments in the external or psychological action. Perhaps if Faber had contented himself with such a précis style he might well have avoided ultimate self-enlightenment. However, it is a measure of the seriousness of his purpose, ill-conceived though this may be, and an indication of nagging doubt, that he attempts something far more comprehensive. This alone is enough to lend support to the view that the decision to write at all constitutes a break with an outlook on life which admits of no doubt and which has hitherto enabled Faber to ignore his basic eccentricity. As Camus puts it : 'Commencer à penser, c'est com-mencer d'être miné,'[16] and there can be little doubt that whatever else is happening in the book, Faber is being forced to *think* and to think in ways hitherto foreign to him, 'thinking about statistics, thinking about Joachim, who had hanged himself, thinking about the future, thinking until I shivered, until I didn't know what I was thinking, it was as though I couldn't make up my mind to recognise my own thoughts' (IV 135, *142 f.*).

In Cuba Faber makes a revealing remark about the problematical nature of a language imperfectly grasped : 'My Spanish is just enough for business negotiations. It's funny : I don't say what I want to say, but what the language wants' (IV 179, *192*). Ironically, this insight could be applied to his narrative as a whole. For by attempting an expanded version of his assessment of the past, Faber's language reveals far more than he bargained for. It appears at times to be escaping his conscious will and delivering a message of its own. To begin with, there are obvious subterfuge and contra-dictions : 'I had told (Ivy) often enough that I definitely wouldn't get married, or anyhow I had made it pretty clear, and in the end I definitely told her so, it was at the airport...' (IV 31, *34*); and in particular every detail of the episode on board the Atlantic liner demonstrates the opposite of Faber's claim that he did not pursue Sabeth—indeed, the arbitrary change of her name from Elsbeth is itself a form of appropriation. But more importantly, his report is full of examples of language taking over from its user. Principally, these can be seen (a) at moments when the conscious will is off-guard (dreaming or drunk); (b) in the peculiarly triadic presentation of crucially significant events (the fiasco with Hanna 1935/36, the 'mirror' motif, the night in Avignon and Sabeth's accident); (c) in recurrent images that unwittingly become symbols; and (d) at moments when *rhythm* subverts meaning to reveal an emotionalism behind apparent objectivity. These must be looked at in turn.

(a) If one discounts the mysterious meeting with Professor O. in Paris Faber gives the content of only one dream, although he mentions dreaming on several other occasions. This occurs at the very start of his narrative and is characteristically introduced by the disarming remark 'dreams don't interest me' (although he cannot help nervously checking his teeth once he is awake!):

Ich träumte von Ivy, glaube ich, jedenfalls fühlte ich mich bedrängt, es war in einer Spielbar in Las Vegas (wo ich in Wirklichkeit nie gewesen bin), Klimbim, dazu Lautsprecher, die immer meinen Namen riefen, ein Chaos von blauen und roten und gelben Automaten, wo man Geld gewinnen kam, Lotterie, ich wartete mit lauter Splitternackten, um mich scheiden zu lassen (dabei bin ich in Wirklichkeit gar nicht verheiratet), irgendwie kam auch Professor O. vor, mein geschätzter Lehrer an der Eidgenössischen Technischen Hochschule, aber vollkommen sentimental, er weinte immerfort, obschon er Mathematiker ist, beziehungsweise Professor für Elektrodynamik, es war peinlich, aber das Blödsinnigste von allem:—Ich bin mit dem Düsseldorfer verheiratet! ... Ich wollte protestieren, aber konnte meinen Mund nicht aufmachen, ohne die Hand davor zu halten, da mir soeben, wie ich spürte, sämtliche Zähne ausgefallen sind, alle wie Kieselsteine im Mund—(IV 15 f.)

I dreamed about Ivy, I think, anyhow I felt depressed, it was in a Las Vegas poolroom (where I've never been in reality), there was a tremendous din and above it loudspeakers kept calling out my name, a chaos of blue and red and yellow automatic machines at which you could win money, a lottery, I was waiting among a lot of stark naked people to be divorced (though in reality I'm

not married), somehow Professor O., my esteemed teacher at the
Swiss College of Technology, was in it, he was wildly sentimental
and kept weeping all the time, although he is a mathematician,
or rather a professor of electrodynamics, it was very embarrass-
ing, but the craziest thing of all, I was married to the man from
Düsseldorf . . . I wanted to protest, but couldn't open my mouth
without holding my hand over it, for all my teeth had just fallen
out, I could feel them in my mouth like so many pebbles—(18)

The dream is full of telling details, pointing both back to the past
and forward into the future: his recent exposure to feeling and
subsequent running away from personal commitment (Ivy), the
sense of guilt ('waiting among a lot of stark naked people to be
divorced'), the emptiness and triviality of his mechanical mode of
existence ('Las Vegas'), the incongruity of life lived one-sidedly
(Professor O.), the hint of perversion ('I was married to the man
from Düsseldorf') and the final image of physical dislocation with
its distinct Freudian overtones.[17] Faber cannot, or will not, appreciate the significance of these details at this early stage, but their
emergence from his subconscious and the fact that he feels the
need to mention them at all point already to the beginnings of a
change in his outlook on life.

The three instances of drunkenness are much clearer. Alcohol
releases Faber's inhibitions and impairs his customary defence
mechanisms with the paradoxical result that he *sees* momentarily
with a frightening clarity. Thus on the first occasion, surrounded
by Ivy and his New York acquaintances (the sum total of eleven
years living in the city), he sees right through the sterility of their
common life-style: ' "In your company a man could die," I said,
"a man could die and you wouldn't even notice, there's no trace of
friendship, a man could die in your company!" I shouted. "What
are we talking to each other at all for?" I shouted. "What's the
point of this party," I could hear myself shouting, "if a man could
die without your noticing?" ' (IV 67, 72).[18] On the second occasion
Faber is aboard ship with Sabeth, and drink saps his will-power,
forcing him to talk about a subject he had wanted to forget, namely
the discovery of Joachim's corpse. For the first time he grasps the
full horror of his friend's death, whereas the original impact of this
event had been controlled by concentrating on photographing
the evidence and wondering where the electricity for Joachim's
radio had come from. The third instance is the most symptomatic.
At Williams' 'usual Saturday-night party' in New York Faber's

escape into drink only brings home to him the full enormity of what happened four days previously to Sabeth, and the episode culminates in a momentary, but nevertheless frightening loss of identity (see above p. 95). These episodes of dream and drunkenness, however, are isolated but nodal points of insight, and it is striking that it is only with conscious will and the habits of a lifetime suspended that Faber comes close to essential truths and his language becomes transparent.

(b) The triadic movement noted in regard to four central episodes in Faber's report follow a roughly similar pattern : from initial obfuscation via a desperate ambiguity towards a greater honesty. The fiasco with Hanna, for example, is first introduced with an air of snappy finality, the facts simply stated, opinions confidently asserted : 'Eine Heirat kam damals nicht in Frage, wirtschaftlich betrachtet, abgesehen von allem anderen. Hanna hat mir auch nie einen Vorwurf gemacht, daß es damals nicht zur Heirat kam. Ich war bereit dazu. Im Grunde war es Hanna selbst, die damals nicht heiraten wollte' (IV 33; *Marriage at that time was out of the question on economic grounds, apart from anything else. Nor did Hanna ever reproach me for not marrying her at the time. I was quite ready to do so. Basically it was Hanna herself who didn't want to marry at that time'*, 36).[19] This is subsequently modified by the second, extended version (IV 45–8, *49–53*) where Faber is at pains to justify himself and rebut possible accusations of cowardice and anti-semitism towards his finacée's half-Jewish family. There is a tell-tale lack of spontaneity in the wooden and rather shame-faced phrases Faber uses, and in fact the more he defends his actions of twenty one years ago, the more plainly does the reader see his vacillation, his bad faith and his callous self-centredness over Hanna's pregnancy : 'I asked : Do you know a doctor you can go to? Of course I only meant, to have an examination.' The phrasing of the question—even after the passage of so many years— belies Faber's gloss. He records her reaction but typically without comment : 'All she said was : It's all over. I had said "your child" instead of "our child". That was what Hanna could not forgive me'. The third and final presentation of this episode (IV 56–7, *61–2*) is delineated with pointed brevity—Hanna's refusal to go through with a farcical marriage does not cover up Faber's basic dishonesty: 'Even if we get divorced, I told myself, Hanna will remain Swiss and in possession of a passport'. But at least on this occasion Faber is less strident in his self-justification with the result that the possibility of guilt on both sides is allowed to emerge from between the lines. A similar gradation can be noted on the three occasions when Faber looks in a mirror. The first is the physical shock at Houston Airport, the impact of which is immediately deadened by the threadbare explanation that his frightful pallor is due to the fluorescent lighting. The warning is unheeded, as is his ensuing physical collapse. The second incident, however, is experienced in a more complex manner : Faber is sitting in a Paris restaurant and sees himself reflected eight times in the room's gilt mirrors :

> Ich hatte Ringe unter den Augen, nichts weiter, im übrigen war ich sonnengebräunt, wie gesagt, lange nicht so hager wie üblich, im Gegenteil, ich sah ausgezeichnet aus. Ich bin nun einmal (das wußte ich ohne Spiegel) ein Mann in den besten Jahren, grau, aber sportlich . . . Was mich irritierte, war einzig und allein dieses Lokal : wo man hinblickte, gab es Spiegel, ekelhaft . . . (IV 98)

> *I had rings under my eyes, that was all, apart from that I was suntanned, as I have said, not nearly so gaunt as usual, on the contrary I looked splendid. I am a man in the prime of life after all (I knew that without a mirror), grey-haired, but athletic . . . The only thing that irritated me was this restaurant with its mirrors wherever I looked—disgusting . . .(104)*

Clear to the reader, if not to the narrator, is the latter's fractured identity and his attempt to disguise from himself the true nature of his illness by the use of what Erich Franzen calls 'this verbal armour of cosmetic adjectives'.[20] The cracks are quickly papered over so that before he leaves the restaurant with its superior waiters he has managed to talk himself into forgetting his intention to have a medical check-up and indeed into feeling 'perfectly normal'. The final variation on this motif occurs during his hospitalisation in Athens. This time Faber cannot escape the truth mirrored before him. His 'natural' gauntness is seen for what it is—emaciation. The cosmetic adjectives no longer work. Weak attempts at explanation recalling his collapse at Houston Airport—'Perhaps it is the whitish light coming through the curtains that makes me look, as it were, pale under my tan; not white but yellow' (IV 171, *184*)—give way to the realisation that man is not replaceable like the worn parts of a machine—'Flesh is not a material, but a curse'. The recollection and recording of his stay in Cuba which immediately follow this handwritten entry prevent any further self-delusion.

The two crucial episodes with Sabeth—Avignon and Akrokorinth—are similarly introduced in a triadic pattern. As Faber is writing with hindsight, this hesitancy can only suggest a refusal to face up to the terrible truth. Thus he first mentions the incestuous night at Avignon in a relatively innocuous manner ('Since Avignon', 'if it hadn't been for Avignon', 'what happened in Avignon', IV 108, *114*), proceeds to render it ambiguous ('Her likeness to Hanna struck me less and less frequently the more intimate we became, the girl and I. After Avignon it no longer occurred to me at all', IV 115, *122*) and finally gives it its full, awful weight in the description of the moon eclipse when the hitherto harmless 'calculable mass which circles our planet' turns into an incalculable and frightening phenomenon, 'an enormous mass, drifting or hurtling through space' (IV 124, *131*).

The account of Sabeth's accident, of course, is the most telling example of Faber's narrative method. The first version of the events on the beach at Akrokorinth points to the snake-bite as the cause of the accident (IV 127, *134*); the second mention of Akrokorinth (IV 150–2, *158–60*) omits the accident altogether, concentrating ironically on their happiness together. It is only in the third account (IV 156–8, *165–6*) that we learn the full extent of Faber's culpability. The language betrays him immediately : 'As regards the accident I have nothing to conceal'. The truth is that as he runs to Sabeth's aid, Faber frightens her with his sudden nakedness and causes her to fall backwards over the embankment, fracturing her skull. The snake-bite is merely what he *wanted* to see.

These four episodes with their characteristic triadic structure are thus key examples of Faber's material slipping between his fingers and turning against his intention. Above all they demonstrate the truth of Frisch's remark in the *Tagebuch 1946–1949* : 'Schreiben heißt : sich selber lesen' (II 361; *'writing means reading one's self'*).

(c) It is a feature of the fundamental irony inherent in the tension between the narrator's situation and what he chooses to narrate that Frisch has Faber introduce numerous motifs and images whose recurrence turns them—without his willing it or even being aware of it—into resonant symbols. Thus the 'Zopiloten', the negress cleaner at Houston whose 'enormous mouth with its black lips and pink gums' is to be echoed in Cuba, the obsession with teeth, and the threefold (!) meeting with Professor O. can all be seen by the reader as harbingers of death. And it is not difficult, although Faber does not appear to see the connection, to interpret the Alfa Romeo which circles Faber and Sabeth's hotel in Rome all night, after he has made his dishonest calculation that Sabeth cannot be his daughter, as a translation of the avenging furies into a modern technological symbol.[21] Similarly, Faber can hardly be aware, as the reader is, of the fear behind his obsessive shaving ('Not being shaved gives me the feeling I am some sort of plant', IV 27, *30*) with its hint of physical malaise, brought out so vividly in the repulsive imagery of the jungle sequence. Such symbols and motifs emerge, as it were, from between the cracks that appear with increasing frequency in the mask Faber wears. It is as if language were taking its revenge on a man who is attempting to stifle its expressive possibilities.

(d) Perhaps the most subtle figuration of language catching Walter Faber out occurs when an underlying rhythm wells up out of his subconscious and defeats the purpose of his words. Two examples will serve to illustrate this common phenomenon. The first is Faber's diatribe against marriage, delivered to impress Sabeth and impose his presence on the festivities before the liner docks in Le Havre. It begins with Faber's annoyance at Sabeth's assumption that being alone made him melancholy. Two short sentences are all that is required to puff him up into a characteristic stance of self-sufficiency : 'I'm used to travelling alone. I live like any real man, in my work. On the contrary, that's the way I like it and I think myself lucky to live alone, in my view this is the only possible condition for men, I enjoy waking up and not having to talk' (IV 90 f., *96*). The speech quickly slips into cynical humour at the expense of female garrulity at breakfast-time, at which moment Sabeth is whisked away to dance, leaving Faber to fall into an interior monologue. At first there is an attempt at judicious weighing of the pros and cons of marriage, but before long familiar features of Faber's style appear : a preliminary defensive admission that solitude is not always fun is followed by a typical string of assertions—people are a strain, feelings are 'fatigue phenomena', fluctuating spirits should be ignored, a good drink can block out minor irritations—until the clear note of self-pity breaks through : 'Sometimes I just fall asleep, the newspaper on my lap and my cigarettes on the carpet. I pull myself together. What for? Somewhere there is a late broadcast with symphonies, which I switch off. What else? Then I just stand there with gin, which I don't like, in my glass, drinking; I stand still so as not to hear steps in my flat, steps that are after all only my own. The whole thing isn't tragic, merely wearisome. You can't wish yourself goodnight . . .' (IV 92 f., *98*). The line of thought set in train by Sabeth—itself defensive—cannot withstand the pressure of the mounting rhythm. The level tone adopted to justify his chosen solitude breaks as he begins to talk to himself, and the nature of his trivial, eccentric life-style emerges clearly as his words reveal the reverse of what he wanted to say.

The second and perhaps most impressive example is the long section, unbroken by paragraphs which is devoted to Faber's defence of abortion (IV 105–7, 111–13). It directly parallels the monstrous passage in *Stiller* where Bohenblust parrots forth the clichés and conventions of Swiss society. The section opens quietly and soberly enough, but as usual it is not long before Faber's repressed emotion, compounded by his sense of guilt, begins to appear. The language takes on a staccato rhythm: 'Mankind has trebled its numbers in a century. Previously hygiene was unknown ... War against puerperal fever, Caesarean operations. Incubators for premature births. We take life more seriously than in earlier times'; it passes through *non sequitur* : 'An end to romanticism. Anyone who rejects abortion on principle is romantic and irresponsible', through cliché : 'But in the last analysis we must face facts', through wild generalisation : 'It is always the moralists who do the most harm', through primitive fear : 'Added to this the feeling of power over the man, motherhood as an economic weapon in the hands of the woman', and on to a rising crescendo of opposition to ideas of 'fate' and the practice of 'idolising nature' :

> Wir leben technisch, der Mensch als Beherrscher der Natur, der Mensch als Ingenieur, und wer dagegen redet, der soll auch keine Brücke benutzen, die nicht die Natur gebaut hat. Dann müßte man schon konsequent sein und jeden Eingriff ablehnen, das heißt : sterben an jeder Blinddarmentzündung. Weil Schicksal ! Dann auch keine Glühbirne, Keinen Motor, keine Atomenergie, keine Rechenmaschine, keine Narkose—dann los in den Dschungel ! (IV 107)

> *We live technologically, with man as the master of nature, man as the engineer, and let anyone who raises his voice against it stop using bridges not built by nature. To be consistent, they would have to reject any kind of operation; that would mean people dying every time they had appendicitis. Because that's fate! No electric light bulbs, no engines, no atomic energy, no calculating machines, no anaesthetics—straight back to the jungle! (113)*

This throbbing, rhythmic language plainly reveals the powerful emotion breaking down Faber's attempt to stick to his criteria of dispassionate judgement. The accelerating rhythms of the passage match the rising panic within him; the words are urgently strung together to form a rampart behind which to hide, but the tempo of construction shakes them all to pieces again. We see Faber's lack of integrity amply demonstrated in linguistic terms—both the mask and the man struggling beneath. The mask attempts to indicate the logical reasons for birth control and abortion, the man's discomfort suggests the real reason behind the tirade : his original fear of commitment to Hanna and refusal to shoulder responsibility.

Most, but not all, of the above analysis has concerned the 'First Stop'. It is true—and it is part of the book's dynamic—that the language of the 'Second Stop' grows calmer and more restrained. This process is helped by the juxtaposition of the handwritten sections which indicate a more tentative, more genuinely enquiring attitude on the part of the narrator.[22] The assertive defensiveness of so much of the first section of his report gives way to a more frequent expression of puzzlement and dismay. It is particularly at two moments in the second part of the report that we see Faber's language drop its mask-like protectiveness and achieve—without any change in its formal properties—a remarkable balance between thought and expression : in Cuba and during the last flight over Switzerland.

In the Guatemala jungle we saw disgust and nausea; at various moments of suspended consciousness or rising emotion we were aware of unwelcome truths emerging and at Akrokorinth we witnessed an all too fleeting lucidity. Now in Cuba we observe Faber's language suddenly gain in equipoise and subtle strength. For it is in Havana that he becomes poignantly aware of the transience of life and begins to correct his faulty relationship to time. The intimation of death brings him paradoxically to life, and not only Faber but his language, too. A profusion of adjectives —'rosa', 'rot', 'schwarz-violett', 'blau', 'lila', 'gelb', 'schwefelgrün', 'braun', 'weiß'—produces a riot of sensual colour, as the narrator discovers new possibilities of expression. For a few brief hours Walter Faber is at one with the world : 'I rock and sing, nothing else, the rocking of the empty chair beside me, the whistling of the cast-iron, the eddy of petals. I sing the praises of life !' (IV 181, *195*).

Once more before the end of his report (and presumably his life) Faber catches this same lyrical simplicity—in the passage beginning 'Die Gletscherspalten : grün wie Bierflaschenglas' (IV 195; '*The glacier's crevasses—as green as bottle-glass*', *210*). In a last farewell to his native land Faber's language mirrors a mental balance, elsewhere largely missing in his report, but a balance gained, it is hinted, like the mountaineer's unique moment of light, at great cost. It registers the moment when Faber's mask at last disintegrates to reveal an unexpected humanity. Thus the act of writing itself can be said in the end to have become the instrument by means of which Faber is able to 'read' himself and recognise the failure of his previous mode of life. It remains to assess the quality of this self-recognition.

5 'RATIO' AND 'MYSTIK': POLARITIES OF FAILURE

When turning our attention to the problem of 'Ratio' and 'Mystik' as manifested in terms of chance and fate, and to the rôle these play in *Homo Faber*, care must be taken to keep the argument within the context of the novel and the temptation to see a metaphysical message behind Frisch's fiction resisted. For it can hardly be Frisch's intention—as a sceptic and ironist fully aware of the problematic nature of a de-mythologised world—to point to a mysterious Absolute which governs men's affairs. If that were so, we should have to say that the agencies he presumably chooses to demonstrate the fact (the Oedipus motif, dreams, symbols, etc.) are unconvincing. Rather does it seem to be Frisch's aim to emphasise, as always in his work, the existence of that mysterious, indefinable element in life which can be approached only through sympathy and love, and which must be preserved in all its unfathomable integrity if life is not to be condemned to a routine of barren repetition. It makes more sense, and certainly creates fewer problems, to see these elements (despite minor reservations) as ways of 'enlarging the expressive dimensions of the novel'.[23]

'Ratio' and 'Mystik' can be seen as two symbolic poles in Faber's report—symbolic of two ways of apprehending the world. The one is associated with electronic brains, the laws of probability and cybernetics, the other with irrational attitudes—myths, gods, furies. The point to be established is that their proponents—Faber and Hanna respectively—are both equally rigid in their stance, and that in isolation neither pole is adequate to express the fullness of life. This can be best seen in a passage where Faber himself notes Hanna's 'déformation professionelle', the fact that 'Gods are part of her job': 'She talked about myths as we talk about the theory of heat, as though she were speaking of a physical law confirmed by daily experience, and hence in a positively casual tone of voice.

Without astonishment. Oedipus and the sphinx, portrayed in child-like fashion on a broken vase, Athene, the Erinyes or Eumenides or whatever they're called, were to her mind facts' (IV 142, *149*). It is a crucial insight: Hanna's belief in her gods, in 'Fate', expressed tellingly in terms of the detritus of a buried civilisation, is one mark of a closed mind, just as much as Faber's tenacious trust in 'chance'. An explanation for life's mysteries is found and petrifies into an unchallenged system. Both ways of looking at the world—'Ratio' and 'Mystik'—are detrimental to real life because of their very exclusivity. Both represent ways of avoiding responsibility and point to personal guilt.

It has become clear that it is part of Faber's intention in writing his report to defend his view of the world and thus to prove that what happened to him was coincidence and that his incest was 'innocent' since he could not have known Sabeth was his daughter. Strictly speaking, of course, Faber is quite correct; for it is part of *Hanna's* guilt that he did not know that he had a daughter. It *is* by chance that he meets his own daughter and becomes the indirect cause of her death. His guilt lies in his whole attitude to life, in particular in his defective relationship to time which causes him to succumb to the temptation of living out his missed opportunities with a girl half his age. This is what Hanna means when she says to a sceptical Faber that his mistake was no chance mistake but one that was part of a life-style which ignored the process of ageing and was hence 'contrary to nature'. Sabeth thus comes to represent both an intensification of guilt and *punishment*.

Despite his reliance on rationality, Faber is peculiarly unaware of his own irrational behaviour (for example, his decision to fly with Herbert to Campeche and his attitude to shaving), and he is certainly inconsistent in terms of the credo he states at the beginning of his report: 'I don't believe in providence or fate, as a technologist I am used to reckoning with the formulae of probability. What has providence to do with it? ... I don't need any mystical explanation for the occurrence of the improbable; mathematics exlains it adequately, as far as I am concerned' (IV 22, *25*). For when the improbable does happen to him, he is thrown completely off course, literally with Herbert, deeply and lastingly by Sabeth's death. The truth of the matter is that his theory is mathematically neat and tidy—effective as long as he is encapsulated in a false centricity—but emotionally unacceptable and incapable of controlling the mysterious chain of chance events, once he has exposed himself to the outside world. The man who criticises Hanna for having 'an unpredictable temperament' (IV 46, 51) develops one himself—one of the book's many ironies. A theory useful for generalisation proves inadequate to deal with the particular. This then is Faber's guilt, that he ignores the incalculable factor in human behaviour, an apprehension of which calls for intuition rather than logic, and that he treats life as if it were a machine and individuals merely interchangeable components. The deepest irony of the novel is that Faber, far from exonerating himself, works a *pattern* into his life by the very nature and arrangement of his memories—a pattern which it is his purpose to deny. Thus each detail he recalls, each interpretation he offers—irrespective of the importance he attaches to them—reveals a mysterious causality that impresses even where it defies analysis.

Whilst writing up his Cuban experience in Athens, Faber himself begins to see the inexorable nature of 'Fate' that his narrative has subconsciously revealed, and in doing so he recognises the gigantic subterfuge he has been busy perpetrating : 'Verfügung für Todesfall: alle Zeugnisse von mir Berichte, Briefe, Ringheftchen, sollen vernichtet werden, es stimmt nichts' (IV 199; '*Arrangements in case of death: all written evidence such as reports, letters, loose-leaf notebooks, are to be destroyed, none of it is true*', 214). This is the true anagnorisis, its genuineness underpinned by the awareness of death. Faber has finally grasped—and it has been a slow process, beginning with the collapse in Houston, not a sudden transformation—the absurdity of his undertaking and the emptiness of his previous life.[24] His case is analogous to Frank Kafka's who also asked for his papers to be destroyed after his death. Both Kafka and Faber arrived at the realisation (though their routes were, of course, very different) that a meaningful coherence must be achieved through living. With T. S. Eliot they know that there is

> At best, only a limited value
> in the knowledge derived from experience.
> The knowledge imposes a pattern, and falsifies,
> For the pattern is new in every moment
> And every moment is a new and shocking
> Valuation of all we have been . . .[25]

The bitter irony here is that Faber appears ready to begin life at the very moment he is being forced to leave it :

Auf der Welt sein : im Licht sein. Irgendwo (wie der Alte neulich in Korinth) Esel treiben, unser Beruf!—aber vor allem : standhalten dem Licht, der Freude (wie unser Kind, als es sang) im

Wissen, daß ich erlösche im Licht über Ginster, Asphalt und Meer, standhalten der Zeit, beziehungsweise Ewigkeit im Augenblick. Ewig sein : gewesen sein. (IV 199)[26]

To be alive: to be in the light. Driving donkeys around somewhere (like that old man in Corinth)—doing our job. The main thing is to stand up to the light, to joy (like our child as she sang) in the knowledge that I shall be extinguished in the light over gorse, asphalt and sea, to stand up to time, or rather to eternity in the instant. To be eternal means to have existed. (214)[26]

Plainly, such coherence cannot be achieved without a balance between the two sides of human nature, here figured as the conflicting poles of 'Ratio' and 'Mystik'. Man's rational desire to control Nature and thus ensure his survival (as the Maya failed to do) must be matched with a respect for the intuitive, emotional sphere of existence. For neither total reliance upon 'Ratio' nor on 'Mystik' is an adequate response to life's complex and ever-changing problems. By insisting on such an either/or position Hanna and Faber succumb to a debilitating extremism, each encapsulated in an isolated and self-contained world.

A possible mediation between these extremes, as has already been suggested, is indicated by Sabeth. Sabeth is a hint, perhaps no more, of 'das wirkliche Leben' which eludes not only Faber and Hanna, but also Jürg Reinhart and Anatol Stiller. Her destruction is the real tragedy, her parents' egocentricity the true measure of their guilt.

Walter Faber can be seen, therefore, as a 'negative' eccentric, his natural reflexes thoroughly blunted by the rôle he has chosen to play in society. From the very first pages we see him as drained, both physically (stomach cancer) and emotionally (Ivy)—a fitting member of Bohnenblust's docile, anonymous society. Faber is the sort of person Bohnenblust wanted Stiller to be, and thus the novel carries forward that particular strand of social criticism. The paradox here is that as Faber becomes aware of his eccentricity, he catches at the same time a glimpse of a possible cure. In doing so he rises above the level of comfortable anonymity and becomes an individual. The centric principle—the reconciliation of opposites indicated in Sabeth—is posited but not achieved. The novel ends, as do *Stiller* and *Die Schwierigen*, pessimistically. Nevertheless, Frisch shares that indomitable humanism of Albert Camus : 'Etre privé d'espoir, ce n'est pas désespérer.'[27] And in *Mein Name sei Gantenbein* he returns yet again to the problem of eccentricity with imagination and irony undiminished.

VI

Mein Name sei Gantenbein

1 INTRODUCTION

The lack of a vital centre which precipitated Stiller's crisis of identity and led to Faber's total dislocation is also the dominant theme of *Mein Name sei Gantenbein*. However, whereas in *Stiller* and *Homo Faber* we witness one man run out of energy and another out of time, as they struggle from opposite points to harmonise their experience of themselves and of the world, here the problem is posed in a radically different manner. The reader is no longer invited to observe the behaviour of a man under stress in a prison cell or of a man caught in a web of habit which fails to sustain his weight at the critical moment. On this occasion he is placed squarely inside the skull of an anonymous narrator who, by an effort of imaginative reflection, endeavours to define and come to terms with his experience. In Frisch's view, the removal of traditional plot structure gives his narrator a better opportunity to explore at will the latent potentialities of his situation. By inventing a number of separate identities the latter achieves an ironic detachment from his fictions which enables him (and the reader) to observe more accurately their relationship to those experiences which triggered off the need to explore in the first place.

In one sense, of course, this technique had been adumbrated in *Stiller*, whose protagonist invents stories to express an existential experience. It is also true that the fundamental experience playfully encircled and probed in *Mein Name sei Gantenbein* is quite as eccentric as any illustrated in the earlier novels. However, in this book the fictive narrator is presented as completely isolated, and the fact that most of what he narrates is put forward unambiguously as fiction leads to a much more radical expression of Frisch's old belief that experience cannot be directly or absolutely captured in language, that truth will always remain fluid and elusive as quicksilver. 'Confessions are more masklike than silence, one can say everything and the secret merely slips back behind our words'

(V 193, *184*). Nevertheless, to try and enmesh the secret of human experience Frisch stakes out a subtle net of verbal fictions. Exploiting humour and irony to the full, he prevents the reader from seizing on any particular fiction and thereby fracturing what is in fact a rich, if unfathomable, totality. Thus he has his narrator construct personae, each of which relativises the other, as the narrator identifies with, and retreats from, each in turn. In this way 'a very ordinary story' (V 313, *297*) is revealed as paradoxically full of extraordinary potentialities, potentialities that were alive enough for, and therefore part of, the individual whose story it is. For it is an essential Frisch insight that 'experience' is not just something that has 'happened' but is also coloured by what has been neglected, by the fact that certain paths, certain decisions have *not* been taken. Frisch here attempts to penetrate the surface level of biography, which is normally all that is accessible to others, in order to reach the underlying pattern of experience ('Erlebnismuster') whose contours are much more fascinatingly varied than the superficial topography would lead one to suspect.[1]

Before the narrator's experience and the fictions which he invents to express it are examined in detail, a word must be said about Frisch's conception of 'experience' and the nature of 'stories'. In a key essay entitled *Unsere Gier nach Geschdichten*, published four years before *Mein Name sei Gantenbein*, Frisch declared: 'Experience is an insight, not a result of external events. A single external event can serve a thousand experiences. Perhaps there is no other way to express experience than by narrating events, i.e. stories, as if our experience sprang from stories. I believe it is the other way round. Stories spring from experience. Experience wants to make itself intelligible and so it invents a reason for itself, preferably a past. Once upon a time... Stories are sketches ('Entwürf') projected into the past, games of the imagination which we pass off as reality.'[2] These 'games of the imagination' are a means of defining the quality of experience more accurately, more openly. If truth cannot be expressed directly (as Stiller knew) because of the subjective nature of perception, then stories must be invented in the hope that they will act as a relatively objective mirror to the reality experienced by the individual. This, for Frisch, is a general and necessary principle: 'There is no other way of coming face to face with our pattern of experience.'[3] Experience is only comprehended and controlled, he goes on significantly, when the story invented to express it has the aura of credibility.

The implications for the narrative technique of *Mein Name sei Gantenbein* are obvious. An experience (or pattern of experience) is searching for stories in which to express itself, much as Pirandello's six characters search for an author who might articulate their particular experience in dramatic form.[4] In this sense fictions as a product of experience have a reality all of their own : 'I believe decisive changes in a person's life can stem from events which have never really happened, from ideas produced by an experience which is there before a story appears to act as a cause. The story merely expresses the experience'[5] It follows that an examination of the stories an individual invents, whether instinctively or deliberately, should lead to the basic pattern of experience that determines their shape and the individual's identity. The more complex the pattern of experience (i.e. the more complex the individual personality and particularly his degree of self-awareness), the greater will be the variety of the stories needed to reflect it. This is the nexus of problems behind *Mein Name sei Gantenbein*. That the pattern of experience at the root of the fictive narrator's inventions is a decidly eccentric one can best be established by a discussion first of the narrator himself and his stance within the book, and then by examining in turn the three personae, Enderlin, Gantenbein and Svoboda, he chooses to adopt in order to give full expression to his fictive identity.

2 PATTERNS OF ECCENTRICITY : THE NARRATOR AND HIS MATERIAL

In one of the answers to a series of imaginary questions on the nature and themes of his new novel, published under the title *Ich schreibe für Leser*, Frisch revealed his intentions vis-à-vis his fictive narrator : 'I wanted to show the reality of a man by having him appear as a white patch ('als weißer Fleck') outlined by the sum of fictional identities congruent with his personality. Such an outline, I thought, would be more precise than any biography which is based, as we know, on speculation. A negative procedure, if you like. There is no investigation of where and when something happened ... The story is not told as if an individual could be identified by his factual behaviour; he betrays himself in his fictions.'[6] And indeed Frisch's narrator does remain 'ein weißer Fleck' at the centre of the book, an ironic non-character searching for a reflected identity in the characters he invents.

Frisch's fictive narrator is thus clearly motivated by that same dissatisfaction with 'biographical' reality which we have already noted in Stiller and which similarly inspires the ironically named Kürmann in *Biografie*. The experience of such men (or perhaps their heightened awareness of it) is plainly too rich to find adequate expression in the mere objective facts of their lives. Nevertheless, although Frisch has his narrator declare : 'I try on stories like clothes!' (V 22, *21*), he makes him at the same time aware of the ironic nature of his enterprise : although these 'clothes' will hide his nakedness and thus protect him against a world which is only too swift to seize on his vulnerability, they will not give him a *new* life—'the same creases always develop in the same places, I know that' (V 21, *20*). Instead the 'clothes' are seen as a possible route to the discovery of his true identity. For they allow playful variations on his static, but fundamentally fragmentary biography.

Examining the fragments of 'static' biography scattered in the novel, two key episodes stand out, centres around which the rest of the novel's material clusters : the vision in hospital of the horse's head emerging from the granite wall and the man sitting in the middle of his deserted home.

The incident of the horse's head and the linked image of cars driving to Jerusalem is puzzling until one recognises that this is the reflection of the 'experience' mentioned in the immediately preceding section of the book ('A man has been through an experience, now he is looking for the story to go with it'). The implication of a central existential crisis then becomes clear :

> Das Morgengrauen vor dem offenen Fenster kurz nach sechs Uhr erschien wie eine Felswand, grau und rißlos, Granit :—aus diesem Granit stößt wie ein Schrei, jedoch lautlos, plötzlich ein Pferdekopf mit weitaufgerissenen Augen, Schaum im Gebiß, aufwiehernd, aber lautlos, ein Lebewesen, es hat aus dem Granit herauszu-springen versucht, was im ersten Anlauf nicht gelungen ist und nie, ich seh's, nie gelingen wird, nur der Kopf mit fliegender Mähne ist aus dem Granit heraus, wild, ein Kopf voll Todesangst, der Leib bleibt drin, hoffnungslos, die weißen Augen, irr, blicken mich an, Gnade suchend—(V 12)

> *The grey of early morning outside the open window just after six o'clock looked like a wall of rock, grey and unfissured, granite. Out of this granite there suddenly comes like a scream, but soundless, a horse's head with eyes wide open, foam on its teeth, whinnying, but without a sound, a living creature, it has tried to jump out of the granite, which it didn't succeed in doing at the*

first attempt and, I can see, never will succeed in doing, only
the head with the flying mane has emerged from the granite,
wild, a head filled with the terror of death, the body remains
inside, hopeless, the white eyes, maddened, look at me, begging
for mercy. (11)

The wild horse is an ancient symbol of virility, and it is not difficult
to interpret its panic leap out of the granite wall as symbolic of
the narrator's own abortive leap out of the grey, featureless petrifi-
cation of his everyday life into a more vital form of existence. The
agony of the horse is that of the narrator himself, for both attempts
to escape the emprisoning wall of external reality are short-lived.
The horse turns unexpectedly into a terracotta figure and is engulfed
by the greyness; everything is 'artistically painted', but the wild
horse has been tamed into a lifeless and harmless piece of sculpture
which itself has no permanence (a hint perhaps at Frisch's own
pessimism about the difficulty of expressing an existential truth in
art). With the concluding vision of a miniature, mechanised 'pil-
grimage' to Jerusalem the associative irony is clear : 'mercy' cannot
be granted to the horse, and the desperate attempt to leap into life
shrinks to an image of an unreal, toy-like progression not towards
a spiritual Mecca, but towards a tourist centre.[7]

This view of an admittedly complex symbol can be supported by
two closely related incidents. First, immediately after the initial
vision of the horse's head, the narrator presents the imagined
episode of the patient's escape from hospital and his attempt to flee
naked through the streets of Zürich (where cars, the reader is
informed, are definitely not Jerusalem-orientated !). On his inevitable capture—in a theatre where, in a pathetic parody of Christ
before His execution, his nakedness is covered with a tattered King's
cloak—he can only offer an inarticulate explanation : 'Er habe
einen Schrei ausstoßen wollen, Man nahm es zur Kenntnis. Einen
Schrei? Er nickte, ja, mit der Dringlichkeit eines Stummen, der
sich verstanden wähnt. Wieso einen Schrei? Das wußte er nicht'
(V 18; *'He had wanted to scream. They took note of the fact. To*
scream? He nodded, yes, in the emphatic manner of a dumb
person who feels he has been understood. Why to scream? He didn't
know', 18). Furthermore, Enderlin's reaction to the discovery of
his imminent death is also one of mute panic : 'If only he could
scream !' (V 152, *145*). Never actually uttered in these fictions, the
'scream' is the strangled expression of human frustration and
existential fear : the granite face is momentarily inhabitable, but at

the cost of any genuine vitality. The spirit, in its search for a centric principle—'mercy', 'Jerusalem'—is overwhelmed and swallowed up in the grey repetitiveness of everyday routine. Yet on the aesthetic level, of course, it can be claimed that the novel itself, taken as a whole, is a brilliant articulation of precisely this soundless, equine scream.[8]

The second piece of supporting evidence is the narrator's own actual visit to Jerusalem, recorded immediately after the repetition of the horse's head vision. The description of this visit as a tourist vividly recalls Stiller's outburst against the modern age of reproduction with its surrogate experiences. But there is an essential difference. This narrator purports to have actually visited Jerusalem —and the experience is *still* characterised as unreal and second-hand. Despite the concrete phenomena of the city (Damascus Gate, machine gun emplacements and sandbags), 'I already know that hours later, when I have been sight-seeing to the point of exhaustion, it won't be true' (V 155, *147*). It can be proved by facts and documents that the journey was indeed made, but the life-giving truth of the Holy City remains ungraspable. The narrator's eccentric stance in a place of traditional centricity ('Jerusalem is the only city under the sky, the sun circles round Jerusalem', V 156, *148*) is mirrored ironically in his observation of a party of Franciscan monks enacting the Stations of the Cross, some of whom rush their devotions in order to have time to film their brothers praying. In short, 'everything remains mere appearance' (V 156, *149*). Even the monks—at least in this framework supposedly at the centre of things—are intent on recording an 'experience' rather than living it.

The second key episode is relatively straightforward. The narrator's marriage has failed and he is unable to match his experience of that failure with the objective data that confirm it, at least for the outside world. He is a man unable to relate to his former environment now presented symbolically shrouded in dust sheets which recall an Egyptian tomb or a 'funeral in a country with alien customs' (V 19, *18*).[9] Time has stopped, surface reality is likened to the preserved but petrified life of Pompeii after its volcanic engulfment. The narrator can register only one inescapable fact: 'As to the people who once lived here, it is clear that one was male and one female' (V 19, *19*). He feels himself an intruder into a strange world, a world as inexplicable to him as the shrouded dusty studio was to Anatol Stiller. The narrator's dislocation is evident: at the centre of his life he sees desolation and petrifaction, on every hand symbols of his failure to relate to the woman he loved. Lacking matches to set fire to the flat, he is ironically forced to *imagine* the destruction of this fragmentary evidence of an unsatisfactory biography. Like Stiller in his former studio, however, he finds that such destruction is beyond his powers. It is not so simple 'to float away without a story'. If the crisis is to be contained, it must be delineated and understood. And it is precisely this task that the fictive narrator sets himself to accomplish in the course of the following four hundred and fifty pages.

To underline its central importance, the episode is recalled on two further occasions. First it reappears immediately after Lila leaves Gantenbein (whose inordinate jealousy has culminated in the farcical Einhorn incident), where its function is to signal the disastrous conclusion of the Philemon and Baucis variation. It serves also as further confirmation of the narrator's honesty of purpose, for even at this late stage he admits 'I don't know what really happened' (V 198, *189*). But the final and most telling repetition is the briefest. It comes after Lila has discovered that Gantenbein is not blind after all. It is introduced by the realisation that, despite all his efforts, the narrator has not been able to capture the exact quality of the experience he has had : 'The awakening (as though all this had never happened) proves to be a deception; something has always happened, but differently' (V 313, *297*). Thus the final vision of his home is coloured by resignation and a sense of *déjà vu*—hence the sharp abbreviation :

> Reste von Burgunder in einer Flasche, ich kenne das, Inselchen von Schimmel auf rotem Wein, ferner Reste von Brot ziegelhart, im Eisschrank krümmt sich verdorrter Schinken, in einer Schüssel schwimmt ein trüber Rest von Kompott, Aprikosenschlamm, Wegzehrung für eine Mumie, ich weiß, ich hocke in Mantel und Mütze, es riecht nach Kampfer, Staub, Bodenwichse, die Teppiche sind gerollt, und ich hocke auf der Lehne eines Polstersessels und spiele mit einem Korkenzieher, weiß nicht, was geschehen ist, alle Polstersessel sind mit weißen Tüchern bedeckt, ich kenne das, Fensterläden geschlossen, alle Türen offen, brauche mich nicht zu erheben, kenne das—(V 313 f.)

> *Remains of burgundy in a bottle, I know what that's like, little islands of mould on the red wine, also remains of bread as hard as brick, in the refrigerator dried-up ham is curling, in a bowl floats the murky residue of stewed fruit, apricot mud, viaticum for a mummy, I know, I sit there in coat and hat, the place*

*smells of camphor, dust, floor polish, the carpets are rolled up
and I am sitting on the back of an easy chair playing with a
corkscrew, don't know what has happened, all the easy chairs
are covered with white cloths, I know what that's like, shutters
closed, all doors open, there is no need for me to get up, I know
what it's like—(298)*

The narrator's protean efforts are seen to end in apparent failure.
The attempt to objectify the unique but ephemeral quality of his
experience has degenerated into a pallid expression of numbed
repetition.

These two key areas in the novel are symptomatic of the fictive
narrator's eccentricity and the crisis which reflects it. So too are the
stories he tells the barman, spurred on by the latter's naïve conviction that 'biography' and 'life' are synonyms. In this connection
it is particularly difficult to know exactly from which perspective
the novel is developing at any given time—that of the narrator
proper or that of one of his personae—and in a sense it does not
ultimately matter. But it seems reasonable to treat the two cameos,
Otto the Milkman and the 'Pechvogel' story,[10] together with the
Piz Kesch episode, as preliminary pointers to the more complex
fictions-within-fiction explored by the narrator's personae—in particular by Gantenbein in his stories for Camilla. That this is likely
can be supported by the fact that the stories for the barman are
prefaced by a number of programmatic statements which are
important for an understanding of Frisch's point of departure. For
example : 'Every story is an invention . . . every ego that expresses
itself in words is a rôle' (V 48, 46); 'One can't see oneself, that's
the trouble, stories only exist from the outside . . . hence our greed
for stories' (V 49, 46 f.); 'Soner or later everyone invents for
himself a story which he regards as his life . . . or a whole series of
stories' (V 49, 47). And it is made very clear in the stories told to
the barman that everything depends on the strength of these inventions to hold together the individual's pattern of experience and
thus his identity. If their elasticity goes, the fabric disintegrates and
with it identity.

Otto the Milkman accordingly ends in a lunatic asylum once the
identity ('story') he has believed in for twenty-one years loses its
cohesion. One Saturday evening Otto is overwhelmed quite
unexpectedly by the utter banality of everyday life : standing on an
identical balcony of an identical terrace-house, he spontaneously

begins to smash his geranium pots. His neighbours react like a line of puppets guided by a single hand : 'All the neighbours immediately turned their heads; they were standing on their balconies, in their shirt sleeves just like him, enjoying their Saturday, or in their little gardens watering the flowers, and they all immediately turned their heads' (V 50, *48*). Secure in an enclosed world of norms and habits, they cannot comprehend Otto's eccentric outburst, and indeed, before the collapse of Otto's identity can threaten their own, he is taken away—'his ego was worn out . . . and he couldn't think of another one. It was horrible.' Because Otto is unable to construct another story for his new and frightening insight, he falls into that extreme form of eccentricity, 'madness'.

The 'Pechvogel' story is a variation of, or pendant to, Otto's. This man, accustomed in his life to being dogged by bad luck, has his identity similarly challenged when one day he wins first prize in a lottery. The event leads him to doubt not only himself but the world, reality itself. Happily for him he avoids Otto's collapse by promptly losing his winnings and thus does not have to face the daunting task of constructing a new personality.

The story of the meeting in 1942 with the mysterious German (presumably a Nazi in view of his praise of the Third Reich) on the Piz Kesch is a further comment on the nature of experience. What fascinates the narrator here, is not what he actually did on that occasion (biographical fact), but rather what he omitted to do, i.e. kill a putative enemy spy in war-time. The world sees the individual in terms of biographical data, and especially in relationship to the deeds he has committed. Only the individual himself is aware that such facts are but a rough approximation to the truth, tedious in their tendency to present a fragment as the whole.

The relevance of these episodes to the narrator's own predicament is as clear as that of the stories told to Knobel was to Stiller's. They are warning indicators, prefigurations of a personal struggle to come. For the search for identity, the attempt to fill in the contours of the 'weiße Fleck', will involve primarily a consideration not of the narrator's 'biography' (by which he exists for others and of whose interpretive powers he can so easily become a victim) but of the alternatives he rejected or which were possible but unclear at the relevant time, alternatives which nevertheless constitute his individuality in all its rich potentiality. It is in this sense that Frisch sees his novel as a search 'not in the direction of the world, but in the direction of the self'.[11] And the first step the narrator takes in the journey towards the self is the invention of the Enderlin persona. For the numerous 'biographical' parallels (pipe-smoking, chess-playing with his friend Burri, for example), together with the paradoxical suggestion of both 'change' and 'finality' in the name itself, link this persona closest to the fictive narrator and justify an examination of 'Enderlin' before 'Gantenbein' and 'Svoboda'.

3   ENDERLIN: 'THE SPLIT THROUGH THE PERSON'

The two nerve centres of the book, discussed above, are linked by an isolated paragraph of singular importance:

> Es ist wie ein Sturz durch den Spiegel, mehr weiß einer nicht, wenn er wieder erwacht, ein Sturz wie durch alle Spiegel, und nachher, kurz darauf, setzt die Welt sich wieder zusammen, als wäre nichts geschehen. Es ist auch nichts geschehen. (IV 18)[12]

> *It's like falling through a mirror, that's all you know when you wake up, like falling through all the mirrors there are, and afterwards, shortly afterwards, the world is put together again as though nothing has happened. And nothing has happened (18)*[12]

Thus the experience in hospital and the visit to the deserted marital home, manifestations of the same inner crisis, are presented in terms of crashing through those appearances which are generally taken to comprise everyday reality. The world itself barely notices such a disturbance—as far as external reality is concerned, nothing has happened. Only the narrator feels that he has to make sense of these brief but crucial insights. And it is the persona of Enderlin which becomes the sharpest lense he invents to bring into focus the true significance of the 'fall through the mirror'. Like Reinhart, Stiller and Faber before him, it is Enderlin who suffers a severe personal dislocation in the face of the inimical nature of time. Impossibly, he wants to live his life in that stasis between past and future which Frisch has elsewhere declared to be 'scarcely open to experience.'[13] The attempt to break out of the prison of time, to grasp the moment and avoid repetition, leads inevitably to a radical loss of personal integrity: 'Was er wirklich erlebt, so oder so, ist der Riß, der durch seine Person geht' (V130; *'What he really experiences, either way, is the split that runs through his person'*, *124*). This 'schizophrenic' experience also lies behind Enderlin's loss of confidence in his rôle in society, and before a closer examination of the time problem and its major expansion into the major theme of ageing is undertaken, this aspect must be dealt with.

The initial shock caused by the sudden loss of confidence in his social rôle as academic occurs significantly in the midst of an intimate party 'where Enderlin knows himself to be valued, and really nothing happens, nothing at all, an evening like many others' (V 39, 37). As with the fall through the mirror, the experience is particular, unique and totally hidden from his environment. The outside agency of a professional appointment to Harvard is enough to act as a catalyst. At a moment of professional success Enderlin becomes abruptly aware of an abyss yawning at his feet. Ironically placed at the centre of attention, caught in a false centricity the longer he remains silent, Enderlin watches an uncomprehending world go on as before, 'only for Enderlin has something happened, not for the first time incidentally and probably not for the last. Before insight comes to him from this occurrence, a lot of little moments of dismay will be needed' (V 41, 39). The Harvard affair is one such moment in a whole series which crystallises in the sudden awareness that the rôle he plays in society is a very tenuous form of centricity indeed. Esteem and respect from others are not won by essential merit but by successful rôle-playing ('even charlatans have been invited to Harvard'). Enderlin realises he has become a prisoner of other people's expectations For the logic of the social rôle he has elected to play reveals its own autonomous laws. Like Graf Öderland, but without the lawyer's primitive vigour, Enderlin calls a halt to the game of 'helpless habit' (V 121, *114*). But the alternative for him proves to be a decline into a passivity, coloured by a longing for the freer, more challenging existence summed up in the Harvard lecture on the God of Ambiguity, Hermes, which he never in fact delivers. God of thieves and rogues, Hermes is also a bestower of fertility, the source of 'the sudden, the improbable, the incalculable and uphoped-for, even the capricious . . . the uncanny element in all gaiety' (V 146, *139*). Unfortunately for Enderlin he has none of the gay cunning which is the strength, for example, of Thomas Mann's great eccentric and swindler, Felix Krull.[14] Krull, indeed, illustrates precisely what Enderlin lacks : the resilient sense of irony which makes rôle-playing and social existence bearable. By contrast, the man who does discover such a quality within himself after a similar crisis of identity, is the Ambassador.

There is little doubt that the fictive narrator and, one suspects, Frisch too, see in this character a possible solution to the fundamental eccentricity which marks out Enderlin. For the Ambassador does not collapse under the impact of his sudden insight into his

true nature, nor does he attempt to escape the consequences by
inventing for himself a multiplicity of identities : 'He chooses that
which is greater : the rôle. His self-knowledge remains his secret'
(V 119, *113*). Aware that he is, at least in his own eyes, an 'impostor'
and a 'charlatan', the Ambassador maintains the dignity of silence,
performs substantial deeds and dies with his secret intact.[15] It is
not an easy solution; the cost is great : in an important area of his
life he is condemned to complete loneliness. But there is grandeur
in the compromise. For the Ambassador does achieve a form of
positive eccentricity whereby he manages to hold together the
centrifugal tensions of his personality. An identity is forged
—imperfectly, one must admit—which renders life in society
possible and indeed might be said in this case to marginally improve
its quality. Anatol Stiller, too, was aware of a possible solution
along these lines : 'One must be capable of passing without defiance
through their confusion of identities, playing a part without ever
confusing oneself with the part; but for this I must have a fixed
point' (III 590, *186*). Frisch's narrator, however, makes no attempt
to delineate the Ambassador's 'fixed point' with the result that this
episode remains a shadowy anecdote, a brief and isolated contrast
to the book's central inventions.

The true significance of the Enderlin persona lies in his search
for a different kind of rôle in which experience retains its immedi-
acy and is not subject to reflection and the disintegrating forces of
time. Enderlin thus tries out the rôle of the detached lover (or
rather the fictive narrator tries out the rôle though Enderlin!)—a
contradiction in terms which is made immediately apparent by the
Doppelgänger device used to explore the rôle's possibilities. A critical
and watchful, although clearly powerless, 'ich' accompanies the
Enderlin 'er' (dubbed frequently 'the strange gentleman') and
comments on his actions. Both 'ich' and 'er', however, share a
common fear of time, both fight against repetition, neither wants a
conventional love affair with all that entails in terms of personal
commitment. But Enderlin, ignoring the warnings of his *alter ego*,
is made to learn that love without commitment can lead only to a
fractured personality, a situation neatly captured in the description
of Enderlin the morning after his first night with Lila as an incon-
gruous figure, dressed for the opera, standing among early shift
workers in a coffee bar : 'The only face in this bar that watched
him from time to time was his own in the mirror behind bottles . . .
Only the two water-grey eyes—they were looking out of the mirror

as though they were really there in the mirror—are such that he recognises himself in them' (V 70, 67).

This image of dislocation is directly related to Enderlin's defective relationship to time. The experience with Lila is already solidifying into a memory which will become an indissoluble part of him, and he flees into a museum 'in order not to be in the world. He wanted to be alone and beyond time' (V 72, 69). But the attempt to escape the past and avoid the future is doomed to failure, as his *alter ego* well knows : 'They wanted what is possible only once: the now . . . because the future, he knew, that's me, her husband, I am the repetition, the story, the finitude and the curse in everything, I am the process of ageing minute by minute' (V 73, 69 f.). The night with Lila cannot simply be added to some absurd number of similar events (cf. the ironic allusion to *Don Giovanni*— 'Mille e tre !'); for it confirms and underlines an experience of transience which renders all relationships problematical. Enderlin feels only too acutely the loss of the exciting possibilities inherent in the potentiality of the moment which is inevitably curtailed as soon as any decision is taken. To be aware of such curtailment as loss rather than as a means of exploiting the chosen possibility creatively, is the root cause of the 'split which runs through his person'.

It is this fractured sensibility which makes Enderlin experience the act of sex, for example, in which man and woman should be most intensely aware of each other, as an anonymous, disembodied phenomenon reflected in a hotel mirror. This is the result of his attempt to defeat the laws of human nature, to thwart the 'demon', time, which 'won't allow any game apart from his own' (V 71, 68). Time ceases to be experienced chronologically (which would give Enderlin a framework of order), but as a pervasive force 'which is forever overtaking us, transience in a trifle' (V 80, 77). And the chief characteristic of transience is shown to be repetition which destroys chronology. This is the reason why the idea of reliving a year of his life 'without the openness, the uncertainty compounded of hope and fear' (V 123, 117) fills Enderlin not with joy but with horror. Only the young—with their hopes and possibilities stretching before them into infinity—are free of this debilitating awareness of transience in the guise of repetition. Thus the young girl on the *via appia antica* answers Enderlin's (and the narrator's) question, 'What can one do with a day-dream?' with the blunt confidence of her years : 'Take it !' (V 138, 132).

Unable to escape repetition with Lila, and having shied away from suicide (the opening death in the novel is only putatively

Enderlin's), the narrator is left with the task of imagining the alternative : 'the process of ageing'. The Enderlin persona is accordingly projected into a future with Lila as 'the couple'. The reader is presented with a depressing picture of the indistinguishable 'endless, swiftly passing years' in which two people with 'bodies dead to love' slowly sink into the granite greyness of 'routine which is truth' (V 136, *129*). The progressive decay of the lovers' bodies is matched by the ebbing of desire, and it is only the possibility of jealousy that can produce a measure of pain to give this relationship a semblance of life. For the mutual respect for and sense of the mysterious otherness of the partner is long since dead. The cold facts of a common biography have submerged, as the ashes buried Pompeii, the excitement of an original, exhilarating unpredictability. All that is left is the shared decline into old age,[16] a process in fact which represents the closing of the 'split which runs through his person' :

> Also altern!
> Morgengrauen—
> aber ohne Pferdekopf—
> Grauen—
> aber ohne Schrei—(V 157)

> *So he'll grow old!*
> *Grey dawn—*
> *but without a horse's head—*
> *grey horror—*
> *but without a scream—(149 f.)*

The featureless rock of routine existence is not inhabitable in any creative way for Enderlin, nor has he the strength to hold the tensions of a fractured personality, as the Ambassador succeeds in doing. The centre does not hold, the gyre widens into an ever-increasing solipsism.

Thus the Enderlin persona culminates in the same area of experience as his inventor's. His 'story' reveals the unmistakable contours of the narrator's pattern of experience. Felix Enderlin has proved not a happy changeling, but a dead end. He has become predictable and therefore dispensable. To match its central significance the decision to give up Enderlin is reached in the very middle of the novel, and we must now turn our attention to the narrator's first invented persona, Theo Gantenbein. Gantenbein has, as it were, shadowed Enderlin all along, and he can now be seen to enjoy the largest scope of all the fictive narrator's 'sketches for an ego'.

4   GANTENBEIN : THE IRONIC PARASITE

Enderlin's difficulty lay in locating a vital centre in relation to which he could find a meaningful rôle. Neither in the private sphere (as lover) nor in the public one (as academic) does he succeed in finding an antidote to the debilitating fear of repetition and the corrosive power of time. The Enderlin persona demonstrates that the basic pattern of the narrator's experience dictates the outcome —'the same creases always appear in the same places'. But alongside Enderlin Frisch's narrator tries out the 'first' Gantenbein model, and indeed this initial experiment is deeply coloured by Enderlin's adventures. It will be seen, in fact, that each half of the novel has its 'own' Gantenbein—the one relating to, and relativising, Enderlin's concerns, the other standing in a similar relationship to Svoboda. The two models pivot neatly on the exact centre of the novel : the story of Ali and Alil. The Gantenbein persona is therefore best discussed in two separate sections : the first, as it were, in a similar orbit to Enderlin, the second to Svoboda. The significance of the central story told to Camilla can then be examined in terms of being a bridge between the two—a bridge which is, in a sense, a mirror facing both ways.[17]

Gantenbein I

The first Gantenbein model is conceived as a counterpoise to Enderlin. It represents an attempt to control the 'prodigious oscillations to which the man who lives aesthetically is exposed'[18] by the deliberate adoption of the stance of a detached ironist. Theo Gantenbein, like the Ambassador, chooses 'that which is greater: the rôle'—his attitude and purpose : 'Life as a game, his freedom by virtue of a secret' (V 21, *21*). This persona, of course, is no less aesthetic in Kierkegaard's sense than that of Enderlin. But clearly the fictive narrator intends to test whether such a peripheral vantage point is in fact at all tenable. Unlike the Ambassador, however, his very parasitic existence, caused by the lie at the centre of his rôle—the Ambassador was at least an Ambassador!— ultimately undermines his resolve. Even humour cannot save him in the long run, for it springs directly out of incongruities which he can only savour solipsistically. His apparent initial success is subtly relativised by Enderlin's concomitant difficulties, his hopes ironically presented in association with a fundamentally spurious relationship with the prostitute Camilla Huber :

Die kleine Begegnung mit Camilla Huber neulich bestärkt ihn in seiner Hoffnung, die Menschen etwas freier zu machen, frei von der Angst, daß man ihre Lügen sehe. Vor allem aber, so hofft Gantenbein, werden die Leute sich vor einem Blinden wenig tarnen, sodaß man sie besser kennenlernt, und es entsteht ein wirklicheres Verhältnis, indem man auch ihre Lügen gelten läßt, ein vertrauenvolleres Verhältnis—(V 44)

His recent brief meeting with Camilla Huber reinforces his hope of making people freer, free from the fear that one sees their lies. Above all, however, Gantenbein hopes, people won't camouflage themselves much against a blind man, so that one will get to know them better, and a more real relationship will come into being as a result of granting validity to their lies, a more trusting relationship—(42)

Gantenbein's adoption of a paradoxical Teiresias rôle is thus aimed at countering the fateful temptation to hide behind defensive clichés, to project graven images on to other people, stunting the growth of genuine relationships. This strategy, of course, is self-delusion. For it is based on deceit. Gantenbein may indeed get to know other people better, but *they* can never get to know *him*. The dialectical nature of human relationships is short-circuited. Gantenbein chooses to ignore the fact that such an eccentric relationship with Camilla, for example, cannot exist beyond the careful limits of their game, the rules of which equally restrict their freedom. Both are playing rôles which do not correspond to empirical reality. Camilla does not cease to be a prostitute—that is, a figure essentially lacking in wholeness on the periphery of society—she merely enjoys living out a private phantasy with her 'blind' client. Gantenbein cannot enable her to lead another life in any true sense. Their conspiracy—'Gantenbein has already understood the rôle she intends to play in his eyes, and he will accept her in this rôle, if Camilla will let him play the part of a blind man in exchange' (V 38, 37)—is turned against the world in which alone authentic existence is to be found. Once the world breaks into this cosy complicity (via Camilla's decision to marry) their relationship promptly disintegrates.

The fascination of this first model lies in Gantenbein's own acute awareness of the inherent disadvantages of his strategem, 'the intro-

version to which his blindness exposes him'. He takes up his blindman's rôle, as it were, with his eyes wide open. What holds the
fictive narrator's attention, and the reader's, is whether he will
manage against the odds to hold the tensions, control the oscillations, within the rôle. In this connection we see him at one point
expressing his admiration for the Roman Catholic sacrament of
confession where for a few moments a man can be himself without
fear and regain the strength necessary to continue his rôle in the
world. Needless to say, what Gantenbein does not appreciate is the
sacramental quality of the confessional, the fact that its efficacy
depends precisely on the existence of a living religious core. His
excursions in the Grunewald, where he can relax with his dog, are
in no way comparable. They are merely—to use Blaise Pascal's
term—'divertissements'. In a sense, a better 'confessional' for
Gantenbein is Camilla's flat. It is there he goes to tell his 'stories'
which represent a method of channelling into an ordered framework
the chaos-threatening tensions of his enterprise.

The crucial test, however, of the Gantenbein persona is not
Camilla, nor for that matter the Zürich welfare authorities whom
he has to convince of his affliction; it is his marriage to Lila.
Whereas Enderlin tries ineffectually to dispense with such a relationship in favour of the permanent freedom of non-commitment,
Gantenbein seeks to live it out. By adopting the position of a
benevolent, idle parasite—Lila works whilst he is left to concentrate
on his rôle—he hopes to render everyday life 'a jolly affair', to
have his cake and eat it. By means of irony and humour (his tricks
as a host, for example, the expert boning of fish, the accurate filling
of glasses until he senses a guest's doubts about his blindness, for
which perfidy the luckless individual receives a measure of wine
over his hand!) he hopes to keep at bay the fears that crippled
Enderlin. 'Only miracles make everyday life bearable' (V 108, *103*).

The source of Gantenbein's temporary magnanimity and success
is what he considers to be their mutual respect for each other's
'secret self'. But here Gantenbein falls into confusion. For *his* secret
is not the central core of his being, which a religious man might
call his soul and which Frisch himself has defined as 'the vital
spark in every man which cannot be grasped'[19]—it is *deceit*. His
secret can only lead him into a false centricity. Likewise, Lila's
secret—in Gantenbein's eyes—is her presumed unfaithfulness, which
is an obvious *barrier* to true understanding. The fragility of his
paradoxical world is most clearly revealed in the one situation in

which he can remove his blindman's glasses with impunity—love-making :

Ein Mann, ein Weib.

Sie kennt vermutlich viele Männer, solche und solche . . . sie küssen mit geschlossenen Augen, um blind zu sein vor Entzückung, aber sie sind nicht blind, haben Angst und sind taub, haben nicht die Hände eines Blinden, Hingabe, aber nicht bedingungslos, nicht unstörbar, Zärtlichkeit, aber nicht die Zärtlichkeit eines Blinden, die erlöst von allem, worüber man erschrickt, wenn man es vom andern auch gesehen weiß; ein Blinder kommt nicht von außen; ein Blinder, eins mit seinem Traum, vergleicht sie nicht mit andern Frauen, nicht einen Atemzug lang, er glaubt seiner Haut—(V 106)

A man, a woman.

She probably knows many men, of various types . . . they kiss with closed eyes in order to be blind with ecstasy, but they aren't blind, they're afraid and are deaf, they haven't the hands of a blind man, surrender, but not unconditionally, not proof against being disturbed, tenderness, but not the tenderness of a blind man which gives release from everything that frightens, even when one knows this has been seen by the other; a blind man doesn't come from the outside; a blind man, at one with his dream, doesn't compare her with other women, not for the space of a breath, he believes his skin—(101)

A blind man may well rely on the primacy of touch, free of doubts as to his ability to satisfy his woman—or so Gantenbein would argue. Because such a man's other senses are sharpened (he is not confused by appearances), he is not tempted perhaps into invidious comparisons which might measure his own performance and find it wanting. He is therefore, in Gantenbein's view, spared the most destructive passion of all : jealousy. For jealousy is essentially 'fear of comparison'.[20] Gantenbein, however, is *not* blind. He cannot thus have developed the 'tenderness of a blind man', and thus he cannot be 'at one with his dream'. The rules of his own game are against him. The aesthetic mode of life is one of absolute neutrality, and absolute neutrality involves total detachment. Gantenbein's game proves an impossible method of bringing about a creative relationship with Lila. The freedom he can grant her because of his assumed blindness he cannot win for himself. His initial gener-osity in the face of the 'fremde Herr" (Enderlin!) who threatens his marriage, gives way to the corrosive power of jealousy.

It is clear from Burri's interpolated story of the Master Baker in O.[21] that Gantenbein has been using Camilla's eagerness for 'true' stories as an opportunity to control his feeling of jealousy by transposing them into an 'alienated' narrative form. Thus he takes over the baker's violent outburst of jealousy, described to him by Burri, as the 'story' which fits his own experience : 'Suddenly some-one performs my deed and it will get him put into prison, and I stand there horror-stricken' (V 113, *108*). The alienated narrative, however, succeeds only in underlining the narrator's dilemma. Gantenbein's 'blindness' inevitably turns against the rôle-player : he adopts a mask in order to achieve a dignified detachment, in short a new life as a husband, and his very blindness plunges him into a vicious circle of doubt : 'If Lila knew that I can see, she would doubt my love, and it would be hell, a man and a woman, but not a couple' (V 103 f., *99*). He is caught in a trap of his own devising. The warnings that Frisch has his narrator place so carefully at the very beginning of the Gantenbein variation now achieve total clarity. When the latter puts on his blindman's glasses for the first time, the world is suddenly deprived of all its colours, all the differentia-tions that give it life. It is reduced to a uniform 'ash-grey with a lilac tint' ('mit einem Stich ins Lila'). In a single trenchant phrase the act of choosing a blind man's glasses is linked both to the metaphor of the rock face which imprisons the wild horse and the telling symbol of Pompeii. The untranslatable 'Stich ins Lila' contains a hint of violence against the woman at whom he stares with increasing impotence. Furthermore, the spectacles do not merely violate Gantenbein's environment, they also have a disturb-ing effect on himself, producing an experience not unlike Walter Faber's sense of personal dislocation :

Im Spiegel, ja, ich sehe gerade noch, daß es keine Tür ins Freie ist, sondern ein Spiegel, sehe ich einen Mann von meiner Gestalt, ohne zu wissen, ob der Mann im Spiegel, dessen Augen nicht zu sehen sind, mich gleichfalls erkennt. Als ich näher trete, um seine Augen zu sehen, kommt der Andere auf mich zu wie ein Blinder, der nicht ausweicht, so als wolle er durch mich hindurchgehen— (V 27)

In the mirror, yes, I see just in time that it isn't a door leading out, but a mirror, I see a man with my figure, without knowing whether the man in the mirror, whose eyes are not to be seen, also recognises me. When I step closer, to see his eyes, the other

man comes towards me like a blind man who doesn't step aside,
as though he were going to walk through me. (26)

Thus even at the beginning of the experiment the first Gantenbein
variation is prefigured as reaching the same impasse of alienation
as Enderlin. Integrity is not achieved, the fractured personality, the
central *Doppelgänger* motif, is seen to be dominant. It is therefore
not surprising to find Gantenbein paying Enderlin a visit in hospital.
From the fictive narrator's point of view the two identities have
come very close together. Neither has escaped into another life;
both are back where they started : Enderlin faced with the problem
of ageing as an alternative to death, Gantenbein with 'both feet on
the ground' but ironically 'without a self' (V150, *142*). With the
Enderlin persona abandoned, the second Gantenbein variation (i.e.
his withdrawal from the blind man's rôle) becomes an irresistible
temptation. Before the narrator embarks upon this experiment,
however, he intercalates between the two halves of his narrative
the 'fairy-tale' of Ali and Alil.

The 'Märchen'

As the name Alil indicates, the novel's central 'story' presents the
mirror image of Lila's situation with Gantenbein. Here it is the
woman who is blind and the man 'seeing'. When Ali has Alil cured
of her blindness, her love remains constant, based as it is on
outward-going affection and gratitude and not on mere appearances. Ali's actions, and in particular his selfless love, have opened
up for her a whole new world in which both live happily. The fictive
narrator is here clearly having Gantenbein indulge in wishful
thinking. The basic ingredients of the persona are being juggled in
view of the unsatisfactory way the first Gantenbein model worked
out. Through his blindness he had hoped to see more clearly, and
thus avoid, the pitfalls that bring human relationships to grief.
But such solutions only work in the miraculous atmosphere of the
fairy-tale, so it is not surprising to find Camilla, for whom it is told,
rejecting this tale with its happy end which offends her taste for
stories which faithfully reflect everyday reality.

Her negative reaction forces Gantenbein to change the fairy-tale's
constituent parts radically, just as the narrator in the larger fiction
is forced to consider varying the Gantenbein persona itself if it is to
remain flexible enough to serve as a vehicle of expression for his
experience. (This is why, of course, the story strikes Camilla—and
the reader—as so improbable : the fiction of a blind woman married

to a seeing man does not correspond in any way to the narrator's pattern of experience. Therefore, like the variation 'Lila as Countess' it does not 'work'). Ali is thus made to 'catch' Alil's blindness and falls a prompt victim to an all-consuming jealousy. Happiness turns to misery, Ali to other women. The 'other women' turn out to be Alil herself. (Gantenbein had tried the same antidote to jealousy, and he, too, discovered that his problem was not how to relate to a particular woman but to Woman as such.) Ali only discovers this ironic fact when he is cured, but he continues to play the blind man in order to spy on his wife. Here the tale breaks off with a clear indication of Ali's, and by extension Gantenbein's, *spiritual* blindness and guilt. There is no 'happy end', no idyllic conclusion. The problem of how Ali restores the balance between himself and his wife is left open. The fairy-tale, in fact, reverses the general movement of the Gantenbein persona : the first half (rejected by Camilla) relates to the second half of the novel, whilst its inconclusive continuation reflects the impasse at which the first Gantenbein model has arrived. It is therefore against an ironically reflecting background that the fictive narrator has Gantenbein explore in the second half of the novel the possibility of dropping his pretence of blindness, and with it his peripheral existence, for an alternative route to the centre—envisioned as a full, genuine relationship with Lila.

Gantenbein II

If the first Gantenbein model is characterised by the attempt to master the rôle of ironic observer, the 'outsider' feeding parasitically on his environment, the second demonstrates the enervating effect of such a stance. Tired of his deception and tempted to confess it, Gantenbein first (tentatively) imagines the consequences—and is immediately exposed to the disintegrating power of jealousy which culminates in the ludicrous episode with the harmless student, Einhorn. As with the Enderlin persona, the narrator has to function at this crucial juncture as a brake on the delicate explora-tion of Gantenbein's new mode of life : 'Since he has stopped playing the blind man, Gantenbein is impossible. I'm getting worried' (V 172, *163*). And in order to distance himself even further from what he foresees as a testing time ahead, he imagines Ganten-bein's life with Lila behind another obfuscation : their old age together in terms of the classical legend of Philemon and Baucis. The purpose of this episode, however, becomes clear : to sound out a possible conclusion to the Ali/Alil fairy-tale.

The result is disaster: The names of Philemon and Baucis, symbols of tranquil old age illuminated by a mutual loving loyalty, come to denote the bitterest irony. Frisch describes brilliantly the complex modulations of jealousy and mistrust as they break up a relationship—the minor irritations avidly seized on to mask the central issues, the comic absurdities of human nature in the grip of a devastating monomania, above all the convincing way his protagonist churns over 'facts' in his mind until he has fashioned them into his own wilful version of 'reality'. Thus Philemon succumbs to his passion, christening his wife's putative lover 'Einhorn' (a phallic nightmare!) and breaking open his wife's personal drawer to read the incriminating love letters it contains, letters which he is then forced to recognise as his own—written to Lila when she was still married to Svoboda. Marital break-up is inevitable and follows promptly on Philemon-Gantenbein's action of locking the bewildered student Einhorn into Lila-Baucis's bedroom.

There is, however, one last and significant twist to the Philemon-Baucis variant which is presented as a story for Camilla and which in fact poses the alternative to Lila's outraged departure, a further possible conclusion to the story of Ali and Alil: Philemon and Baucis live out their lives together. The picture the narrator paints is one of the clearest expressions of physical and spiritual dislocation in the book. In an atmosphere of boredom, where love and sex have sunk to a mere repetitive confirmation of long-known facts, where crises are restricted to revolving round trivialities, the calm flow of everyday routine is punctured only rarely by moments of awareness: 'Sometimes it happened that he saw their lovemaking, while it was taking place, as though from outside, as though he were sitting in an armchair beside them or just standing by the window' (V 233, 222). Pretence and hypocrisy take the place of warmth and love. We are left with the vision of a man 'alone with the love of his life', but one whose balance and wholeness are merely the ironic reflections of a solipsistic phenomenon.

With such stark premonitions of the risks attached to telling Lila the truth it is not surprising that Gantenbein shrinks back into his blind man's rôle with the cry 'What help is it to see!' As Anatol Stiller found out to his cost, people quickly establish a vested interest in one another's rôles; what may appear a relatively insignificant change in one's own life can cause a veritable upheaval in others'. The decision to remain blind, however, forces Ganten-

bein into an ever deeper hypothetical labyrinth of alternative identities, for a simple return to the game of the novel's first part is
hardly possible. The dangers of such multiplicity were clearly
pointed out by Kierkegaard. If life is treated as a masquerade, an
inexhaustible material for amusement, one risks the disintegration
of the self : 'If your nature were resolved into a multiplicity . . . you
really might become many . . . and you thus would have lost the
inmost and holiest thing of all in a man, the unifying power of
personality.'[22] To obviate this danger the fictive narrator has
Gantenbein decide to remain 'himself' and to try and change *Lila's*
rôle.

Lila, however, is not a character at all, as Frisch himself has
explained : 'Lila is a name for the female principle, the other sex
as the book's narrator sees it, a name from which he cannot free
himself. That's why she alone exists and yet does not exist. There's
the comedy. What the narrator tells us of Lila portrays only him.
Lila is a phantom, therefore impossible to grasp—hence his
jealousy.'[23] It is accordingly pointless to change her rôle into that
of 'countess', 'scientist' or 'doctor' because such variations effectively
remove her from the scope of the narrator's pattern of experience,
which is obviously not an infinite one. The result is seen, for
example, in the extended version of 'Lila as Countess : why it does
not work' where she simply disappears altogether, leaving an empty
space at the breakfast table surrounded by mocking mirrors.

It is an essential feature of the 'second' Gantenbein persona that
he is made aware of the limits placed on his hypothetical enterprise.
For example, he tells Camilla a story about a man who attends his
own funeral.[24] The man—an eccentric figure in his light-coloured
raincoat and 'always the black sheep of the family'—had never
succeeded in changing his way of life despite his constant resolve
to do so. Change for him comes solely with 'death', when he can
jettison 'like old clothes' the various rôles he has played in life.
Having observed his own obsequies and visited his empty home for
the last time, the man is content to slip away into thin air. This
gentle slide into oblivion will be Gantenbein's fate, too, as he well
knows. Death puts a term on all rôle-playing.[25] But this is no
answer to the question of how life can be lived or understood.
Such 'freedom' from private and public obligations via a merely
presumed death does not reflect the pattern of experience which
articulates the Gantenbein persona. Indeed, the more the narrator
feels his persona slipping from him into a vortex of gyrating inventions, the more he has him struggle to maintain some contact with

the world around him. This struggle becomes increasingly urgent once the safety-valve of Camilla's flat has been closed by her return to social conformity. With her achievement of 'respectability' she no longer needs Gantenbein's 'blindness', and their conspiratorial meetings cease—albeit with a solemn promise not to reveal the other's secret. (That Camilla has never in fact been taken in by Gantenbein's pretence is a typical touch of Frisch humour : people who wear masks self-consciously are clearly well-attuned to their fellow ironists!)

It is now that Gantenbein begins to appreciate more clearly his *own* propensity to fix false images on other people. He remarks, for example, that in the company of others 'it is not the party in which I am interested, but a party of masks for which I am to blame' (V 268, 254). At another moment, he verges on the paranoic and buys a taperecorder in order to eavesdrop on his friends' conversation when he is not in the room in the hope that their malicious gossip, at least, will confirm his identity : 'I am hankering after betrayal. I should like to know that I exist . . . I should like to come out from my imagination, I should like to be in the world. I should like to be betrayed in my innermost being' (V 270, 256). This is Gantenbein's (and the fictive narrator's) basic predicament: both are imprisoned in their own minds, victims of their own imaginations, both desire 'to be in the world', to fix their identities if need be, like Christ, through suffering. For Christ, argues Gantenbein, talked of betrayal at the Last Supper not just to shame Judas, but 'to appoint one of his disciples to betray him in order that he should be in the world, in order to bear witness to his reality in the world'. The comparison is a startling illustration of Gantenbein's one-sidedness. Christ gave witness to his reality in the world, of course, through *love* not by inviting betrayal. Suffering and death were the consummation of that love. And it is precisely the impossibility of such love, the outward going devotion to other people, which is fundamental to the pattern of experience which the fictive narrator is trying to capture and understand through his multi-facetted inventions.

In this context 'jealousy' is the outward sign of a far deeper malaise than mere sexual inadequacy; it is the ground bass of the eccentric experience :

Eifersucht als wirklicher Schmerz darüber, daß ein Wesen, das uns ausfüllt, zugleich außen ist. Ein Traumschreck bei hellichtem Tag. Eifersucht hat mit der Liebe der Geschlechter weniger zu tun, als es scheint : es ist die Kluft zwischen der Welt und dem Wahn, die Eifersucht im engern Sinn nur eine Fußnote dazu, Schock : die Welt deckt sich mit dem Partner, nicht mit mir, die Liebe hat mich nur mit meinem Wahn vereint. (V 270 f.)

Jealousy as real pain that a being who fills us completely is at the same time outside. A dream-terror in broad daylight. Jealousy has far less to do with the love of the sexes than appears; it is the chasm between the world and madness, jealousy in the narrower sense is only a footnote to this, a shock: the world is identical with my partner, not with me, love has merely made me one with my madness. (256)

This insight, however, only serves to strengthen Gantenbein's resolve to play out his rôle to the end despite the guilt it involves. He survives the symbolic disaster of the Flood in his flat which threatened to destroy his relationship with Lila once and for all, and he tries a final, desperate invention : Gantenbein as a father.

From the early play *Santa Cruz* (1944) to *Die Schwierigen* and *Homo Faber* the 'child' has been posited by Frisch as a possible guarantee of centricity. Conversely, Stiller saw the arrival of the child-substitute, the dog Foxli, as a symbol of the negative forces within his marriage to Julika. It is not surprising therefore to find Gantenbein expressing paternal pride that he 'is in the world through this glorious creature', his daughter Beatrice. And indeed the child does form a momentary bond between him and Lila, but only in the sense that by living through the child they are able to avoid each other. The pleasures of fatherhood are not sufficient to check the destructive power of jealousy, the irrational persistence of which even leads Gantenbein to suspect that the child is not his. In his shifting, obsessive world only the child's existence itself is a central certainty, but its very growth emphasises Gantenbein's continuing dissolution. The brief contact with a reality outside his own mind merely underlines his increasing isolation. A surrogate life through his child proves an illusion, a false centricity, and he is driven back to his peripheral stance in the relationship with Lila, where the final shock awaits him : he discovers at long last that Lila in fact has no lover—and for that contingency, the negation of all his anxieties, like the 'Pechvogel', 'he has no rôle', and the Gantenbein persona necessarily disintegrates.

The fictive narrator has thus been led by his fictions back to his point of departure : the surface banality of an everyday experience eventually stifles the attempted expression of its true complexity.

As both Enderlin and the Gantenbein models in this way prove inadequate 'stories' for the narrator's purpose, it remains for the Svoboda persona to complete the pattern. If Enderlin is the deceiver, Gantenbein both deceiver and deceived, Svoboda is the deceived—thus the book's shape imitates its central motif : the mirror.

5   SVOBODA : THE CIRCLE CLOSED

If Enderlin was the persona invented to explore the conflicting pressures of love in its initial stages and Gantenbein the persona to examine how that love might nevertheless be kept alive, Svoboda's function is to articulate the experience of that love actually coming to an end. The Svoboda model is logically necessary to close the circle. And just as the 'first' Gantenbein's attempt to imagine a different life is mirrored and ironised by Enderlin's vain search for the same possibility, so too the 'second' Gantenbein's desire to drop his mask and live 'in the world' is echoed and commented upon by the concomitant Svoboda persona. For Svoboda is presented as an architect, a man very much 'in the world' and, on the surface at least, at one with it.

If Enderlin shares some of the traits of Anatol Stiller, Svoboda can be seen as related to Walter Faber. Like Faber he is imagined with a clearly defined (and socially useful) rôle, a man used to controlling his environment by decisive action. He also shares Faber's initial naïve acceptance of appearance as reality. The collapse of his marriage with Lila, however, opens up a similar abyss to the one Faber experiences momentarily in the airport lavatory at Houston. In both cases the congruity of the man and his world suddenly and without warning disintegrates. There, however, the comparison ends. For Svoboda does not lose touch with concrete reality. In the terms of the book's dominant motif, 'he doesn't like looking at himself in the mirror' (V 234, 222).

Because the Svoboda persona is conceived as a straightforward biographical entity, that is, a man who sticks to the facts of his life, who does not experience time as a problem nor have any sense that possibilities can be as real as actuality, the narrator is forced to admit that reality cannot be treated like a dramatic text, altered at will or cut off with a neat curtain-fall. For this reason he finds the Svoboda rôle so uncomfortable. And indeed it is noticeable how he keeps the Svoboda variation very much at arm's length by the use of the third person pronoun, whereas when trying out the Enderlin and Gantenbein models, first and third person pronouns were constantly interweaving in an intricate pattern of irony. The alternatives for Svoboda in the face of Lila's desertion are consequently relatively perfunctory. Five possibilities are briefly sketched : suicide, a policy of wait-and-see, drowning his sorrows in nightclubs, the maintenance of nerve and dignity or flight to Salamanca. For painful though the situation is, Svoboda recognises soberly that the belief 'one cannot live without someone' is mere self-delusion. Thus he is clear-headed enough to realise that his marriage is over and separation is inevitable. Despite the fact that he is prey—like Gantenbein—to explosions of wild jealousy, hitting out around him like an injured bear, his sense of life's continuity does not desert him.

The fictive narrator's reluctance to assume the Svoboda identity stems from precisely this fact that Svoboda comes to terms with the situation. It is Svoboda, for example, who appears to absorb most readily Burri's analysis of man's basic inferiority vis-à-vis woman. The sexual act, Burri declares, reveals man for what he is, whilst woman can choose to remain an infinite enigma. The biological difference (which, for example, enables the woman to be a whore but not the man) grants woman a permanent superiority; for only male vanity compels her to counterfeit orgasm where she fails to achieve it, and the knowledge that this is so leaves the man forever uncertain of his potency and the genuineness of his partner's emotions. Furthermore, in so far as man struggles against this natural state of affairs, his relationships with women will always prove destructive.[26] Paradoxically, by accepting this bleak view (its first expression in Frisch's narrative world centred on Yvonne in *Die Schwierigen*), by letting go of his particular image of Lila, Svoboda is the only one who comes close to seeing her objectively. The implications are neatly encapsulated on board the liner sailing to New York, where for the first time the narrator, by speaking in the first person, directly acknowledges his affinity with his invention. The image is presented of individual solitude in a shaky world where no paint can ever cover up the corrosive rust, a self-contained world moving heedlessly towards its predestined goal. Time is the master, imagination a means to momentary, but illusory, freedom. In such a world the meeting with the woman who could be 'Lila from the outside' can only be perfunctory, interesting but without lasting consequence. When the ship (at one point significantly likened to a labyrinth) eventually reaches its destination, all that is left of Lila is a memory of 'her face in a mirror'.

In essence the Svoboda story can be seen as an extended echo of the narrator's frightening experience of nearly drowning in the sea—the sudden panic at losing contact with ground, the desperate struggle in the breakers and the final, rather sheepish regaining of his footing on a crowded beach of unknowing sun-bathers. But unlike the narrator, Svoboda recovers rapidly from his attack of vertigo and returns to the ostensibly stable world whose solidity he had never really doubted. For Svoboda is one of the great majority who have no difficulty in adapting to their environment, who experience reality in an unproblematic way. He is the sort of man of whom Frisch once said that he remains happily unaware that 'a fixed number of identical occurrences could produce seven different life-stories to be told and indeed lived through merely by the self inventing a new identity as their basis. It's uncanny. Anyone who knows this, finds life difficult. Anyone who doesn't, and luckily very few do, has no choice to face, since he does not see through the fact that his self is an invention.'[27] The fictive narrator can find no point of contact with such a behaviour pattern, indeed he fears it as a form of living death. Thus even as the Svoboda persona is evolving, he begins the drift back to Gantenbein and what appears to be the latter's richer possibilities. Nevertheless, the Svoboda persona is an important part of the total structure. His pattern of behaviour represents a norm which serves to offset the eccentricity of the more dominant personae. This does not imply, however, that the 'freedom' indicated by the simple translation of the Slav name 'Svoboda' is anything other than a deeply ironical one. The pattern of experience that the fictive narrator is seeking to express in the novel is too radically complex to be subsumed in the relative simplicity of the Svoboda figuration.

*   *   *

It has become clear from the preceding analysis of the narrator's three 'sketches for an ego' that, faced with the problem of defining and recreating his experience of reality on the basis of his imagination, the narrator has a simple choice : either he could cut himself off altogether from empirical reality and enter a world of fantasy or he could keep alive his roots in that reality with the hope that his inventions would then produce that sense of personal integrity which he lacks in his everyday life. Although the variations, the stories he tries on like a man tries on clothes, are openly presented as fictions, it is obvious the narrator has chosen the second course.

For the stories gain in credibility the more they approximate to his fundamental experience—that is, acts of pure imagination become a method of defining a pattern of experience which is rooted in a clear fictive reality.

Although Krolevsky's remark to Kürmann in *Biografie,* 'ab posse ad esse valet, ab esse ad posse non valet', is obviously correct, such a law is inadequate to grasp an experience whose rich ramifications require imaginative interpretation if it is to be fully understood. By giving form to such experience, exploration and delineation of the fictive narrator's identity becomes a viable proposition. The process of writing thus becomes a method of revealing the true self in all its contradictions, and *Mein Name sei Gantenbein* can be seen accordingly to link up closely with the earlier narratives *Stiller* and *Homo Faber.*[28] The novel demonstrates Frisch's belief that 'the individual is a sum of various possibilities, not an unlimited sum, but one which goes beyond his biography. Only the variations reveal the common centre.'[29] Paradoxically, the 'common centre' which fuses the separate biographies of Enderlin, Gantenbein and Svoboda is a sense of lost centricity—loss of resilience in the face of time and loss, above all, of Lila. And yet the sum total of these stories culminates in an all-pervasive ambiguity which effectively ensures that the narrator does not succumb to a final, unchanging image of himself nor present one to the reader. The essential person behind the fictions remains as unfathomable as the Limmat corpse which tried 'to float away without a story'. For in the last analysis, the problem of identity is a profoundly private one. Other people are only concerned with 'law and order', and a man fleeing from his biography presents a threat to their stability in so far as they have a stake in that biography. The corpse's escape is thwarted, just as Stiller's attempted flight was—and just as in the final pages of the novel the fictive narrator himself is brought to account by an inquisitor who will not accept that reality is any other than a logical sequence of facts. But at least one can say that all these reluctant detainees led their respective pursuers a merry dance before the end.

The grotesque episode of the Limmat corpse closes the narrative proper; it also subtly relativises the final scene of *al fresco* pleasure. The apparent breakthrough on the last page of the novel can only be understood as a welcome, but momentary, pause in a continuing struggle for stability. The book's final sentence, after all, does not end with a full-stop, but a dash—a symbol indicating a pause in a continuity, not a rounded conclusion. Although this final scene appears to represent, both formally and thematically, a break out of eccentricity into a simple, naïve wholeness, all the evidence points to the temporary nature of this phenomenon. The 'notes of the flute', for example, are not quite as idyllic as they sound, for they are merely 'wind in the telegraph wires'; the car stands 'grey with dust and burning hot'—a faint, but unmistakeable, echo of the Pompeii metaphor; the sunlight after emerging from the tomb is decidedly autumnal. Nevertheless, the novel's conclusion, with its irony and humour, is a long way from the bleakness of the final pages of *Die Schwierigen*, *Stiller* or *Homo Faber*. What the fictive narrator (and with him Frisch) has achieved, however precariously, can perhaps be summed up in Nietzsche's words as 'a kind of peace amidst hostile forces'.[30]

VII

Conclusion: Montauk

A close analysis of Max Frisch's novels has demonstrated that the
concept of eccentricity is the key to the understanding of his narrative world. In all five works the theme of lost centricity can be seen
to be of prime importance. Such thematic consistency over thirty
years is remarkable in itself, but Frisch's achievement is best gauged
by the fact that he has been able to treat the theme of eccentricity
in such a complex and continually fascinating way. It has proved
indeed to be a starting point for an intense exploration of problems
that have shown themselves to be endemic in contemporary German
literature. His heroes, whilst retaining their essential individuality,
can be seen as symptomatic of a whole society. Their acute sense
of dislocation, their feeling of crisis in terms of personal identity
—whether caused by the collapse of marriage as a centric principle
or by scepticism towards the claims of language to express experience adequately or by the inevitability of old age and death—are
magnificently caught in narratives of extraordinary diversity.

It is true that Jürg Reinhart, Anatol Stiller, Walter Faber and
the fictive narrator of *Mein Name sei Gantenbein* never attain 'das
wirkliche Leben' which they all, sooner or later, acknowledge to be
the only goal worth striving for. They are all brought face to face
with the same central dilemma : surface reality is simply not
adequate to reflect human experience and values. Realisation of this
fundamental truth separates them from their fellows, turns them
—irrespective of their wishes—into 'Sonderlinge' and reveals
dimensions to life that are wholly unsuspected by an apparently
centric majority. Their uneasy narratives bear witness to the fact
that they cannot escape from the pain of being alive. They have
each had a glimpse of the meaning of integrated personality, and
there can be no going back to the unreflective life represented at
its most positive by the Oberst in *Die Schwierigen* and at its most
negative by Dr Bohnenblust in *Stiller*.

All five models are informed by this concern for personal centricity and affirm essential human values in a world which appears

itself to have lost its centre. Frisch himself is well aware of the difficulties of writing such novels in a situation where personality is constantly under attack from increasingly fearsome abstractions. In *Mein Name sei Gantenbein*, for example, he has his narrator remark—significantly in parenthesis : 'I, too, often have the feeling that any book which isn't concerned with the prevention of war, with the creation of a better society and so on, is senseless, futile, irresponsible, tedious, not worth reading, inadmissible. This is no time for ego stories.' Yet he goes on ruefully : 'And yet human life is fulfilled or goes wrong in the individual ego, nowhere else' (V 68, 65). As a novelist, therefore, Frisch sees his work as asserting itself in that ironic tension which is generated between two polar opposites : the absurdity of 'ego stories' and the necessity for their existence. Thus he is led to re-affirm the importance of the individual personality and proclaim what he once called his 'individuelles Engagement an die Wahrhaftigkeit'.[1] This 'personal commitment to truthfulness' has enabled him in an age of widespread depersonal-isation to put forward a consistent body of fiction which has thrown a sharp, critical light on those pressures within the individual and within society that threaten integrity and prevent the attainment of genuine centricity.

* * *

When asked once to define 'die Domäne der Literatur', Frisch gave an entirely characteristic reply : 'The sphere of literature? I would almost say : the private world which sociology and biology cannot comprehend—the individual being, the self, not my self, but a self, an identity which experiences the world as self, which dies as self, an identity in all its biological and social limitations, the representa-tion of that identity which is contained in statistics but is never articulated and which is irrelevant in relation to the totality.'[2] It is in this context that Frisch's latest work *Montauk* (1975) is to be seen. In no other book—not even in the two major Diaries—has Frisch kept so closely to his own person as object and source of a literary text. *Montauk* (the name of a small fishing resort at the tip of Long Island) is the story of a weekend spent with Lynn, a chance acquaintance thirty years younger than the author. Frisch's professed design is to locate 'eine einfältige Erzählerposition' (VI 671; '*a naive narrative standpoint*') from which to capture the quality of this brief and uncomplicated affair, to write autobiographically 'without escaping into inventions, without justifying writing, without any responsibility towards society, without a message' (VI 719).

Frisch has always been a writer whose autobiography has been closely interwoven in his fiction, and it is not difficult to relate the candid discussion of his two marriages, the relationship with Ingeborg Bachmann, the problems of ageing and the sense of guilt and remorse in *Montauk* to the obsessions which motivated Reinhart, Stiller, Faber and the various personae of *Mein Name sei Gantenbein*. Yet unwary readers are warned both by the book's subtitle—'Eine Erzählung'—and by the preface taken from Michel de Montaigne, against any temptation to indulge a prurient curiosity:

> Reader, loe-here a well-meaning Booke. It doth at the first entrance fore-warne thee, that in contriving the same I have proposed unto myselfe no other than a familiar and private end . . . It is myselfe I pourtray. My imperfections shall therein be read to the life, and my naturall forme discerned, so farr-forth as publike reverence hath permitted me . . . Thus, gentle Reader, my selfe am the ground-worke of my booke : it is then no reason thou shouldest employ thy time about so frivolous and vaine a subject.[3]

To read the book as a guide to Frisch's private life would indeed be an idle occupation, just as it would be an error to ignore the ironic implications pointed to by the subtitle. What in the hands of a lesser stylist might have proved at best sentimental, at worst embarrassingly indiscreet, is here fashioned into an impressive meditation on the pattern of an individual's life. Because this individual is Max Frisch, mawkishness is prevented by a characteristic irony which informs a self-analysis conducted without rancour and with an artist's detachment.

For despite Frisch's desire to write 'naïve' autobiography as directly as possible in *Montauk*, he knows from the outset that he will not and cannot succeed. All creative writing, all expression, is a form of abstraction, a process of selection and suppression determined by the artist's sensibility. Accordingly, *Montauk* is no merely factual, mimetic account of a weekend affair between an old man and a young woman, but a *story*, a complex fabric of associations and memories woven by a quite particular imagination. The empirical, lived reality is certainly closer to the surface than in any previous book by Frisch, but it is his skill in the selection and arrangement of his material which gives *Montauk* its specific charm and wider interest. Fundamental preoccupations of Frisch's earlier fiction reappear : the problematic nature of experience in a world which seems to have lost its axis (Montauk is presented on its deserted peninsula, as it were, outside time); the acute awareness of human transience; and the extreme difficulty of establishing balanced personal relationships which allow each partner, whether a wife or a wealthy benefactor, that independence without which mutual growth is impossible. The significance of Lynn lies not in any primal sexuality or feminine warmth (indeed, like Frisch himself, the reader discovers very little about her), but in the fact that she grants the author a momentary sense of liberation and personal renewal. For Lynn has never read a word of Frisch's *oeuvre*; she has therefore no preconceptions, no ready-made judgements that could pin him insect-like against the backcloth of his fame. Although their conversation never rises above the trivial, the young American is recorded as demonstrating an uncomplicated and undemanding affection which succeeds in outweighing even the narrator's frankly admitted impotence on their final night together. Her presence, her strange mixture of openness and reserve, not only offer Frisch a few moments suspended from time, but also release in his mind the bitter-sweet recognition of how much he is a part of the past—a person with a historic continuity—and importantly, how much he (the author of *Stiller*!) is an uneradicable part of the past of other people.

Thus the books unfolds themes long familiar to readers of Frisch's fiction, but in *Montauk* they are presented with a lightness of touch which helps him to maintain a delicate balance between art and confessional diary. The most personal and private of Frisch's books to date succeeds in expressing a central paradox : the author does not 'float away without a story' any more than the corpse did at the end of *Mein Name sei Gantenbein*, and yet, despite the accumulation of autobiographical detail, the open naming of names, the essential Max Frisch remains obstinately hidden—a 'Rumpelstilzkin who does not betray himself' (VI 657). Like Goethe's *Dichtung und Wahrheit*, *Montauk* is in its own small-scale way a poetic balance sheet[4] in which Frisch, too, refuses to pose 'poetry' and 'truth', 'fact' and 'fiction' as alternatives or antinomies. For Frisch, experience can only be expressed and grasped as a subtle mixture of the two. Formally, *Montauk*—together with the *Tagebuch 1966–1971* published three years before—marks a return to the mosaic structure of his first major work, the seminal *Tagebuch 1946–1949*[5]; it is also a product of an insight first recorded in that book : 'Schreiben heißt : sich selber lesen'—or as Frisch puts it in this latest work : 'I can understand my experience only when I write' (VI 624). The fascination and profit for the reader lie not in achieving a glimpse into a writer's intensely private world, but, as with the *Essays* of Montaigne, of achieving through his reading a perception of the obscure richness of his own self.

The five novels which have formed the basis of this study all underline this essential perception : human reality is too complex and the individual's transient experience of it too fluid to be captured either in a neat set of statistics or in a simple 'story'. Each human being has to come to terms with the consequences of this predicament in his own way. For Frisch offers no global solutions to the problems he delineates so clearly in his books. The vital, integrating centre is not finally located but remains tantalisingly beyond his protagonists' grasp.

What the reader witnesses and recognises, however, when confronted with Max Frisch's narrative world, is a unique and creative paradox : in an eccentric environment only those eccentric individuals, the 'Schwierigen', who are alive to their condition and who strive to find the lost centre, come close to personal integrity. Like Camus' Sisyphos, Jürg Reinhart, Anatol Stiller, Walter Faber and the protagonist of *Mein Name sei Gantenbein* realise their essential identity only to the degree with which they commit themselves to the struggle to make sense of their lives and their environment. Though they fail, the nature of their failure is both impressive and illustrative of their common humanity. Max Frisch's verstaile and imaginative handling of the theme of eccentricity, with its characteristic irony, humour and subtlety, has established for the Swiss novelist a strong claim to a position of central significance in the history of post-1945 German fiction.

Notes

(Where references are given in abbreviated form, see Bibliography for full details.)

I INTRODUCTION

1 Bienek, *Werkstattgespräche mit Schriftstellern*, p. 27.

2 For an important study of the eccentric in German literature up to Naturalism, see Herman Meyer's *Der Sonderling in der deutschen Literatur* (Munich, 1963).

3 Cf. Erich Heller's remark that when tradition loses its coherence, when the centre no longer holds, 'eccentrics become the norm ... when the limits of a pattern are reached, what else can there be but borderline cases?' *The Ironic German, a Study of Thomas Mann* (London, 1958), p. 49. What is required in such a situation is a subtle differentiation between 'positive' and 'negative' eccentricity. This is what Frisch provides in his novels.

4 Stiller's frightening experience of his 'angel' is not unlike Rilke's in the *Duineser Elegien*. Both use the term as a metaphor for an insight into, and guarantee of, a deeper, richer mode of existence—although Stiller's angel does not have the complex mythical implications of Rilke's formulation. It would be interesting to pursue the parallel in other ways; for example, Stiller can be seen to share some features with Rilke's 'prodigal son' in *Die Aufzeichnungen des Malte Laurids Brigge* who returns to his family as a consciously alienated child, 'der Entfremdete'.

5 'Lack of destiny.' Schmid, *Unbehagen im Kleinstaat*, p. 6.

6 Wehrli, 'Gegenwartsdichtung der deutschen Schweiz', p. 113.

7 For years out of print, Zollinger's work has been collected and re-published under the editorship of F. Hindermann and with a Preface in the form of a 'Nachruf' by Frisch: Albin Zollinger, *Gesammelte Werke*, 4 vols. (Zürich, 1961–2). References are to this edition.

8 Zollinger, *Pfannenstiel*, p. 122. Frisch uses the identical image when he describes the efforts made by 'der andorranische Jude' to make contact with his fellows: 'Er redete in ein Schweigen hinein, wie in Watte.' *Tagebuch 1946–1949*, II 373. A recent book confirms the difficult nature of the relationship between Swiss German writers and their society: Dieter Fringeli, *Dichter im Abseits. Schweizer Autoren von Glauser bis Hohl* (Zürich/Munich, 1974). Fringeli concentrates on those neglected writers who fall into the no-man's-land 'nach Keller und Meyer' and 'vor Frisch und Dürrenmatt'. He entitles his Introduction after Zollinger, 'Die große Unruhe', declaring: 'This novel's title not only characterises the social and political tensions

which mark out Zollinger's autobiographical artist-novels; it could also be taken as the key concept in any study of Swiss literature in the twentieth century', p. 8

9 Zollinger, *Bohnenblust*, p. 252. Frisch has recently commented on the ironic fact that foreigners who live in Switzerland have a happier relationship with the country than the native Swiss: 'What they enjoy is a feeling of comfort generated by the country's lack of history' ('Geschichtslosigkeit als Komfort'). *Tagebuch 1966–1971*, VI 12.

10 'Nachruf auf Albin Zollinger, den Dichter und Landsmann nach zwanzig Jahren' in Zollinger, *Gesammelte Werke*, vol. 1, p. 12. (Reprinted : IV 265–71.)

11 *Emigranten*, IV 239. The point is expressed more forcibly by Frisch's younger colleague and compatriot, Jörg Steiner: 'I, too, am a victim of autism; I, too, live in isolation, unable to integrate myself into this or any other society.' W. Bucher and G. Ammann, *Schweizer Schriftsteller im Gespräch*, vol. 2 (Basel, 1971), p. 215.

12 The process has proved, in fact, intermittent and incomplete. Cf. Böll's definition of the writer's task in 1963 as 'the search for an inhabitable language in an inhabitable country'. *Frankfurter Vorlesungen* (Munich,[2] 1973), p. 45.

13 In a list of items for which Frisch recently declared himself permanently grateful, he included 'the tension between dialect and written language'. *Tagebuch 1966–1971*, VI 235. See also Schenker's study, *Die Sprache Max Frischs in der Spannung zwischen Mundart und Schriftsprache* (1969).

14 'Someone who has been spared', Preface to the *Tagebuch 1946–1949*.

II Jürg Reinhart

1 The reference is to Goethe's *Selige Sehnsucht*: 'Und so lang du das nicht hast, /Dieses: Stirb und Werde!/Bist du nur ein trüber Gast/ Auf der dunklen Erde.' ('And until you possess it, this commandment: Die and become! You will be but a troubled guest on the dark earth.')

2 Frisch is well aware of such weaknesses in his early work: 'What I dislike now in my early works, which were in fact written under the influence of Albin Zollinger, is the exhibition of feelings, the use of the so-called poetical metaphor... The metaphor compares something inaccurate with something even more inaccurate... the result is nothing more than a slightly bombastic elevation.' Kieser, 'An Interview with Max Frisch', p. 11 f. (Kieser's translation) Frisch's initial enthusiasm for Zollinger's lyrical prose expressed in the *Tagebuch 1946–1949* (II 436–9), which records his sole (chance) meeting with the older writer, had yielded over a decade before this interview to a more sober assessment of Zollinger's talent—see his 'Nachruf auf Albin Zollinger'.

III Die Schwierigen

1 In the *Neue Zürcher Zeitung*, Nr. 1837, 1934, Frisch discusses the

general complaint that there was a lack of recruits in the field of contemporary Swiss fiction and adds: 'And now that the recruits are there, there is a lack of recruiting officers.'

2 Two short prose works, however, did appear: *Antwort aus der Stille* (1937), a further exploration of the themes of *Jürg Reinhart* but not a novel, and the first 'military' Diary, *Blätter aus dem Brotsack* (1940).

3 See Schenker, *Die Sprache Max Frischs in der Spannung zwischen Mundart und Schriftsprache*, p. 30, and I 667.

4 The association between 'life' and 'danger' is already explicit in the earlier *Blätter aus dem Brotsack* where Frisch declares: 'All life has its roots in danger' (I 115).

5 This image of the frightening nature of time is a favourite Frisch device. It is at the root of his fascination by the Rip van Winkle tale alluded to later in the novel (I 559) and overtly used in *Stiller*. He has returned to the theme again in his *Tagebuch 1966–1971* (VI 398–400). See also the opening of *Gantenbein* (V 11 and 133). Perhaps the most radical example of the telescoping of time and the resultant confusion of identity is Rilke's vision at the beginning of *Die Aufzeichnungen des Malte Laurids Brigge*: 'Is it possible that one has had centuries of time to look, reflect and note down, and that one has let the centuries pass like a school break in which one eats an apple and a sandwich?/Yes, it is possible.'

6 Stiller uses the same image to describe the architect Sturzenegger whose cynical *bonhomie* reminds him of an automaton (III 591). In the *Tagebuch 1946–1947* (II 357) Frisch has his puppeteer Marion's awareness of the ubiquitous nature of 'puppet strings' contribute directly to his suicide; in a world of automata the independent man cannot survive.

7 For Frisch, the Lawyer is the archetypal symbol of 'Ordnung', of laws, conventions and habit that restrict the full development of the personality. Graf Oderland, for example, is a Staatsanwalt who rebels against societal rigidity represented by his calling; in *Stiller* Dr Bohnenblust, the defence counsel, is the vehicle for a series of satirical attacks on Swiss society and its narrow conformism and smugness; and at a more subtle level there is the Staatsanwalt, Rolf, who stands against the struggling 'Sonderling', Anatol Stiller.

8 Jurgensen misses the irony completely when he sums up this marriage as 'lasting and meaningful'. *Max Frisch: Die Romane*, p. 52. Doris Merrifield also describes Yvonne as happy and her marriage to Hauswirt as successful—a mistake she is led into by her method of attempting individual studies of Frisch's female characters too isolated from their context. *Das Bild der Frau bei Max Frisch*, p. 46.

9 Frisch gives the identical thought to the narrator of his next work, *Bin oder die Reise nach Peking* (1945), see I 604.

10 The whole scene with its complacent and self-righteous atmosphere lends weight to the analysis of the Swiss character essayed by Karl Schmid, 'Versuch über die schweizerische Nationalität' in his *Aufsätze und Reden* (Zürich & Stuttgart, 1957), pp. 10–133.

11 The Oberst's admonition strongly recalls similar sentiments expressed by Konsul Buddenbrook in his letter to his daughter Tony in which he made *his* attempt to dissuade her from an 'unsuitable' match: 'My child, we are not born for that which, with our short-sighted vision, we reckon to be our small personal happiness. We are not free, separate and independent entities, but like links in a chain, and we could not by any means be what we are without those who went before us and showed us the way, by following the straight and narrow path, not looking to right or left.' *Buddenbrooks*, translated by H. Lowes Porter, Penguin edition, p. 114.

12 Frisch returned to a discussion of the consequences of this attitude for the artist/intellectual in his *Tagebuch 1946–1949*: 'The aim is to produce a society which does not make the intellectual into an outsider, nor into a martyr, nor into a court jester. But in so far as this is not the case, we must remain outsiders in our society' (II 397). Cf. the Zeremonienmeister in *Die Chinesische Mauer*: 'It is an old custom, your Majesty: the man who defends innocence before the Emperor has always been the Fool' (II 190). Social criticism is only permitted when it is filtered through the innocuous mask of the Fool. That society in general has still not lost its skill in controlling its 'Schwierigen' can be gleaned from Ralf Dahrendorf's article, 'Der Intellektuelle und die Gesellschaft: Uber die soziale Funktion des Narren im 20. Jahrhnudert', *Die Zeit*, 29.3.1963.

13 Cf. Wendel Bach, the central character of Zollinger's *Der halbe Mensch*.

14 Reich-Ranicki, *Deutsche Literatur in West und Ost*, p. 87.

15 The critical meridian of thirty is a tradition going back to Christ and beyond. It occurs frequently in literature: Villon was 'en l'an trentiesme' of his age when he set down his *Testament*; Nietzsche's Zarathustra is the same age when he leaves home for the mountains and meditation; Büchner's Woyzeck, Benn's Dr. Rönne, Roquentin in Sartre's *La Nausée*, Meursault in Camus' *L'Etranger* and Grass's Oskar are all thirty, to name a few striking examples. For an interesting discussion of this phenomenon, see Theodore Ziolkowski's chapter 'The Novel of the Thirty Year Old' in *Dimensions of the Modern Novel* (Princeton, 1969).

16 In Frisch's next novel Stiller will in fact have a crucial 'meeting with his angel'.

17 See his essay, *Uber das Marionettentheater*.

18 Wilson, *The Outsider* (London, 1956), p. 105 f. (Italics in text)

19 The same note is struck at the end of Frisch's first play, *Santa Cruz* (1944), where despite the reconciliation between Elvira and the Rittmeister, we are left with the vision of their daughter, Viola, 'who will experience everything afresh, who will begin everything again' (II 75).

IV STILLER

1 Respectively, R. Sanders in *Die Welt*, 18.12.1954, and Thilo Koch in *Die Zeit*, 2.12.1954.

2 Respectively, Herbert Ahl, *Literarische Portraits*, p. 85, Hans Mayer, *Dürrenmatt und Frisch*, p. 48, and Philip Manger, 'Kierkegaard in Max Frisch's Novel *Stiller*'.

3 The English version of quotations from *Stiller*, *Homo Faber* and *Mein Name sei Gantenbein* are by Michael Bullock. All other translations are mine unless otherwise indicated.

4 This was a criticism raised by Dürrenmatt, among others. 'Fragment einer Kritik', quoted from *Uber Max Frisch*, ed. T. Beckermann, p. 11.

5 See Frisch's remark to Bienek: '... the novel *Stiller* presented as the diary of a prisoner trying to escape his identity.' *Werkstattgespräche mit Schriftstellern*, p. 24.

6 Walter Jens, 'Nachwort' to *Max Frisch: Erzählungen des Anatol Ludwig Stiller*, p. 53. The stories of Rip van Winkle and Jim White, along with other substantial sections of Frisch's text, are unaccountably omitted from Bullock's translation, the Penguin edition of which is erroneously described as 'complete' and 'unabridged'.

7 Frisch returned to the comic possibilities of the theme of a hen-pecked husband fleeing to the Foreign Legion in his short farce *Die große Wut des Philipp Hotz* (1958). The very sight of a 'double room as a permanent arrangement' (IV 91, 97) is enough to make Walter Faber think of joining the Legion!

8 Cf. Werner Stauffacher: 'Ce cauchemar du labyrinthe humain qui est bien l'image du désarroi de Stiller à la recherche de sa véritable identité.' 'Langage et Mystère', p. 334.

9 The symbolic significance of this flight is echoed in the scene where Stiller attempts to destroy his studio. He himself makes the connection when he notices a dripping tap: 'It was dripping, and I wondered whether it had been dripping like that for six years, a passing idea that somehow irritated me, reminding me of the dripping in the Carlsbad caves' (III 104 f, *286*). The reference can hardly be understood by readers of the English version.

10 Stiller himself later makes the Little Grey/Julika identification explicit (III 726, *307*). It is characteristic of Bohnenblust's blindness to meanings beneath the level of surface facts that he ignores the cat episode entirely.

11 Schmid, 'Versuch über die schweizerische Nationalität', p. 29.

12 Ibid., p. 45 (italics in text).

13 In his recent compilation *Max Frisch: Stich-Worte* Frankfurt/Main, 1975), produced to celebrate the Suhrkamp Buchwoche in September 1975, Uwe Johnson included excerpts from Frisch's most important statements on Switzerland and the Swiss under the heading 'Nationalität: Schweiz'. (Johnson's intentional splitting of the word 'Stichwort'—'key-word' or 'cue'—points neatly to the double-edged nature of language in Frisch's work: on the one hand, a means of orientation; on the other, an unpredictable goad and frequent source of hurt. See note 23 below!)

14 *Tagebuch 1946–1949*, II 629. See also Frisch's essay 'Kultur als Alibi' (1949), II 337–43.

15 The words are the Doktor's in *Andorra*, see IV 511. The two doctors have a great deal in common besides the title.

16 Dürrenmatt, 'Fragment einer Kritik', p. 14 f.

17 The Sturzennegger pages are among those omitted in a drastically abbreviated version of the fifth Notebook in Bullock's translation.

18 Frisch, the architect, expanded this theme a year later in an amusing, dramatised 'Funkgespräch', *Der und die Architektur* (1955), reprinted: III 261–89. His professional experience in this field has helped Frisch to avoid in his own work that 'moral schizophrenia' which culminates in an 'aesthetic culture' divorced from politics and everyday reality. (See the *Tagebuch 1946–1949*, II 629.)

19 One is reminded of Reinhart's decision to become a gardener. Exactly the same criticism was made in the previous century by Conrad Ferdinand Meyer: 'Swiss life has much of value, honourable in character, the bourgeois virtues of hard work, efficiency and prosperity. But Switzerland is too small, too narrow, too limited. Thus all Swiss writers are driven to the miniature: they end up in the idyll.' Quoted by Karl Schmid, *Unbehagen im Kleinstaat*, p. 83.

20 Cf. Goethe's very similar views on Swiss 'freedom', expressed almost 200 years ago in his *Schweizer Reisen*. The criticisms of Swiss attitudes Frisch has Stiller articulate are by no means idiosyncratic or peculiarly Swiss German. Cf. C. F. Ramuz's essay *Besoin de Grandeur* (1938) in which he undertakes a thorough analysis of how in a small country conformism can be mistaken for order, inertia for moral certitude and resignation for self-confidence. There is a wry note on Ramuz in the *Tagebuch 1946–1949*: 'C. F. Ramuz, the poet of French Switzerland, who died recently, is already being worn as a feather in our national cap: Gotthelf, Keller, Meyer, Spitteler. Ramuz . . . Eh bien! All that one can say to that is a few months ago when Ramuz was facing his final operation, he had to ask the Authors' Society to give him 2000 francs for it' (II 562).

21 Karl-Heinz Braun. *Die epische Technik in Max Frisch's 'Stiller'*, p. 84.

22 III 477–82 are omitted from Bullock's translation.

23 That even a stray remark can thrust a decisive image on a person is central to Frisch's 'Bildnis' theme. Cf. the story of his mother's formidable knitting prowess developed in response to a teacher's comment—never forgotten, never forgiven—that she would never master the skill! *Tagebuch 1946–1949*, II 371.

24 Exactly the same irony can be observed in *Andorra* where Pater Benedict delivers a similar homily to Andri. The truth of what he says (here the necessary corollary of 'self-acceptance') is belied by what he does (or in this case fails to do). It is an interesting fact that Frisch puts some of his deepest convictions into the mouths of highly ambivalent characters—a point to be borne in mind when assessing Rolf's rôle in the novel.

25 The significance of this attitude, apart from the fact that it is also a defence mechanism employed by Julika, was revealed in the analysis of Yvonne's relationships in *Die Schwierigen*.

26 See, for example, Emil Staiger's review in *Neue Zürcher Zeitung*,

17.11.1954, and H. Boeschenstein, *Der neue Mensch: die Biographie im deutschen Nachkriegsroman*, p. 107.

27 We know from the *Werkstattgespräch* with Bienek that the radio play was not a preliminary study for *Stiller*: 'I was working on the novel and needed money. I couldn't think of an idea for a radio play, so I stole the material from the novel in progress' (p. 28). Klaus Haberkamm is therefore clearly wrong in stating: 'A year later Frisch's first novel of world rank appeared : *Stiller* which had evolved out of the radio play *Rip van Winkle* (1953).' *Deutsche Literatur seit 1945*, ed. Dietrich Weber, p. 335 f.

28 Cf. Enderlin's similar experience in *Gantenbein* (V 18, *18*). See above p. 130.

29 The 'Engel' symbol occurs also in the Marion sections of the *Tagebuch 1946–1949*, where it is a figure beckoning a reluctant Marion to realise his full potentialities via self-knowledge—a process that needs the sort of faith required to walk on water. Marion refuses the call and commits suicide. (See II 359 and 500 f.)

30 Soren Kierkegaard, *Repetition, An Essay in Experimental Psychology* (New York, 1964), p. 35 : 'If God himself had not willed repetition, the world would never have come into existence... Repetition is reality, and it is the seriousness of life.'

31 Mayer, *Dürrenmatt und Frisch*, p. 40. The motto, in fact, is not placed before the *book*, but after the title, 'Erster Teil: Stiller's Aufzeichnungen im Gefängnis'. The fact that the two quotations are placed in reverse order from that in which they appear in *Either/Or* may be an ironic pointer to the lack of progression from Part One to Part Two.

32 Laing, *The Politics of Experience* (Harmondsworth, ⁴1967), p. 24.

33 Kierkegaard, *Either/Or*, vol. 2 (London, 1944), p. 193.

34 Cf. Bin's remark: 'I almost believe that what all of you are lacking in your lives is a little experience of God, that's all.' *Bin oder die Reise nach Peking*, I 633. Hans Bänziger is quite right in calling Bin 'ein Stiller in nuce'. *Frisch und Dürrenmatt*, p. 48.

35 *Repetition*, p. 48.

36 Jurgensen is incorrect in stating: 'Rolf at no time questions his narrative. He remains the authoritative, omniscient narrator.' *Max Frisch: Die Romane*, p. 76. In general, it is clear in the 'Nachwort' that Rolf's relationship with Stiller in 'freedom' is an uncomfortable one. Although aware of Stiller's continuing need of his friendship, he admits to neglecting him and Julika totally, to being embarrassed by Stiller's phone calls and to being somewhat afraid of a reunion. His sympathy seems fully engaged in prison, where he plays a dominant rôle and where he has his own problems to talk out, but he shrinks from the much more demanding commitment posed by friendship with Stiller on an equal footing in 'freedom'.

37 C. G. Jung, *The Development of Personality* (London, 1954), p. 174.

38 'Zwei Männer sinds, ich hab es lang gefühlt,
Die darum Feinde sind, weil die Natur
Nicht Einen Mann aus ihnen beiden formte.' (III, ii)

('They are two men, I have long felt it, who are enemies because Nature did not make one man of them.')

39 *Bin oder die Reise nach Peking*, I 645.

V HOMO FABER

1 And fruitfully so. The entries in the *Tagebuch 1946–1949* relating to Frisch's design and construction of the open-air swimming pool in Letzigraben (Zürich) reveal delight and excitement in such work. See especially II 634, where he touches on his dual creativity as architect and dramatist: 'Reality: the tension between them.'

2 Cf. Frisch's remark: 'Fate becomes credible to the extent that it is denied. That was the conscious method in *Homo Faber*.' *Dramaturgisches. Ein Briefwechsel mit Walter Höllerer*, p. 28. This point will be discussed more fully in the final section of the chapter.

3 Rolf Geißler takes too superficial a view of 'anagnorisis' when he writes: 'With Oedipus anagnorisis (recognition) is the result of his analysis; with Walter Faber the presupposition.' *Möglichkeiten des modernen deutschen Romans*, p. 195. Faber's true anagnorisis is achieved not at the outset of his report, but gradually in the course of his composing it.

4 Beckett, *Proust* (London, 1965), p. 18 f.

5 Ibid., p. 19.

6 Faber's narrative situation must not, of course, be forgotten. It is perfectly possible—in fact, likely—that knowledge of his incest causes him to present his memories in these terms. This is not to say, however, that he is reading significance into the past that is not already there. Rather is he beginning to recognise the true meaning of events and impressions which were at the time vague or repressed. Frisch uses very similar language in describing the narcissistic corruption of love by that traditional eccentric, Don Juan. See his 'Nachträgliches zu *Don Juan*', III 169. For a comparison of the novel and the play see Herta Franz's article 'Der Intellektuelle in Max Frischs *Don Juan* und *Homo Faber*'.

7 This aspect of the Cuban interlude is too often overlooked—for example, by Günter Bicknese, 'Zur Rolle Amerikas in Max Frischs *Homo Faber*', p. 60. There is an inherent imbalance in the apparently happy and beautiful negroes and negresses of Havana.

8 Camus, *Le Mythe de Sisyphe* (Paris, ⁴1961), p. 18.

9 Ibid.

10 It is this feature that makes it clear that the primary recipient of the report is Faber himself. For much of what he writes, ostensibly in lieu of a letter to Hanna (IV 170, *183*)—for example, the facts concerning Hanna's life between 1933–57—is only relevant in terms of an explorative, interior monologue.

11 Beckett, *Proust*, p. 14.

12 Cf. Ursula Roisch, 'Max Frischs Auffassung vom Einfluß der Technik auf den Menschen', p. 963.

13 Cf. Mary Cock, *The Presentation of Personality in the Novels of Max Frisch and Uwe Johnson*, p. 169.

14   Cf. Eduard Stäuble, *Max Frisch: Gesamtdarstellung seines Werkes*, p. 193.

15   Geulen, *Max Frischs 'Homo Faber'*, p. 86. It is interesting to compare this opening with that of *Stiller*. The same technique is at work: a staccato beginning followed immediately by a complex and lengthy sentence which tends to undermine the surface confidence of the opening phrases. A further similarity catches the eye in the use in both long sentences of the would-be assertive 'einzig und allein'—twice in the case of *Stiller* where panic is even closer to the surface. In both novels the opening rhythms thus indicate the basic movement and direction the stories are to take.

16   Camus, *Le Mythe de Sisyphe*, p.17.

17   Freud records that teeth falling out is a common symbol for fear of castration. In puberty such dreams are also associated with the desire to masturbate, whereas in folklore 'Zahnausfall' is linked with death in the family. *Traumdeutung* in *Gesammelte Werke* II/III (London, 1942), p. 390 ff. The parallels with Faber's situation can be drawn easily enough. The symbol obviously fascinates Frisch. He uses it again for Felix Enderlin in *Gantenbein* ('Only his teeth, which have often fallen out already in dreams, we know what that means, only his teeth shock him', V 158, *150*), and he gives the same dream to Kürmann in *Biografie*. It also introduces the major theme of growing old in his *Tagebuch 1966–1971*. Günter Grass, indeed, weaves a whole novel, *Örtlich betäubt* (*Local Anaesthetic*, 1969) around his hero's decaying teeth!

18   The English translation cannot capture the pun on 'Gesellschaft'— 'party' or 'society'.

19   The underlying tone of shiftiness as Faber tries to wriggle out of responsibility 'damals' is unmistakable. Frisch catches exactly the same cadences in the speeches he gives to the citizens of Andorra when they appear at the witness box to whitewash *their* murky past.

20   Franzen, 'Homo Faber', p. 983. In Mann's *Der Tod in Venedig* Aschenbach actually does use cosmetics in a desperate attempt to rejuvenate himself and escape death.

21   It must be admitted that this particular invention, together with Faber's fear of being struck down in his bath by Hanna-Clytemnestra and the moment when he desires, Oedipus-like, to put out his own eyes, are not only a little melodramatic but also strictly speaking a *Stilbruch*. For it is not credible that Faber would light on such literary allusions at random, and that he should be aware of them goes against not only his strictly prosaic stance, but quite specifically against his own declared lack of interest in such matters: 'My ignorance of mythology and *belles lettres* in general' (IV 142, *149*).

22   The temporary removal of his typewriter is keenly felt by Faber, which befits a man whose past life has demonstrated his preference for machines over human beings. However, being forced into a more *direct* contact with what he is writing is an essential part of the now quickening process of enlightenment.

23   Brigitte Bradley, 'Max Frisch's *Homo Faber*', p. 281.

24 By misreading the book's characteristic irony W. G. Cunliffe succeeds in turning its meaning on its head: '(Faber) is to be understood as the sympathetic portrait of a man who tries, and fails, to exist by being honest and avoiding illusions.' 'Existentialist Elements in Frisch's Works', p. 117.

25 Eliot, *East Coker* II, lines 82–7.

26 Eighteen years later in *Montauk*—the story of a brief weekend of love between a man of sixty-four and a woman of thirty-one—Frisch identifies himself closely with these sentiments, see VI 685.

27 Camus, *Le Mythe de Sisyphe*, p. 124.

VI MEIN NAME SEI GANTENBEIN

1 Frisch and his fictive narrator show a desire to explore the implications of Nietzsche's reflection: 'We contain within ourselves the sketch ('Entwurf') of many different people. The poet reveals himself through the characters he invents... Each moment of our lives presents us with many possibilities. Chance always plays a part.' *Gesammelte Werke*, Musarionausgabe, vol. 16 (Munich, 1925), p. 304. This insight into the multiplicity of personality is reflected in the work of a large number of twentieth-century novelists, both before and after the Second World War—two disparate examples to stand for many: Hermann Hesse's *Der Steppenwolf* (1927) and Walter Jens' *Herr Meister* (1963).

2 IV 263. First published in *Weltwoche*, 4.11.1960. Many of the ideas expressed in this short essay appear almost verbatim in *Gantenbein*. See also Frisch's replies to an imaginary interviewer, *Ich screibe für Leser* (V 323–34), first printed in *Dichten dun Trachten* 24 (Frankfurt/Main, 1964), and the *Werkstattgespräch* with Bienek, p. 24 and passim.

3 IV 263. Cf. the Bishop's remark in *Don Juan oder die Liebe zur Geometrie*: 'Truth cannot be demonstrated, only invented' (III 165).

4 It is an odd fact that, whilst most critics have pointed to Frisch's diary entry (*Tagebuch 1946–1949*, II 573 f.) which notes his admiration for Dürrenmatt's *Der Blinde* as the probable germ for the idea of the Gantenbein rôle, none have mentioned Pirandello's *Enrico IV* (1922), which must surely have served as the model for Dürrenmatt's play and which would yield some interesting parallels with Frisch's handling of what he calls 'the interplay of perception and imagination'.

5 IV 264. Martin Walser has expressed a very similar idea which has direct relevance to the concerns of Frisch's fictive narrator: 'There are stories which reality does not allow to happen because they would reveal reality too plainly. These are the stories one has to tell. In this way reality might be compelled to admit: yes, that's me.' 'Eine winzige Theorie der "Geschichte" ', *Dichten und Trachten* 24, p. 31.

6 V 325.

7 To highlight the existential nature of this symbolic crisis, the narrator repeats the sequence as Enderlin's reaction to his mistaken discovery in hospital that he has only one year to live (V 153 f.).

The narrator has just 'visited' Enderlin and thus the 'weiße Fleck' is at this point very close to its invented identity.

8   One of the most powerful images in contemporary German literature of a similar existential crisis is to be found in Grass's *Die Blechtrommel* where a dead horse's head is used as bait for catching eels, a piece of repulsive carrion which 'screamed instead of whinnying'.

9   The final paragraph of the novel recalls the image: 'Everything is as if it had never happened ... It is a day in September, and when we come up into the light again out of the gloomy and not at all cool tombs, we blink, so bright is the day'. This 'emergence from the tomb' comes immediately after the abortive attempt of the corpse 'to float away without a story'. In a sense, the whole novel can be said to be an emergence from the 'tomb' of the existential and marital crises represented by the two key episodes under discussion.

10 The 'Pechvogel' story appears for the first time in the *Werkstattgespräch* conducted by Bienek in the summer of 1961, and thus belongs to the earliest stages of the novel's composition.

11 *Ich schreibe für Leser*, V 328.

12 The 'Spiegel' motif is by far the dominant one in the novel. With the exception of the section which deals with Gantenbein's initial experiments with his dark glasses and the narrator's stories for the barman, the word 'Spiegel' occurs every few pages. Stiller's experience of his angel is couched in similar terms: 'There was nothing but falling, a falling that was actually no falling, a state of total powerlessness accompanied by total wakefulness, only time had disappeared' (III 725 f., *308*). Don Juan, too, is acutely aware of the fragility of surface reality once it is called into question : 'Once we quit the lie which shines like a glittering surface and see this world as something more than a mirror of our desires, when we want to know who we are ... then there is no limit to our fall, there is such a whistling in our ears that we no longer know where God dwells' (III 133). The experience of this 'Spiegelsturz' is seen by Wolf Marchand as fundamental to all Frisch's protagonists. 'Mein Name sei Gantenbein', p. 517.

13 *Tagebuch 1946–1949*, II 710: 'We can only experience expectation or memory. The present, where these intersect, is scarcely open to experience.' See also the entry: 'The present somehow remains unreal, a void between presentiment and memory which are the true spheres of our experience; the present is merely transitory, the well-known void we do not like to admit to ourselves' (II 452).

14 For the significance of the Hermes figure in Mann's novel, see Frank J. Kearful's article 'The Role of Hermes in "The Confessions of Felix Krull"', *Modern Fiction Studies* XVII, 1 (1971), pp. 91–108. Kearful argues that Felix, like Hermes, is 'an image of the paradoxical unity of the Self' (p. 101). Frisch appears here to be continuing that hint of affectionate parody of Mann's fiction which is also discernible in *Stiller* vis-à-vis *Der Zauberberg*.

15 Kierkegaard speaks of the young man 'whose soul lacked elasticity' thus: 'He had not the strength to take irony's vow of silence, not the

power to keep it; and only the man who keeps silent amounts to anything.' *Repetition*, p. 48.

16 The bitter ironies involved in the process of ageing provide one of the major themes of Frisch's *Tagebuch 1966–1971*. His latest story *Montauk* is also in part an elegy on the same subject.

17 The most frequent criticism levelled at the novel has been its formlessness. It is not possible within the limitations of this study to undertake a rigorous structural analysis of the book, but a close reading of the text reveals a remarkable symmetry of design: it opens and closes with an anonymous death; the Enderlin/Gantenbein pole dominates the first half, Gantenbein/Svoboda the second–both pairs reflected in the central Ali/Alil story. The basic 'Erlebnismuster' of the fictive narrator holds the whole together via a flexible technique of verbal and ideational associations. For a thorough examination of the novel's structure: cf. Hans Wolfschütz's thesis: *Die Entwicklung Max Frischs als Erzähler von 'Mein Name sei Gantenbein' aus gesehen.*

18 Kierkegaard, *Either/Or*, p. 193. Kierkegaard declares that 'aesthetic existence' is the rejection of continuity in favour of living in the moment. This is what Enderlin longs to do. By running the two personae side by side in the first half of the book, Frisch is able to make each reflect ironically on the other. Irony ironised!

19 *Tagebuch 1946–1949*, II 374: 'Das Lebendige in jedem Menschen, das, was nicht erfaßbar ist.'

20 *Tagebuch 1946–1949*, II 713. According to Frisch, this fear lies at the heart of Shakespeare's classic tragedy of jealousy *Othello*. The Moor's tragedy has its roots in his 'otherness': 'Jealousy is representative of the more general fear of inferiority, the fear of comparison, the fear that one is the black sheep' (II 716).

21 The allusion to Heinrich von Kleist's famous story *Die Marquise von O.* is apt. Kleist, too, was a writer preoccupied with the problem of illusion and reality. In particular, obvious associations can be made between the Gantenbein/Enderlin configuration and, say, *Amphitrion*. (Frisch actually refers to Kleist's play in the same context of jealousy and *Othello* noted above.)

22 Kierkegaard, *Either/Or*, p. 135.

23 *Ich schreibe für Leser*, V 333 f. Hans Mayer, among others, misses the point when he complains that the character of Lila defeated Frisch's narrative skill. 'Mögliche Ansichten über Herrn Gantenbein', p. 211.

24 Frisch re-worked this story into a film scenario. The project was never completed, and Frisch published the text under the title *Zürich-Transit. Skizze eines Films* (Frankfurt/Main, 1966), reprinted: V 401–52.

25 *Ich schreibe für Leser*: 'Was keine Variante mehr zuläßt, ist der Tod' (V 331). See also the 'Schillerpreisrede', V 367.

26 It is, however, characteristic of Frisch's irony that he has Svoboda repeat Burri's views with such conviction, when Burri's views themselves are originally neither presented nor accepted unambiguously by the fictive narrator. Svoboda's ready adoption of second-hand

opinions recalls Julika's similar parrot-learning from the young Jesuit in the Davos sanatorium. Neither Svoboda nor Julika can therefore be taken wholly seriously. Their 'views' are equally ironised and presented as primarily defensive rather than deeply felt.

27 Bienek, *Werkstattgespräch*, p. 25.

28 In this connection replies given by Frisch in an interview on the subject of his play *Biografie* are highly pertinent to *Gantenbein*, too: 'I didn't want to demonstrate something premeditated, but to carry through a game in order to discover how I experience things. Writing as a method of discovering one's identity ... Writing a play or carrying through a game, you can be as arbitrary as you like; anything is allowed if it works. But things only work if I can follow them through to the end, if they strike me as credible in terms of my play. It's in this limitation that the self is revealed and experienced.' 'Noch einmal anfangen können', *Die Zeit*, 22.12.1967.

29 *Ich schreibe für Leser*, V 327.

30 'Mastery over the self consists of striking a balance between many accumulated memories and motives—a kind of peace amidst hostile forces.' *Gesammelte Werke*, p. 306.

VII CONCLUSION: MONTAUK

1 *Emigranten*, IV 243.

2 'Noch einmal anfangen können', *Die Zeit*, 22.12.1967. See also *Max Frisch. Dramaturgisches. Ein Briefwechsel mit Walter Höllerer*, p. 34.

3 Preface to Montaigne's *Essais* in John Florio's translation of 1603.

4 Cf. Marcel Reich-Ranicki's review 'Mein Name sei Frisch', *Frankfurter Allgemeine Zeitung*, 7.10.1975, and Rolf Michaelis, 'Love Story—und mehr', *Die Zeit*, 19.10.1975.

5 In a recent interview Frisch explained his early and continuing predilection for the Diary form precisely in terms of 'the permanent confrontation between fact and fiction' it affords. By presenting objective 'fact' and subjective 'fiction' contrapuntally, Frisch generates an ironic tension between the two and thus comes closer to a true expression of his experience of reality. Technically, the Diary offers 'a formal counter ('eine Antwortform') to the general scepticism about the claims of narrative fiction and its mode of illusion which has been, and still is, widely felt, if today less acutely than before.' 'Gespräch mit Max Frisch' in Heinz Ludwig Arnold, *Gespräche mit Schriftstellern*, p. 41 f.

Bibliography

PRIMARY LITERATURE

Edition used

Max Frisch: Gesammelte Werke in zeitlicher Folge, 6 vols. (Frankfurt am Main, Suhrkamp Verlag, 1976). This edition is textually identical with the simultaneously published *werkausgabe edition suhrkamp*, 12 vols.

Translations

I'm not Stiller, trans. Michael Bullock (Harmondsworth, Penguin Books, 1961). First published by Abelard-Schuman (London, 1958).
Homo Faber, trans. Michael Bullock (Harmondsworth, Penguin Books, 1974). First published by Abelard-Schuman (London, 1959).
A Wilderness of Mirrors, trans. Michael Bullock (London, Eyre Methuen, 1967). First published : 1965. (= *Mein Name sei Gantenbein*)

SECONDARY LITERATURE

This bibliography lists only those items which bear directly on Frisch as a novelist. Two anthologies of critical essays on Frisch have appeared: Thomas Beckerman (ed.), *Uber Max Frisch* (Frankfurt/Main, 1971) and Albrecht Schau (ed.) *Max Frisch—Beiträge zu einer Wirkungsgeschichte* (Freiburg im Breisgau, 1971). Where a listed item is reprinted in these volumes, this is indicated by the abbreviations *TB* and *SCHAU*. The fullest bibliographies on Frisch and his work generally are to be found in the Beckermann anthology and in the special number of *Text+Kritik* 47/48 (October 1975) devoted to Max Frisch compiled by Klaus-Dietrich Petersen and Thomas Beckermann respectively.

A. *Frisch and his Novels generally*

AHL, Herbert, 'Homo Ludens—Homo Faber—Homo Sapiens: Max Frisch', *Literarische Portraits* (Munich/Vienna, 1962), 83–92.
ARNOLD, Heinz L., 'Gespräch mit Max Frisch', *Gespräche mit Schriftstellern* (Munich, 1975), 9–73.
BADEN, Hans-Jürgen, *Der Mensch ohne Partner. Das Menschenbild in den Romanen von Max Frisch* (Wuppertal-Barmen, 1966).
BANZIGER, Hans, *Frisch und Dürrenmatt* (Berne/Munich, ⁶1971).
BANZIGER, Hans, *Zwischen Protest und Traditionsbewußtsein. Arbeiten zum Werk und zur gesellschaftlichen Stellung Max Frischs* (Berne/Munich, 1975).
BARLOW, D., ' "Ordnung" and "Das Wirkliche Leben" in the Work of Max Frisch', *German Life & Letters*, XIX, 1 (October, 1965), 52–60.

BECKERMANN, Thomas, ' "Einmal möchte er es wissen". Zur Ästhetik des Engagements im Prosawerk von Max Frisch', *Text+Kritik*, 47/48 (October, 1975), 27–36.

BIENEK, Horst, 'Max Frisch', *Werkstattgespräche mit Schriftstellern* (Munich, 1962), 21–32.

BLOCH, P. A. and BUSSMANN, R., 'Geespräch mit Max Frisch', *Der Schriftsteller in unserer Zeit. Schweizer Autoren bestimmen ihre Rolle in der Gesellschaft* (Berne, 1972), 17–35.

BURGAUNER, Christoph, 'Versuch über Max Frisch', *Merkur*, XXVIII, 5 (May, 1974), 444–63.

BURGER, Hermann, 'Des Schweizer Autors Schweiz. Zu Max Frischs und Peter Bichsels Technik der Kritik an der Schweiz', *Schweizer Monatshefte*, 51 (1971/2), 746–54.

BUTLER, Michael, *The Theme of Eccentricity in the Novels of Max Frisch* (Council for National Academic Awards, London, unpublished Ph.D. dissertation, 1973).

BUTLER, Michael, 'Das Problem der Exzentrizität in den Romanen Frischs', *Text+Kritik*, 47/48 (October, 1975), 13–26.

CAUVIN, Marius, 'Le Chemin de Max Frisch', *Etudes Germaniques, XV*, 1 (Janvier/Mars, 1960), 59–63.

COCK, Mary, *The Presentation of Personality in the Novels of Max Frisch and Uwe Johnson* (University of Oxford, unpublished D.Phil. dissertation, 1968).

COCK, Mary, ' "Countries of the Mind"—Max Frisch's Narrative Technique', *Modern Language Review*, LXV, 4 (October, 1970), 820–8.

CUNLIFFE, W. G., 'Existential Elements in Frisch's Works', *Monatshefte*, LXII, 2 (1970), 113–22.

DESCHNER, Karl Heinz, 'Max Frisch: "Stiller" und andere Prosa', *Talente. Dichter. Dilettanten* (Wiesbaden, 1964), 125–55.

EDFELT, Johannes, 'Max Frisch', *Moderna Sprak*, LVI, 3 (1962), 284–91.

ESSLIN, Martin, 'Max Frisch', *Swiss Men of Letters*, ed. Alex Natan (London, 1970), 241–58. Expanded version of chapter first published in *German Men of Letters III*, ed. Alex Natan (London, 1968), 307–20.

HABERKAMM, Klaus, 'Max Frisch', *Deutsche Literatur seit 1945 in Einzeldarstellungen*, ed. Dietrich Weber (Stuttgart, 1968), 332–61.

HEISSENBUTTEL, Helmut, 'Max Frisch oder die Kunst des Schreibens in dieser Zeit' (previous unpublished 'Radio-Essay', now in *TB*, 54–67).

HILLEN, Gerd, 'Reisemotive in den Romanen von Max Frisch', *Wirkendes Wort*, XIX, 2 (1969), 126–33.

HOEFERT, S. P. 'Zur Sprachauffassung Max Frisch', *Muttersprache*, LXXIII, 9 (1963), 257–9.

HOFFMANN, Charles, 'The Search for Self, Inner Freedom and Relatedness in the Novels of Max Frisch', *The Contemporary Novel in German*, ed. R. Heitner (Austin/London, 1967), 91–113.

HOLLERER, Walter, *Max Frisch. Dramaturgisches. Ein Briefwechsel mit Walter Höllerer* (Berlin, 1969).

JURGENSEN, Manfred, 'Die Entmythologisierung der Freiheit oder die Umschulung des Geistes', *Schweizer Monatshefte*, 51 (1971/72), 755–62.

JURGENSEN, Manfred, *Max Frisch. Die Romane. Interpretationen* (Berne/Munich, 1972).

KAISER, Joachim, 'Max Frisch und der Roman. Konsequenzen eines Bildersturms', *Frankfurt Hefte*, 12 (1957, 876–82 (*TB*).

KIESER, Rolf, 'An Interview with Max Frisch', *Contemporary Literature*, XIII, 1 (January, 1972), 1–14.

KIESER, Rolf, 'Man as his own Novel: Max Frisch and the Literary Diary', *The Germanic Review*, XLVII, 2 (March, 1972), 109–17.

KIESER, Rolf, *Max Frisch—Das literarische Tagebuch* (Frauenfeld/ Stuttgart, 1975).

KINGSBURY, Jane, *Crisis in the Novels of M. Frisch and H. E. Nossack* (University of Cambridge, unpublished M.Litt. dissertation, 1973).

KJAER, Jorgen, 'Max Frisch, Theorie und Praxis', *Orbis Litterarum*, XXVII, 4 (1972), 264–95.

KURZ, P. K., 'Identität und Gesellschaft. Die Welt des Max Frisch', *Uber Moderne Literatur 2* (Frankfurt/Main, 1969), 132–89.

KUSTOW, Michael, 'No Graven Image. Some Notes on Max Frisch', *Encore*, IX, 3 (May/June, 1962), 13–24.

LIVINGSTONE, R. S., 'The World-View of Max Frisch', *Southern Review*, I, 3 (1965), 32–45.

MARCHAND, Wolf, 'Max Frisch', *Deutsche Dichter der Gegenwart*, ed. Benno von Wiese (Berlin, 1973) 231–49.

MAYER, Hans, 'Max Frischs Romane', *Zur deutsche Literatur der Zeit* (Hamburg, 1967).

MERRIFIELD, Doris, *Das Bild der Frau bei Max Frisch* (Freiburg i.Br., 1971).

MULLER, Joachim, 'Das Prosawerk Max Frischs—Dichtung unserer Zeit', *Universitas*, XXII, 1 (January, 1967), 37–48 (SCHAU).

PETERSEN, Carol, *Max Frisch* (Berlin, 1966).

REICH-RANICKI, Marcel, 'Uber den Romancier Max Frisch', *Deutsche Literatur in West und Ost* (Munich, 1963), 81–100.

SCHAU, Albrecht, 'Max Frisch. Dichtung der Permutation', *SCHAU*, 353–6 (= 'Nachwort' to the anthology).

SCHENKER, Walter, *Die Sprache Max Frischs in der Spannung zwischen Mundart und Schriftsprache* (Berlin, 1969).

SCHMID, Karl, 'Max Frisch: Andorra und die Entscheidung', *Unbehagen im Kleinstaat* (Zürich/Stuttgart, 1963), 169–200.

STÄUBLE, Eduard, *Max Frisch. Gesamtdarstellung seines Werkes* (St. Gallen, 1967).

STÄUBLE, Eduard, *Max Frisch. Gedankliche Grundzüge in seinen Werken* (Basel, 1967).

STAUFFACHER, W., 'Langage et mystère: à propos des derniers romans de Max Frisch', *Etudes Germaniques*, XX, 3 (1965), 331–45 (*SCHAU*).

STEINMETZ, Horst, *Max Frisch: Tagebuch, Drama, Roman* (Göttingen, 1973).

STROMSIK, Jiri, 'Das Verhältnis von Weltanschauung und Erzählmethode bei Max Frisch', *Philologica Pragensia*, 13 (1970), 74–94.

WEHRLI, Max, 'Gegenwartsdichtung der deutschen Schweiz', *Deutsche Literatur in unserer Zeit,* ed. W. Kayser (Göttingen, 1959), 105–24.

WEISSTEIN, Ulrich, *Max Frisch* (New York, 1967).

WELZIG, Werner, *Der deutsche Roman im 20. Jahrhundert* (Stuttgart, 1967), 68–78.

WERNER, Markus, *Bilder des Endgültigen. Entwürfe des Möglichen. Zum Werk Max Frischs* (Berne/Frankfurt, 1974).

WINTSCH-SPIESS, Monika, *Zum Problem der Identität im Werk Max Frischs* (Zürich, 1965).

WOLF, Christa, 'Max Frisch, beim Wiederlesen oder: Vom Schreiben in Ich-Form', *Text+Kritik*, 47/48 (October, 1975), 7–12.

ZIMMER, Dieter, 'Noch einmal anfangen können. Ein Gespräch mit Max Frisch', *Die Zeit*, 22.12.1967.

B. Stiller

BOESCHENSTEIN, H., *Der neue Mensch. Die Biographie im deutschen Nachkriegsroman* (Heidelberg, 1958), 104–10.

BONNIN, Gunther, 'Stiller—Swiss Don Quichotte', *Queensland Studies in German Language and Literature*, 2 (1971), 103–6.

BRAUN, Karl-Heinz, *Die epische Technik in Max Frischs 'Stiller' als Beitrag zur Formfrage des modernen Romans* (Frankfurt/Main, D.Phil. dissertation, 1959).

BUTLER, Michael, 'The Ambivalence of "Ordnung" : the Nature of the "Nachwort des Staatsanwaltes in Max Frisch's *Stiller*', *Forum for Modern Language Studies*, XII, 2 (April, 1976), 149–55.

DEMETZ, Peter, 'The Swiss Establishment and Anatol Ludwig Stiller: 1950–1960', *Postwar German Literature. A Critical Introduction* (New York, ²1972), 17–20.

DURRENMATT, Friedrich, ' "Stiller", Roman von Max Frisch. Fragment einer Kritik', *Theaterschriften und Reden* (Zürich, 1966), 261–71 *(TB)*.

EMMEL, Hildegard, 'Paradie und Konvention: Max Frisch', *Das Gericht in der deutschen Literatur des 20. Jahrhunderts* (Berne, 1963), 120–50.

FRANZEN, Erich, 'Der gescheiterte Traum vom neuen Ich', *Aufklärungen. Essays* (Frankfurt/Main, 1964), 168–70 *(TB)*.

GONTRUM, Peter, 'The Legend of Rip van Winkle in Max Frisch's "Stiller" ', *Queensland Studies in German Language and Literature*, 2 (1971), 97–102.

HARRIS, Kathleen, 'Stiller (Max Frisch): Ich oder Nicht-Ich?', *The German Quarterly*, XLI, 4 (November, 1968), 689–97.

HELMETAG, C. H., 'The Image of the Automobile in Max Frisch's "Stiller" ', *The Germanic Review*, XLVII, 2 (March, 1972), 118–26.

HENNING, Margrit, 'Die Ich-Erzähler als Medium der Verfremdung in Max Frisch's "Stiller" ', *Die Ich-Form und ihre Funktion in Th.Manns 'Dr. Faustus' und in der deutschen Literatur der Gegenwart* (Tübingen, 1966), 159–71.

HESSE, Hermann, 'Uber Max Frischs "Stiller" ', *Gesammelte Werke*, XII (Frankfurt/Main, 1970), 564–5.

HOLL, Oskar, *Der Roman als Funktion und Uberwindung der Zeit* (Bonn, 1968), 167–86.

HORST, K. A., 'Bildflucht und Bildwirklichkeit', *Merkur*, IX, 2 (February, 1955), 190–3 *(SCHAU)*.

JENS, Walter, 'Nachwort', *Max Frisch: Erzählungen des Anatol Ludwig Stiller* (Frankfurt/Main, 1962), 50–7 *(TB)*.

KOCH, Thilo, 'Auf den Spuren Dostojewskijs', *Die Zeit*, 2.12.1954.

KOHLSCHMIDT, W., 'Selbstrechenschaft und Schuldbewußtsein im

Menschenbild der Gegenwartsdichtung. Eine Interpretation des "Stiller" von Max Frisch und der "Panne" von Friedrich Dürrenmatt', *Das Menschenbild in der Dichtung*, ed. A. Schaefer (Munich, 1965), 174–93.

MANGER, Philip, 'Kierkegaard in Max Frisch's Novel "Stiller"'. *German Life & Letters*, XX, 2 (January, 1967), 119–31.

MARTI, Kurt. 'Das zweite Gebot im "Stiller" von Max Frisch', *Kirchenblatt für die reformierte Schweiz*, 5.12.1957.

MAYER, Hans, 'Anmerkungen zu "Stiller"', *Dürrenmatt und Frisch. Anmerkungen* (Pfullingen, 1963), 38–54 (TB). (Reprinted in H.M., *Zur deutschen Literatur der Zeit*.)

Pfanner, H. F., 'Stiller und das "Faustische" bei Max Frisch', *Orbis Litterarum*, XXIV, 3 (1969), 201–15 (*SCHAU*).

SANDERS, R., 'Der Mensch in Untersuchungshaft', *Die Welt*, 18.12.1954.

STAIGER, Emil, ' "Stiller". Zu dem neuen Roman von Max Frisch', *Neue Zürcher Zeitung*, 17.11.1954 (*SCHAU*).

WEIDELI, Walter, 'Stiller or Le Malaise Helvétique', *Adam*, XXVII, 275 (1959), 67–8.

WHITE, Andrew, 'Labyrinths of Modern Fiction. Max Frisch's *Stiller* as a Novel of Alienation and the "Nouveau Roman" ', *Arcadia*, II, 3 (1967), 288–304.

C. Homo Faber

BICKNESE, Günther, 'Zur Rolle Amerikas in Max Frischs "Homo Faber" ', *The German Quarterly*, XLII, 1 (January, 1969), 52–64.

BRADLEY, Brigitte, 'Max Frisch's "Homo Faber": Theme and Structural Devices', *The Germanic Review*, XLI, 4 (1966), 279–90.

BOESCHENSTEIN, H., *Der neue Mensch* (see under *Stiller*), 123–6.

BUTLER, Michael, 'The Dislocated Environment: the Theme of Itinerancy in Max Frisch's "Homo Faber" ', *New German Studies*, IV (1976).

FRANZ, Herta, 'Der Intellektuelle in Max Frischs "Don Juan" und "Homo Faber" ', *Zeitschrift für deutsche Philologie*, XC, 4 (1971), 555–63.

FRANZEN, Erich, 'Homo Faber', *Aufklärungen* (see under *Stiller*), 171–7 (*TB*).

GEISSLER, Rolf, 'Max Frisch. Homo Faber', *Möglichkeiten des modernen deutschen Romans* (Frankfurt/Berlin/Bonn, 1962), 191–214.

GEULEN, Hans, *Max Frischs 'Homo Faber'. Studien und Interpretationen* (Berlin, 1965).

HENZE, Walter, 'Die Erzählhaltung in Max Frischs Roman "Homo Faber" ', *Wirkendes Wort*, XI, 5 (September, 1961), 278–89 (*SCHAU*).

JENS, Walter, 'Max Frisch und der homo faber', *Die Zeit*, 9.1.1958 (*SCHAU*).

KAISER, G., 'Max Frischs "Homo Faber" ', *Schweizer Monatshefte*, XXXVIII, 10 (1958/59), 841–52 (*SCHAU*).

LIERSCH, Werner, 'Wandlung einer Problematik', *Neue Deutsche Literatur*, 7 (1958), 142–6 (*TB*).

MULLER, Gerd, 'Europa und Amerika im Werk Max Frischs. Eine Interpretation des Berichts "Homo Faber" ', *Moderna Språk*, LXII, 4 (1968), 395–9.

ROISCH, Ursula, 'Max Frischs Auffassung vom Einfluß der Technik auf

174 THE NOVELS OF MAX FRISCH

den Menschen—nachgewiesen am Roman "Homo Faber" ', *Weimarer Beiträge*, 13 (1967), 950–67 *(TB) (SCHAU)*.

SALIS, J-R. de, 'Zu Max Frischs Homo Faber', *Schwierige Schweiz: Beiträge zu einigen Gegenwartsfragen* (Zürich, 1968), 148–52. English translation: *Switzerland and Europe. Essays and Reflections*, ed. C. Hughes (London, 1971), 281–4.

SCHURER, Ernst, 'Zur Interpretation von Max Frischs "Homo Faber" ', *Monatshefte*, LIX, 4 (1967), 330–43.

WAIDSON, H. M., 'Max Frisch: "Homo Faber" ', *Twentieth Century German Literature*, ed. A. Closs (London, 1969), 150–5.

WEBER, Werner, 'Max Frisch 1958', *Zeit ohne Zeit. Aufsätze zur Literatur* (Zürich, 1959), 85–101.

WEIDMANN, Brigitte, 'Wirklichkeit und Erinnerung in Max Frischs "Homo Faber" ', *Schweizer Monatshefte*, XLIV, 8 (August, 1964), 445–56.

D. *Mein Name sei Gantenbein*

ARNOLD, Heinz L., 'Möglichkeiten nicht möglicher Existenzen. Zu Max Frischs Roman: Mein Name sei Gantenbein', *Eckhart Jahrbuch 1964/65*, ed. K. L. Tank (Witten/Berlin, 1964), 298–305.

BAUMGART, Reinhard, 'Othello als Hamlet', *Der Spiegel*, 36 (1964) *(TB)*.

BIER, Jean Paul, ' "Mein Name sei Gantebein". Ein Beitrag zur Deutung von Max Frischs letztem Roman', *Revue des Langues Vivantes*, 33, 6 (1967), 607–14.

BIRMELE, Jutta, 'Anmerkungen zu Max Frischs Roman "Mein Name sei Gantenbein" ', *Monatshefte*, LX, 2 (1968), 167–73 *(SCHAU)*.

BLOCKER, Günter, 'Max Frischs Rollen', *Literatur als Teilhabe. Kritische Orientierungen zur Literatur der Gegenwart* (Berlin, 1966), 15–19.

BOTHEROYD, P. F., *Aspects of First- and Third-Person Narration and the Problem of Identity in Three Contemporary German Language Novels:* Günter Grass' 'Die Blechtrommel', Uwe Johnson's 'Das dritte Buch über Achim' and Max Frisch's 'Mein Name sei Gantenbein' (University of Birmingham, unpublished Ph.D. dissertation, 1970).

BRINKMANN, Hennig, 'Der komplexe Satz im deutschen Schrifttum der Gegenwart. Der komplexe Satz bei Max Frisch und Günter Grass', *Sprachkunst als Weltgestaltung*, ed. A. Haslinger (Salzburg/Munich, 1966), 13–21 *(SCHAU)*.

BURGAUNER, Christoph, 'Max Frisch oder die Liebe zur Dramaturgie', *Frankfurter Hefte*, XXIII, 6 (1968), 439–42.

CAUVIN, Marius, 'Max Frisch, l'absolu et le nouveau roman', *Etudes Germaniques*, XXII, 1 (January/March, 1967), 93–8 *(SCHAU)*.

EMRICH, Wilhelm, 'Die "goldenen Früchte" der Literaturkritik', *Polemik. Streitschriften, Pressefehden und kritische Essays um Prinzipien, Methoden und Maßstäbe der Literaturkritik* (Frankfurt/Bonn, 1968), 65–70.

FARNER, Konrad, 'Mein Name sei Frisch', *Sinn und Form*, XVIII, 1 (1966), 273–8.

HARTUNG, Rudolf, 'Max Frisch: "Mein Name sei Gantenbein" ', *Die Neue Rundschau*, LXXV, 4 (1964), 682–6.

HEISSENBUTTEL, Helmut, 'Ein Erzähler, der sein Handwerk haßt? Zu

Max Frischs drittem (sic) Roman: "Mein Name sei Gantenbein"',
Die Welt der Literatur, 3.9.1964.

HOLTHUSEN, H. E., 'Ein Mann von fünfzig Jahren', *Merkur*, XVIII,
10/11 (October/November, 1964), 1073–7 (*SCHAU*).

KAHLER, Hermann, 'Max Frischs "Gantenbein"-Roman', *Sinn und Form*,
XVII, 1/2 (1965), 299–303 (*TB*).

KRAFT, Martin, *Studien zur Thematik von Max Frischs Roman 'Mein
Name sei Gantenbein'* (Berne, 1969).

KRATTLI, Anton, 'Max Frisch: "Mein Name sei Gantenbein"', *Schweizer
Monatshefte*, XLIV, 10 (1965), 975–9.

KURZ, P. K., 'Mein Name sei Gantenbein', *Stimmen der Zeit*, CLXV, 1
(1964), 57–61.

MANTHEY, Jürgen, 'Prosa des Bedenkens', *Frankfurter Hefte*, XX, 4
(April, 1965), 279–82.

MARCHAND, Wolf, 'Max Frisch: "Mein Name sei Gantenbein"', *Zeitschrift
für deutsche Philologie*, LXXXVII, 4 (1968), 510–34 (*TB*).

MERRIFIELD, Doris, 'Max Frischs "Mein Name sei Gantenbein": Versuch
einer Strukturanalyse', *Monatshefte*, LX, 2 (1968), 155–66 (*SCHAU*).

REICH-RANICKI, Marcel, 'Max Frisch: "Mein Name sei Gantenbein"',
Literatur der kleinen Schritte (Munich, 1967), 79–89.

SCHNEIDER, Peter, 'Die Mängel der gegenwärtigen Literaturkritik', *Neue
Deutsche Hefte*, 107 (1965), 98–123.

SCHROERS, Rolf, 'Max Frisch oder das Mißtrauen', *Christ und Welt*,
18.9.1964 (*SCHAU*).

SEEBA, H. C., '"Erfahrung" und "Geschichte" bei Max Frisch', *Kritik
des ästhetischen Menschen* (Bad Homburg/Berlin/Zürich, 1970), 12–15.

STONE, Michael, 'Max Frisch oder der Konjunktiv im Hirn', *Christ und
Welt*, 18.9.1964 (*SCHAU*).

STROMSIK, Jiri, 'Max Frisch, Mein Name sei Gantenbein. Eine Interpretation', *Germanistica Pragensia*, 5 (1968), 111–31.

VIN, Daniel de, 'Max Frisch: Mein Name sei Gantenbein. Eine Interpretation', *Studia Germanica Gandensia*, 12 (1970), 243–63.

VORMWEG, Heinrich, 'Max Frisch oder Alles wie nicht geschehen', *Die
Wörter und die Zeit. Uber Neue Literatur* (Neuwied/Berlin, 1968),
80–6.

WOLFSCHUTZ, Hans, *Die Entwicklung Max Frischs als Erzähler von 'Mein
Name sei Gantenbein' aus gesehen* (Salzburg, D.Phil. dissertation, 1972).

Index